France Encounters Globalization

France Encounters Globalization

Peter Karl Kresl
Bucknell University

Sylvain Gallais
Université François Rabelais

Edward Elgar
Cheltenham, UK • Northampton, MA, USA

Published by
Edward Elgar Publishing Limited
Glensanda House
Montpellier Parade
Cheltenham
Glos GL50 1UA
UK

Edward Elgar Publishing, Inc.
136 West Street
Suite 202
Northampton
Massachusetts 01060
USA

A catalogue record for this book
is available from the British Library

Library of Congress Cataloguing in Publication Data
Kresl, Peter Karl.
  France encounters globaliztion / Peter Karl Kresl, Sylvain Gallais.
    p. cm.
  Includes bibliographical references and index.
  1. France–Economic conditions–1945–2.France–Economic policy–1945–3. France–Foreign economic relations.4.Globalization.I.Gallais, Sylvain.II.Title

HC276.2 .K73 2002
337.44–dc21   2001055545

ISBN 1 84064 542 3

Printed and bound in Great Britain by MPG Books Ltd, Bodmin, Cornwall

Contents

Tables

Figures

Maps

The Authors

Peter Karl Kresl has been Professor of Economics and International Relations at Bucknell University (USA) since 1969. His teaching and research interests are in European and North American economic integration, urban economies and globalization, and cultural policy. He has published in, among others, *Urban Studies*, *The Journal of European Integration*, *The American Review of Canadian Studies* and *Ekistics*, and his book *Urban Economies and Regional Trade Liberalization* was published in 1994. He has been visiting professor at the Norwegian School of Economics, the University of Lund and McGill University and has lectured throughout Europe, North America and Asia.

Sylvain Gallais has been Professor of Economics and Political Science at Université François Rabelais (France) since 1969. His research specialization had been in International Trade and Microeconomics, and is now in Institutionalism, Austrian Economics, Europe and Democracy. He has been published in *Le Journal des Economistes et des Etudes Humaines*, *La Revue de l'Aleps* and he published in 1982 *Autour de Pigou et Coase*, and various working papers in Public Choice in Science Politique, Paris (FNEP). He is a co-founding member of research teams Jerico-st and CEDP (Center for Studies on Public Debate). He has lectured in France, in London and at Bucknell University where he has also been twice as a visiting professor.

Preface

Jointly authored books are always a learning experience and we both have learned and benefited much in this collaboration. One is an outsider with a great deal of affection for France while the other lives there. We hope that the combination of the perspective of the outsider and the deep insights of the insider have combined to produce a book that will prove to be informative to the reader.

The story of France and its encounter with globalization is fascinating in itself, given France's historic sense of self and of its role in the international community of nations. In some sense, globalization is the great leveler, in that there are powerful forces of homogenization that go hand in hand with it. The opening of national economies, deregulation of markets, and ascendancy of economic liberalism have generated endorsement and protest in virtually all parts of the globe. But the debate in France has been at the same time heated and rational, and the interaction of these two responses is what drew us to write this book. While we do not agree on all aspects of the implications of globalization, we have very much enjoyed and benefited from the discussions that have accompanied the forging of a common position on which we could both agree. We earnestly hope the reader will find this to be an informative and stimulating text.

Chapters 1, 4, 5 and 7 were written by Kresl, and Gallais wrote Chapters 2, 3, 6 and 8. The Gallais chapters were written in French and were translated by Kresl, with the assistance of Laura Ryan. It would take a far more skilled translator to do full justice to the Gallais chapters, but we have aspired to give the reader a text that has a reasonable consistency of prose style.

We sincerely want to express our great appreciation to our wives, Lois and Françoise, for their understanding that while our attention was often devoted to this project our love and affection remained where they belong.

1 France Encounters Globalization

France is in the midst of a public policy debate focused on the conflict between the exceptionalist French model of an economy which is characterized by a close, structured political economic relationship between labor, capital and the state, and the pressing need to make accommodations to the demands of an emerging universalist model of liberal market economic relations. This debate occurs at different levels of sophistication: the popular press, serious public affairs journalism, and academic scholarship. It is a fascinating discussion as it takes place in a society which celebrates discussion within a highly segmented political culture and which takes seriously serious discussion. The French debate, while interesting in and of itself, is also one which captures the intensity of concern felt in the rest of the continental European countries regarding the complex of benefits and costs of further globalization and, in particular, monetary union and the other objectives of the (Maastricht) Treaty on European Union.

In this introductory chapter we will examine the major positions and publications in this public policy debate. Once this context has been established we will treat the issue that is at the front of the French, and European, debate, that of a generalized sense of economic malaise and its relationship to globalization. The challenge for all of continental Europe is that of finding a model of political economy that both allows European producers to compete successfully on global markets on terms that benefit both capital and labor and can be accommodated by the social structures and cultural values Europeans so obviously wish to preserve. First, however, we must examine the impacts globalization has had on various aspects of the French economy.

THE ELEMENTS OF GLOBALIZATION

Following the conclusion of the Second World War France experienced what is referred to as *les trente glorieuses*[1], a period of 30 years in which gross national product grew by over 5 per cent annually and unemployment remained below 3 per cent of the total labor force.[2] This was a period marked by post-war reconstruction, an opening to the external world principally through adoption of the Treaty of Rome (1957) which established the European Economic Community, a growing role for the state through planning and nationalization, and an occasional devaluation of the currency. It was also a period in which the labor needs of the growing manufacturing sector were met by substantial migration from rural areas to towns and cities, and by immigration. Between 1946 and 1975 the percentage of the population living in rural areas declined from 47 per cent to 31 per cent, and the number of immigrants doubled from 1.7 million to 3.4 million and their share of the French population rose from 4.38 per cent to 6.54 per cent. The geographical origination of immigrants also changed, with Europeans declining from 89 per cent to 61 per cent, and Africans rising from 3 per cent to 35 per cent during the same period. By 1982 the European/African mix of immigration was 48 per cent/43 per cent.[3] Finally, the labor participation rate for females rose from 48.5 per cent in 1970 to 59 per cent in 1993.[4]

Les trente glorieuses were followed by a period of Euro-pessimism triggered by the economic stagnation which affected most of Western Europe during and immediately following the OPEC oil price hikes of 1973 and 1979. The collective response of the member states of the European Economic Community was to complete the internal market with adoption of the Single European Act (the 1992 process) in 1986. While there was an on-going internal logic to pushing forward the European integration process, based on the desire to achieve both prosperity and peace, Axford is right to see this as 'also a defensive strategy, based on the recognition that the European economy was and is losing out to the more dynamic, expansionist and technologically efficient Japanese, and to the still massive economies of scale seen in the United States.'[5]

The importance of globalization to the French economy can be made clearer if we examine individually the two components of this process, trade liberalization and technological change. The accomplishments of the integration process in Europe to date have been: a reduction of tariff and quantitative barriers to trade; a common external tariff; progress toward the four freedoms, that is, free movement of goods, services, capital and labor; considerable standardization of industry practices and harmonization of government policies; progress toward common policies regarding agriculture, transportation, and competition; and a persistent, if controversial, effort to reduce regional economic disparities. This has involved a process whereby individual member states have imposed constraints on their ability to intervene in their own economies to address the needs of some elements of their population. While most of the continental member states have been willing to proceed down this path, the United Kingdom has chafed at the notion that decisions made in Brussels by a deliberative body which was not controlled by Her Majesty's Government, such as the Social Charter or the European Monetary Union, would determine the economic life of its citizens.

France has been a more enthusiastic supporter of EU integration, in part because of the long-term economic benefits to be derived, but also because of the need to achieve Franco-German *rapprochement,* to confront the challenges posed by the Cold War, and to reduce European dependence on the United States.[6] Nevertheless, participation in the regional integration agenda has posed a clear challenge to the cherished notion of French exceptionalism and the ability of France to maintain a distinctive national approach to questions of social, economic, political and cultural institutions and practices. To take just one example, the relative political autonomy and strength of the German *Länder* resulted in their having a significant role in decision-making processes in Brussels,[7] beginning with a formal participation agreement between the Federal Chancellor and the Conference of *Länder* Prime Ministers in 1979.[8] Decentralization in France began with legislation introduced shortly thereafter during 1982-4 and involved both institutional-structural changes and devolution of some responsibilities.[9] While there were some changes in mentalities and behaviors internal to France,[10] the example of sub-national governments in other member states contributed powerfully to the demand for similar freedom of action on the part of French regions and cities. While continuing to resist seduction by the liberal, Anglo-American approach to policies and institutions, France has accepted immersion in the more congenial harmonization and standardization processes of the continent-dominated European Union.

In addition to trade liberalization through the European Community/Union, a similar process has been occurring at the global or multilateral level through the General Agreement on Tariffs and Trade. Between 1947 and the Uruguay Round (concluded in 1993) there were eight rounds of trade liberalization which lowered tariffs by 21 per cent (1947), and by 33-35 per cent in 1967, 1979 and 1993. At the conclusion of the Uruguay Round, European Union external tariffs had been lowered from prohibitive post-war rates to a rather insignificant 3.6 per cent. The GATT, now the World Trade Organization, either forbade or standardized other protectionist international trade practices and international disputes were made subject to impartial dispute resolution procedures. While there is some disagreement as to whether trade liberalization at the global and regional levels are mutually reinforcing or conflicting strategies, there is no disagreement that together they have profoundly affected the environment in which national economies function and have posed challenges to national governments, such as that of France, that seek to retain their ability to shape the evolution of their economies and to safeguard national distinctiveness.

The other component of globalization, technological change at an exponentially increasingly rapid pace, has greatly enabled firms and local economies to respond to the opportunities and the challenges inherent in the new economic spaces that have been created by trade liberalization. This is a very complex topic with its own extensive literature; given the limitations of this chapter only a superficial review of the major consequences will be examined here. Dramatic advances in the technologies of production, transportation, and communication have resulted in reconsideration of traditional views as to the relationship between center and periphery, the advantages of industrial districts, the effects of agglomeration, and the locational advantages of regions rich in resources, factors of production and consumer demand.[11] It has also led to industry demands for deregulation of markets, and relaxation of strictures against mergers and acquisitions, that in the pre-globalized economy would have given rise to concerns about market power. The requirements of this new economy have created a polarization in the demand for labor, with demands for highly skilled, technologically literate workers soaring and many traditional jobs being downgraded to low-skill assembly work.[12] In the context of an 'open economy' this has led to a geographic restructuring of global production and distribution activities. As Third World countries have become increasingly attractive to producers needing low-skill labor, workers in countries such as France who lack the capacity to interact with new technologies have seen their employment opportunities and job security erode over time. The consequences of this are: reduction in the power of industrial labor unions; widening of the gap between rich and poor; increase in racist and anti-immigrant sentiment; and increase in a variety of social pathologies.[13]

Taken together, global and regional trade liberalization and rapid advances in technology have put national governments on the defensive. They are torn between the positive benefits of efficiency and the higher standards of living promised by the liberal agenda of freer trade and open markets, and the negative consequences these changes clearly impose on significant portions of their citizens and some of their industries and regions.

In Chapter 5 we will present data that will demonstrate that in the years since 1973, the year of the first OPEC price hike and the conclusion of the three decades of post-war reconstruction and growth, total employment has remained almost stagnant while increases in population show up in higher rates of unemployment. The inability of France to create jobs is indicated by a reduction in job vacancies. Workers who have lost their jobs have experienced longer periods of unemployment and French youth have found it increasingly difficult to gain access to lasting employment. It will also be made clear that France has had a sharper rise in the rate of unemployment, between 1970 and 1995, than any of the other Group of Seven countries, with the exception of Italy. France shares with the other European countries the inability to create jobs. This is striking when one compares the European record on employment growth with that of Japan, but especially with that of Canada and the United States. During this 25-year period, employment in the European Four grew by 6.7 per cent while in North America this figure was 59.8 per cent; in France employment grew by 7.9 per cent.

The weak performance in job creation and the high levels of unemployment experienced by France in recent years by no means give a full picture of the basis for the concern in France, and in other European countries, regarding the impacts of globalization. However, they should be sufficient to suggest that there is something valid to the reservations that have been raised by those who fear for the well-being of individuals and for democratic processes in the post-modern, globalized society and economy that, in their view, neo-liberals are intent on imposing on all countries and all individuals.[14] Not all who have reservations about the impact of globalization on France would express their position as stridently as has just been done but, as we shall see, for many the difference is only one of degree. It is to this debate that we must now turn our attention.

THE FRENCH DEBATE ABOUT GLOBALIZATION

As was indicated earlier, the debate in France on globalization has been extensive, with contributions at all levels of analysis from popular press to scholarly journals. In this examination of that debate we will limit ourselves to several recent books and articles that have gained some publicity and circulation in France and which offer a serious analysis of the process. Our intention is less to provide an estimate of the economic impacts of globalization than it is to explore the reaction of French political economists to the notion of France being integrated into, and perhaps dominated by, a globalized economic environment.

The best place to start this examination is at one of the extremes with the book *L'horreur économique* by the literary critic of the newspaper *Le Monde*, Viviane Forrester.[15] This attack on globalization by a non-economist was on the French best-seller list for months and generated considerable controversy among economists. Written in an elegant prose, the analysis is inspired by *élan vital* rather than by either data or theory, the mainstays of social scientists whose prose, as compensation, is invariably comparatively pedestrian. In addition to the processes of globalization, which have been enumerated above, Forrester includes in her polemic the *pensée unique*, which in the French discourse refers to the set of values, assumptions and policy prescription that accompanies post-modernist globalist thinking. It places the emphasis on free markets, deregulation, profit maximization and a minimal role for government on the assumption that a properly functioning private sector will accomplish the objectives of efficiency and equity that society desires. In an analysis that finds affinity to both the anti-capitalist left and the extreme right of Jean-Marie Le Pen, Forrester ascribes virtually all of the contemporary economic failings to the processes of and thinking behind globalization. Whereas economists see profit as a signal which directs both the allocation of capital and distributive shares, Forrester admits only the latter and poses rhetorical questions such as: '[i]s it useful for one to live if this is not beneficial to profit?'.[16]

Central to her critique is the notion that in the globalized economy French workers, and those of other industrialized economies, will no longer be needed. The combination of cybernetics, robotics and access to production sites in low-wage Third World countries means that 'for the first time the mass of human beings is no longer materially or economically necessary to the small number of individuals who hold power and for whom others outside their intimate circle have interest or existence only from a utilitarian point of view.'[17] The consequence of this is the set of economic and social problems that have been noted by many observers: the inability of young people to find employment; the persistence of high levels of unemployment; the social exclusion of racial minorities and immigrants and the social pathologies that result from their concentration in *banlieus*, the ghetto suburbs which are situated on the periphery of large French cities; and the state of anxiety regarding job security of those who have been able to find employment.

Many would agree with Forrester that France suffers from these and other difficulties; however, few would accept as not unthinkable her scenario of 'from exploitation to exclusion, from exclusion to elimination, indeed to disastrous unimagined exploitations.'[18] What the social scientist finds lacking is establishment of a causal relationship between what could conceivably be considered to be two parallel series of events. As will be elaborated later in this chapter, this question of causation is hotly discussed in France, and determination of the proper answer is too important, for the French economy and French working people, to be left hanging. A second shortcoming of Forrester's analysis is that no real policy prescription is offered. One of the most succinct sentences written in reaction to Forrester's polemic is that of Jean-Claude Milner who wrote: 'The denunciation, heard more and more frequently today, of *L'horreur économique* is nothing more that the moaning of the salaried bourgeoisie upon discovering with considerable shock that it is from this time on a class that is condemned economically.'[19] Forrester's offering to the anxious middle class is: 'Why not seek before all a method of distribution of income and of survival which will not be a function of remuneration for employment?' But the details of this approach or a strategy for its accomplishment are left to be developed. To his credit, the writer who initiated much of this concern for the end of work, Jeremy Rifkin, wrote of the need for a new social contract in which the Third Sector, that is the independent or volunteer sector, would make up for the failings of the market and government sectors to provide employment for increasing numbers of workers.[20]

While *L'horreur économique* offers neither a satisfying analysis of the problem nor a policy solution to it, Forrester does provide a summary of the emotional reaction of many French people, and indeed Europeans, to the complex of challenges and threats that globalization requires them, either as individual national economies or collectively as the European Union, to confront.

As should be expected, the contributions of political economists to this discussion are more analytical, more focused on causation and, as will be seen later, of more use with regard to policy formulation. The majority seek to make some accommodation to the rationality of globalization while at the same time rejecting endorsement of the Anglo-American model of liberalism. They reject the notion that globalization is the causal factor behind France's current economic and social problems, and they argue that France can find its own policy approach to adjusting to the evolving economic environment, an approach that will be in conformity with France's unique national values. A good example to begin with is Forrester's colleague at *Le Monde*, economics editor Erik Israelewicz, who has written a book explicitly in response to hers, *Ce monde qui nous attend.* Israelewicz argues that under the government of Lionel Jospin 'globalization has become in the space of several months not just THE cause but absolutely the explanation of everything.'[21] He agrees with Robert Reich who has so compellingly analyzed the transformation of the work place with emphasis placed on the rise of what he calls the 'symbolic analysts' and the fall of traditional manufacturing and personal service jobs.[22] In Israelewicz's words: 'the third phase of the industrial revolution, globalization, modifies the economy of production and of trade as well, naturally, as that of work.'[23] As a consequence of this transition, France must expect to see rising regional inequality, a growing disparity of income, persistent unemployment among workers who do not have the required education and skills, and insecurity of employment.

For Israelewicz the problem is not globalization, but rather the political leadership of France whose thinking, along with that of Forrester, is marked by 'extreme confusion with regard to the economic revolution under way,'[24] and who seem to be convinced either that France need not change its policies and its mentality or that the world will adopt France's approach. In either case, the leadership ignore the need to respond positively and actively to a developing economic environment which places a premium on flexibility and the ability to adjust to evolving production and distribution needs and to rapidly changing consumer demands. This same point is made by Alain Minc who finds it incredible that France can think itself to have a better approach (to globalization) than the rest of the world and to think it possible to continue its Colbertist model (of subsidies and state intervention) in a global context of deregulation and privatization.[25] Hans-Peter Martin and Harald Schumann, two Germans whose recent book was translated into French and has been widely circulated, argue the more general case, which nonetheless has relevance for France, that the globalization process has been the product of government action and that recognition of its negative consequences on social conditions and the ability of the state to look after the basic needs of its citizens requires that political leaders 'reestablish the primacy of politics over the economy.'[26] Alain de Benoist agrees that states themselves have created the globalized environment in which they 'no longer have any choice but to fall back on policies of pure competition, to the detriment of social cohesion.'[27] While these writers do not, as we shall see, agree on the most appropriate policy response for the government of France, they are in general agreement as to the nature of France's encounter with globalization.

Another point on which they agree is revulsion for the Anglo-American policy response to globalization and the need for France to find its own way. Even the self-proclaimed liberal Alain Minc finds that 'Capitalism has triumphed, but it leaves place for national variants,' and then examines the differences between the British, German, Dutch and American models of capitalism.[28] France, he states, must seek a path between total state and total Wall Street. Other writers reject the applicability to France of the disembedded self-regulating market in which everything: labor, land, goods, services and capital, are mere commodities to be bought and sold in markets that was so powerfully depicted by Karl Polanyi in 1944 in *The Great Transformation.* Israelewicz states that 'globalization is not the dictatorship of ultraliberalism.'[29] Martin and Schumann seek a viable and powerful European alternative to Anglo-Saxon free market extremism.[30] Philippe Arondel asserts it is necessary to renew the ties of social amity and to call forth the image of another France, of another nation based on the imperatives of justice and of solidarity rather than on dogmatic liberalism.[31] Minc argues that globalization imposes no single model on national economies: 'it allows us to be free to determine the terms of our social contract, the type of society we choose, the degree of solidarity that pleases us, with the sole condition that we continually strive not to deceive ourselves or to cheat.'[32]

Several writers have observed that while France experienced higher rates of unemployment than did the United States, this was for them more than off-set by the stagnant incomes and growing income inequality which have plagued the US in recent decades. As Daniel Cohen puts it: 'Never in the history of the US, nor elsewhere in the industrial world, has such an explosion of inequality been registered, with the salary of a corporate Chief Executive Officer rising from 30 to 150 times the salary of a worker during the period 1970 to 1990.'[33] These tendencies for growing inequality are manifest in France as well, but whereas Forrester would consider this to be the consequence of globalization, Cohen argues: '[i]t is manifestly absurd and demagogic to characterize as a failure what is in reality the difficulty industrialized countries have in resolving their internal conflicts over redistribution of the gains from globalization.'[34]

While this has in no way been a comprehensive survey of the thinking of French political economists with regard to globalization, it does convey the main features of their analysis at the most general level of abstraction. Globalization is seen to be clearly a feature of the current economic environment, but it should be seen as just the latest phase of a process of economic evolution. They are critical of those who would try to shield France from its effects through protectionism or through attachment to Colbertism, which in France is a reference to the policies of heavy-handed state intervention introduced by Louis XIV's comptroller general of finances in the latter part of the seventeenth century. They also argue that it is both possible and desirable for France to seek its own path or set of policies to adapt to these evolutionary changes since they explicitly include in their notion of the French welfare function arguments for both economic maximization and preservation of a distinctly national value set and way of life.

A second round of salvos was fired in 1999 and 2000. Forrester changed her critique from that of globalization to 'the fiasco of ultra-liberalism,' in *Une étrange dictature*, published in 2000.[35] Indeed, she argues that globalization does not require ultra-liberalism, defined as 'self-regulation of the economy through the mechanism of the market.' Rather ultra-liberalism was a conscious political choice exercised at the global level. It is not that the economy has triumphed over politics, but rather the reverse, with the culprit being 'the world of business, which has itself evolved into speculation.'[36] The key words in this world, as she sees it, are casino, competitiveness, Asian miracle, derivatives, and so forth. The result is a world in which 'all is sacrificed so that one exploiter is able to conquer another exploiter, essential infrastructure is destroyed, social programs are suppressed, a reactionary and regressive revolution is unleashed, and cynicism and de-industrialization are the rule.'[37] The dictatorship of the quest for profit also destroys democratic processes as power is transferred to a cartel of like-minded corporate leaders.

Much of her critique focuses on the events that have taken place in the United States during the past two decades, which are marked by massive unemployment and a slashing of government expenditure and the social programs it supports. She argues that they are the result of ultra-liberalism. The truth, of course, is that ultra-liberalism had its impact during the Reagan years in the form of an almost three-fold increase in the national debt that financed a tax cut and increased defense expenditures. The experience of the 1990s was one of economic growth, a reduction in the debt and falling unemployment, with Reagan's ultra-liberalism banished from center stage. Not only have millions of jobs been created, but the quality of those jobs has become a positive factor during the past three or four years.

When Forrester examines the French economic and political situation she has a clear preference for the so-called old economy of stability and little change. Caught in the transition from the status quo that privileged the managed economy of *les trente glorieuses* and the new information technology services economy with which France is trying to come to grips, for which she uses the term globalization, she resorts to an ideal-type of ultra-liberal capitalism that bears little relation to the mixed versions of capitalism found in, for example, the Netherlands, Scandinavia, Asia or, for that matter, North America – all of which have been reasonably successful in providing growth and employment for their citizens. Even in France unemployment has fallen by 25-30 per cent during the past two years while at the same time France was meeting the convergence criteria for monetary union: a reduction in both the government budget deficit and the government debt, and a lowering of the rate of inflation. So essentially Forrester fails to distinguish between the transition period and the end state.

While Jacques Généreux published his *Une raison d'espérer* a few months before the second Forrester book, his critique of her position is as relevant for that book as it is for the first. Looking backward, he argues, there is no *horreur économique* but rather an *horreur sociale*; looking forward, he concludes that this is not caused by economics but rather by politics. Specifically, what is involved is a lack of political will rather than the operation of economic laws.[38] He asks: 'Who deregulated financial markets? Who introduced the European Monetary System? Who gave priority to reducing inflation rather than to reducing unemployment? Of course, in all instances it was national governments responding to the wishes of the electorate.'[39] All economic change or transformation should be understood to involve costs, and it is the role of the political process to impose the compensatory mechanisms that bring us to Pareto optimality. Rather than halt the introduction of the economic rationality that Adam Smith demonstrated was available to us, as would Forrester, Généreux would have us reform the political processes and institutions and assert the political will that would generate a result that is acceptable to all.

Jacques Régnier poses the question whether we are in the first stages of an *horreur économique* or of a *nouvel âge d'or*, that is, a period of hordes of unemployed or one of robust economic growth.[40] Régnier opts for the latter in each pair of alternatives. He follows Généreux by also asking whether the unsatisfactory aspects of the current economic situation in France and throughout the world are the result of the principles upon which the relatively liberal global economy is based or of human failings.[41] For him, human failings in policy implementation have been and will continue to be crucial. As an example, he argues that the policy of refusing to accept change, flexibility and openness, *à la* Forrester, was followed by British governments during the 1960s and 1970s, that this led to the economic and social catastrophe which led to the right-wing policies of the Thatcher government. Both the catastrophe and the ensuing right-wing revolution can be avoided by a complex of government actions that promote the development of new goods and services and a flexibility and adaptability of institutions and processes. These actions must ensure macro-economic conditions favoring growth and micro-economic conditions that promote new supply.[42]

In a second book published in 2000, Daniel Cohen tries to put closure to the critics of globalization by reminding us of two things. First, the contemporary economic transformation is as yet unachieved. What it lacks is a set of social regulations and rules that is appropriate to the age. Cohen tells us, first, that as long as the influence of financial capital obscures the importance of human capital, to the degree that the conflict between private consumption and public consumption persists we will fail to enter this new age and, second, rather than work blindly to have more than our neighbor, he argues that even though technology liberates us progressively from need, it does not liberate us from technology itself. We must come to understand that 'health, education and sport are no less worthy as objects of consumption than an automobile or a washing machine.[43] Hardly new thoughts, but thoughts nonetheless that put this discussion in a proper perspective. The differences among these writers concerning the details of their preferred policy mix will emerge when we examine more closely the important question of France's economic performance in the context of globalization. It is to this that we now turn our attention.

THE FRENCH ECONOMY AND GLOBALIZATION

The concern over French economic performance is broadly focused on competitiveness, job creation, economic growth, several aspects of unemployment and, ultimately, France's position in the global economy. This chapter is not the place to examine all of these manifestations of unsatisfactory performance, so in this section we will relate the analysis of the economists included in this survey to the question of unemployment. Economists have identified a wide array of conditions that can be taken as the cause of high rates of unemployment, ranging from the fairly benign frictional and seasonal versions to those which indicate a profound challenge to existing economic activity.[44] In the broadest representation of the positions taken on this issue, there are two primary schools of thought. The first focuses on the understanding that if perfect competition obtained there would be no unemployment as the wage would rise and fall in response to changes in the demand for and supply of labor, with the equilibrium wage being the wage that equalized the number of workers who wish to work at that wage and the number of offers of employment employers are willing to make at that wage. From this point of view, any unemployment other than normal frictional or seasonal unemployment must by definition be due to some constraint on the ability of wages to fall to the full employment equilibrium wage. The second approach argues instead that since perfect competition is never attainable in the real world, actual unemployment is the consequence of macro-economic failures or of fundamental changes in the global economy. The latter include deindustrialization (transfer of industrial activity to Third World economies), technological unemployment, restructuring (a shift in the structure of production from manufacturing to services) and deteriorating competitiveness; clearly these could be subsumed under the rubric of globalization.

The array of positions that have been taken on unemployment is too extensive to be considered here and, as has been stated above, we will limit this discussion to the positions of the French economists included in this survey for the purpose of gaining a better understanding of their response to the phenomenon of globalization and the extent to which they relate unemployment to globalization. That is to say, we will at this time consider neither the argument of the Organization for Economic Cooperation and Development (OECD) that France's unemployment is caused by micro-economic factors such as labor market inflexibilities, high employee benefits and imperfect goods markets,[45] nor the academic debate about unemployment in Europe as a whole[46] since neither is germane to the focus of this introduction.

A brief *tour d'horison* shows that the economists referred to in the previous section, who would appear to represent the middle of the political spectrum from social democrat to liberal, are united in their general view on this question. Israelewicz is categorical in his conclusion that 'it is impossible to establish a serious relationship between the explosion of unemployment in Europe and the rise in economic power of Asia' and states that his intention in writing his book was 'to attempt to respond to the great fears that globalization has engendered in popular opinion.'[47] Minc is even blunter when he states that 'no one can demonstrate with quantitative argumentation that globalization has a decisive role in the rise in [French] unemployment.'[48] Cohen takes the somewhat softer position that in addition to globalization one must look to the shift to services, immigration, the weakening of trade unions, and deregulation as causes of France's unsatisfactory employment situation and states that 'the empirical relation between international trade and inequality is weak, indeed nonexistent.'[49] Lesourne rejects as the cause of France's unemployment two of the primary elements in globalization, international trade and the *franc fort* policy of linking the currency to the strong German Mark in the early 1990s.[50]

The consensus position of this group, then, is that France's problems with economic performance are not closely tied to globalization; each looks to factors internal to France, either to its structure or to its political philosophy. For Israelewicz, '[t]wo great needs confront France,...,first, individual mobility and, second, collective solidarity,... Without mobility one is economically dead,...,the new economy is, it is said, an economy of movement;'[51] without solidarity, stability will be fundamentally threatened by growing economic inequality both within and between nations. Cohen emphasizes the third industrial revolution, the information revolution, and argues that 'behind the screen of globalization or of the shift to services is a revolution in the technology of production which is the origin of the formidable explosion of inequality which is observed today,'[52] to which France must respond by adjusting to its new comparative advantage in more sophisticated goods. Minc locates France 'between antiquity and modernity, between an impossible retreat and a prosperous globalization,' and dreams of a France in which the political choice is 'between left-wing liberalism and right-wing liberalism.'[53] According to Lesourne: '[t]he increase in the number of unemployed is not at all mysterious. It results from the inadequate responses of French society to demographic, economic and technological phenomena that are clearly identified' and it is 'necessary [for France] to choose resolutely a path of moderate liberalism.'[54] However, Martin and Schumann warn that 'the policy of laissez faire demolishes permanently all social stability'[55] and Arondel adds that it is necessary 'to dare to escape the "new speak" of false prophets of neoliberalism and to offer to people the possibility of founding an existence emancipated from market totalitarianism.'[56] Thus, among these economists whose work has gained wide distribution in France, there is hardly agreement on the fundamental critique of France's economic performance, but none of them would agree with Forrester's assertion that globalization is the root cause of this unsatisfactory performance.

Globalization does, however, feature prominently in the analysis of these economists and it is of interest to examine how they see France in the context of this phenomenon and how it shapes France's future. The most striking feature they hold in common is their commitment to the notion that France can adapt to globalization without giving up what has become referred to as French exceptionalism. That is, France can seek a new comparative advantage and introduce such efficiency-enhancing measures as deregulation and privatization without attacking in a fundamental way *l'état providence,* France's combination of market interventions and generous social benefits. Israelewicz reminds us that 'France has succeeded [during the first two industrial revolutions] to manage the attendant changes while preserving the principle elements of its identity, the elements which constitute *l'exception française.*'[57] At some points they argue that the solution rests within France itself, while at others the importance of a collective European Union response is stressed. For Minc, the Euro, the common currency projected for some members of the European Union and the institutional changes that accompany it are the accelerator of change and the ultimate avatar of reform for France.[58] However, whereas Minc considers the market to be a state of nature and that to deny this is to invite the experience of the Soviet Union and Mao's China, Martin and Schumann argue that Europe must find a model that is closer to the managed capitalism of John Maynard Keynes and Ludwig Erhard than it is to free-marketeers Milton Friedman and Friedrich von Hayek. For them the choice is between the 'Anglo-Saxon path of social cannibalism' and 'the European Union which represents a unique opportunity to reestablish the capacity of the state to take action for the common good.'[59] Israelewicz believes that the European Union offers France and the other member states 'the opportunity to seek in common a European model.'[60] Cohen takes this a bit further, arguing that it is naive to think that markets in themselves are sufficient to create an international social cohesion and suggesting that 'Europe can play a fundamental role: in seeking a cohesion to offer to an international equilibrium, in offering itself as an example in this regard, and in giving its support to a set of rules of the game which should accompany globalization.'[61]

Others see dangers to France in a European integration process that is dominated by financial interests. Arondel, for example, argues that the monetarist-inspired Euro and the convergence criteria impose on those states aspiring to membership a fiscal austerity which will completely destabilize the European social model and pose a strong threat to *l'exception française.*[62] Milner considers the forces of globalization, and specifically the Maastricht treaty, as an attack on the well-being of working people, but argues that the expanding bureaucracy he sees as one of its consequences offers hope for the professional classes - the salaried bourgeoisie.[63]

A POSITIVE NOTE

Throughout this chapter we have examined the critiques of the impacts of globalization on the French economy and society that have been offered in a set of economics writings which have been given wide circulation in France during the past couple of years. Most of their analysis has been made public in specific reaction to what Israelewicz referred to as *l'erreur économique* in obvious reference to the title of the book by Forrester. Beyond this critique they do offer some thoughts about the positive side of globalization and the economic strategy that should be followed by France, and by Europe, in the new globalized context, and we would like to close this chapter with reference to this aspect of their work.

While certain aspects of the American model are admired, specifically its appropriateness for the development of new technologies,[64] its stable and homogeneous space and 'strategic serenity,'[65] and its good fortune in having a large domestic market,[66] all are repelled by the growing inequality in the United States and the ideologically based destruction of the ability of the state to take action for the common good. In addition to expressing the opinion that the days of US dominance are over, Israelewicz argues that the German economic model is also in crisis due to its incapacity to deal successfully with new technologies and new competitors; his conclusion is that 'globalization tends in reality to favor an economic re-equilibration between [France and Germany].'[67] Martin and Schumann see the material advantages of globalization but are also keenly aware of its threat to democratic processes. They state that in the Europe of the Euro, the choice lies in the history of the two great European powers: 'the democratic current shown in the Paris of 1789 or the totalitarian current which swept through Berlin in 1933.'[68]

Globalization for these French economists, then, is seen not so much as a threat as an opportunity for France, and Europe, to fashion a collective response which is nonetheless in conformity with traditional French, or European, values. With regard to unemployment the solution lies not at all in some new form of protectionism. Cohen argues that '[t]his new revolution carries with it a formidable deconcentration of activities which stimulates the quest for specific comparative advantages,' and warns of the dangers of the protectionist strategy, whether by the nation or, as in the example of Apple Computers, by its major companies.[69] Canadian economist Robert Lacroix states that the inability of France and Germany, and Quebec, to introduce the institutional changes required for a globalized economic environment, and so readily accepted by the United States, is precisely why these economies have not been able to replicate the transition to full employment experienced by the US.[70]

This, of course, is the challenge to France. Throughout the writings that have been examined here one cannot help but notice a powerful reluctance to stray far from the traditional centrality of the state as a decision-maker. Without an explicit recognition of the need to consider a fundamental rethinking of this aspect of French economic policy an outsider cannot help but wonder whether the hope placed in a European solution to France's unsatisfactory economic performance is not just a response to an inability to find solutions within France itself.

Before we begin our examination of how globalization has affected France in the major areas of economic policy, we would like to discuss the evolution in thinking, in the broadest sense, of its most recent governments. It is always an interesting exercise to try to relate the approach taken by a nation's leadership to the debate among its intellectuals.

NOTES

1. This period of growth, given its name by Jean Furastié, has been characterized as an 'anomaly' by Moses Abramovits, *Thinking about Growth*, Cambridge, MA: Harvard University Press, 1989.
2. André Straus, 'La croissance en France de 1945 à la crise,' *Histoire économique de la France au XXe siècle*, Les Cahiers Français, No. 255, March-April, 1992, pp. 22-32.
3. Vincent Gourdon, 'Les étrangers en France,' *Histoire économique de la France au XXe siècle*, Les Cahiers Français, No. 255, March-April 1992, p. 103.
4. *OECD Country Surveys: France*, 1995, Paris: Organization for Economic Cooperation and Development, 1996, p. 158.
5. Barrie Axford, *The Global System: Economics, Politics and Culture*, New York: St. Martin's Press, 1995, p. 121.
6. Alain Buzelay, *Intégration et désintégration européennes*, Paris: Economica, 1996, p. 5.
7. For a review of the concerted pressure exerted by the *Länder* begun in 1987, see Joachim Bauer, *Europa der Regionen*, Schriften zum Europäischen Recht, Band 9, Berlin: Duncker & Humblot, 1992, pp. 5 to 9, and especially the '10 Münchner Theses zur Europapolitik,' p. 13 to 17.
8. Rudolf Hrbek, 'The German Länder and EC integration,' *Journal of European Integration*, Vol. XV, Nos 2 & 3, 1992, p. 180.
9. Claude de Granrut, *Europe, le temps des Régions*, Paris: Librairie Générale du Droit et de la Jurisprudence, 1994, p. 44.
10. Ibid., pp. 42 and 43.
11. See, for example: Peter Hall, 'Forces shaping urban Europe,' *Urban Studies*, Vol. 30, No. 6, 1993, pp. 883-898.

12. Jacques Lesourne, *Vérités et mensonges sur le chômage*, Paris: Editions Odile Jacob, 1995, esp. chs 1 and 6.
13. For a review of the less dramatic but nonetheless important consequences of deteriorating economic opportunity see: Amartya Sen, 'Inequality, unemployment and contemporary Europe,' *International Labour Review*, Vol. 136, No. 2, Summer 1997, pp. 155-172.
14. For one such analysis, see Benjamin Barber, *Jihad vs. McWorld*, New York: Balantine, 1996.
15. Viviane Forrester, *L'horreur économique*, Paris: Fayard, 1996.
16. Ibid., p. 22.
17. Ibid., p. 193.
18. Ibid., pp. 23 and 14.
19. Jean-Claude Milner, *Le salaire de l'idéal*, Paris: Éditions du Seuil, 1997, p. 116.
20. Jeremy Rifkin, *The End of Work*, New York: G.P. Putnam, 1995, chs 16 to 18.
21. Erik Izraelewicz, *Ce monde qui nous attend,* Paris: Grasset, 1997, p. 19.
22. Robert Reich, *The Work of Nations*, New York: Vintage, 1992, esp. Part Three.
23. Izraelewicz, *Ce monde qui nous attend*, p. 131.
24. Ibid., p. 17.
25. Alain Minc, *La mondialisation heureuse*, Paris: Plon, 1997, p. 196.
26. Hans-Peter Martin and Harald Schumann, *Le piège de la mondialisation*, Paris: Solin-Actes Sud, 1997, pp. 18 and 22.
27. Alain de Benoist, 'Confronting globalization,' *Telos*, no. 108, Summer 1996, p. 123.
28. Minc, *La mondialisation heureuse*, p. 221.
29. Israelewicz, *Ce monde qui nous attend* ,p. 261.
30. Martin and Schumann, *Le piège de la mondialisation*, p. 300.
31. Philippe Arondel, *L'homme-marché*, Paris: Desclée de Broulwer, 1997, p. 125.
32. Minc, *La mondialisation heureuse*, p. 10.
33. Daniel Cohen, *Richesse du monde, pauvretés des nations*, Paris: Flammarion 1997, p. 67.
34. Ibid,, p. 127.
35. Viviane Forrester, *Une étrange dictature*, Paris: Fayard, 2000.
36. Ibid., p. 22.
37. Ibid., p. 30.
38. Jacques Généreux, *Une raison d'espérer*, Paris: Pocket, 2000, pp. 41 to 42.
39. Ibic., p. 53.
40. Jacques Régniez, *Nouvel âge d'or ou horreur économique?*, Paris: Presses Universitaire de France, 1999, p. 175.
41. Ibid., p. 8.
42. Ibid., p. 184.
43. Daniel Cohen, *Nos temps modernes*, Paris: Flammarion, 1999, pp. 150 to 151.
44. For a review of most of these potential causes, see: Lesourne, *Vérités et monsonges sur le chômage*, ch. 2.
45. *OECD Economic Surveys: France, 1997*, Paris: Organization for Economic Cooperation and Development, 1997, Part III.
46. See Stephen Nickell, 'Unemployment and labor market rigidities: Europe versus North America,' *Journal of Economic Perspectives*, Vol. 11, No. 3, Summer 1997, pp. 55 to 74.

47. Israelewicz, *Ce monde qui nous attend*, pp. 131 and 17.
48. Minc, *La mondialisation heureuse*, pp. 30 and 31.
49. Cohen, *Richesse du monde, pauvretés des nations*, p. 69 and 67.
50. Lesourne, *Vérités et monsonges sur le chômage,* ch. 4.
51. Israelewicz, *Ce monde qui nous attend*, pp. 253 to 255.
52. Cohen, *Richesse du monde, pauvretés des nations*, p. 74.
53. Minc, *La mondialisation heureuse*, pp. 227 and 222.
54. Lesourne, *Vérités et monsonges sur le chômage*, p. 202.
55. Martin and Schumann, *Le piège de la mondialisation*, p. 293.
56. Arondel, *L'homme-marché*, p. 126.
57. Israelewicz, *Ce monde qui nous attend*, p. 252.
58. Minc, *La mondialisation heureuse*, p. 225.
59. Martin and Schumann, *Le piège de la mondialisation*, pp. 301 to 305.
60. Israelewicz, *Ce monde qui nous attend*, p. 247
61. Cohen, *Richesse du monde, pauvretés des nations*, p. 99.
62. Arondel, *L'homme-marché*, p. 36.
63. Milner, *Le salaire de l'idéal*, pp. 111 and 112.
64. Israelewicz, *Ce monde qui nous attend*, p. 205.
65. Minc, *La mondialisation heureuse*, p. 36.
66. Martin and Schumann, *Le piège de la mondialisation*, p. 278.
67. Israelewicz, *Ce monde qui nous attend*, pp. 245 and 247.
68. Martin and Schumann, *Le piège de la mondialisation*, p. 306.
69. Cohen, *Richesse du monde, pauvretés des nations*, p. 155.
70 Robert Lacroix, 'Mondialisation, emploi et chômage,' *L'Actualité économique, Revue d'analyse économique*, Vol. 73, No. 4, December 1997, p. 639.

2 The French Economy since the Second World War

The wonderful growth of *les trente glorieuses* had focused attention on technological innovation and progress in economic management. The events of recent years suggest a longer-term perspective and to better understand the long term, we must consider changes in ideologies to be the most powerful determinants.[1] The progress of individualism during the second millennium is the final triumph of a conception of the relationship of humans and their Creator, and that of men and society.

These are the words of Henri Mendras.[2] Actually, the primary motor of economic growth for France has in essence been the array of technical innovations between 1945 and 1974; and then, after 1971, the West transformed itself under a renewal of liberalism, [3] a movement in which France participated albeit with some delay. The spread of technological progress throughout the world accelerated following the Second World War, principally under the aegis of the support of the United States.[4] In France, this diffusion of technology took a unique path since it was orchestrated by the state, consecrating the 'triumph of a model of voluntarist management of technological change.'[5] Here, then, is how during the third quarter of the century the French approach can be characterized: technological and ideological innovations and state management. The fundamental trait of the French at the end of the century is ideological innovation in which the market is rediscovered, an innovation that is truly destructive of the traditional French ideal of the economic role of the state.

This radical double transformation of the French, of the managers of their economy (through innovation and the role of the state), which appears only with the perspective of the distance of time, can be seen in the cyclical context that is characterized by three distinct forms of transformation: (a) an industrial economy dominated by the state that is replaced by a service economy which is more open to external contact, (b) a social-protectionist state that has had to reorient itself toward an economy of the market and competition and (c) the replacement of inflation as a policy concern by that of unemployment. These three changes schematically characterize the apparent evolution of the French economy. It is however necessary that one not ignore the political desire to regulate everything, which remains a feature of French culture until today, even in the face of the objective of the European Union to affirm a liberalized, competitive, single market.

In order to show accurately what has happened and what is to take place in the French economy, we will begin with an overview of the structural evolutions of the period 1945–98. Central to this discussion will be the succession of countercyclical measures or plans to struggle against inflation, to assure economic growth and to treat unemployment. These fundamental economic-social roles of the state will be the object of more extensive treatment in a later chapter. After briefly presenting the entire period of 1945–2000, we will focus more precisely on 1965–73 as an introduction to a deeper study of the last quarter of the century.

THE PERIOD 1945–98

After the Second World War, it was necessary to reconstruct the French economy. Industry was far less active than before the war. The steel industry of Lorraine produced only 10 per cent of what it produced in 1939. A similar situation existed in the coal industry where the productivity per miner had fallen to half of its pre-war level. Industrial capital was old (25 years of usage on average) and transportation was in a desperate strait. For one example, only one railroad locomotive in six was operable. Much of France's capital equipment had been pillaged by Germany. In France, many villages and towns had been destroyed (2.5 million buildings had been destroyed), and the war resulted in the death of over 600,000 individuals; 3.5 million French citizens had been obliged to work for Germany; 1 million prisoners (out of 2 million that had been taken to Germany) returned to France in 1945 unable to obtain clothing or food. There was a shortage of manpower for at least 20 years following the war in France, but in this period individuals were ready to work in whatever kind of employment they could get. The underground economy (the black market, the 'D' system and the traffic with the American military) became as important in 1945 as the official rationed economy (with one ration coupon providing 1500 calories per day). The GDP fell 50 per cent between 1938 and 1945. Scarcity reigned until the beginning of the 1950s of the basic products of consumption and, until the 1970s, of housing. As always following a period of conflict, this situation explains how the French state was able to expand its powers to take command and to direct the economy and to increase both taxes and public expenditure. This controlling and centralizing orientation was reinforced by the political weight of the *Conseil national de la résistance* but was tempered by intellectuals such as those of the less powerful *Comité général d'etudes*. The state established after the Second World War as the chief operating officer of France the planner and the capitalist, it made the fundamental allocational and distributional choices of society, and it named the bosses of the large state owned or controlled enterprises. France had become, more than before, a Jacobin centralized republic. Despite this, the French economy caught up rapidly with those of the United States, the United Kingdom, and Germany.

During the 1950s, the French discovered the mass-consumption society and modernity at the same time, and there was a true revolution and an economic and industrial transformation of the economy in all aspects. During this decade, the hours of work diminished gradually, largely through the effect of changes in the law, which was characteristic of both France and Europe as a whole. Unfortunately, towards the end of the 1960s and the beginning of the 1970s, the increase in productivity slowed (the marginal productivity of capital eventually became negative) and the French economy lost its competitiveness. The global economic crisis developed in 1974 following the first great petroleum shock. The French were captured by the anxieties of facing a new world, of meeting competition from the rest of Europe, of the emerging technologies of information and communication, of globalization of consumption, enterprises and markets. This was becoming a world in which everything had become flexible and precarious and where legal monopoly rents were replaced by competitive profits.[6]

In the 1970s, there were profound social changes following this astonishing phase of growth, *les trente glorieuses*: a social revolution succeeded an economic revolution. In the late 1990s and the early 2000s, France is at the heart of a period of transition, so to speak, sitting between two chairs. The past has gained for the French a taste for transfers of revenue and a preference for security of employment and of activity. Anxiety comes when the immediate future threatens instability, internationality, the exodus of more and more of the young to jobs abroad, and the incomes that come from new but also more interesting employment possibilities. As a response, the reply is demands for protectionism, xenophobia, anti-Americanism and the condemnation of the market, which increases in the popular layers of French society. To take one example, there is an economic consequence of the very weak rate of creation of new enterprises.

This half-century of the economy can actually be divided into two great sub-periods that are quite distinct: the period after the war to the crisis (1945–73) and during the economic crisis (1974–97). Chapter 8 will be devoted to a more detailed analysis of the two years 1998–2000. The distinction between these two periods is evident with regard notably to the rates of economic growth, as is shown in Table 2.1. For 2000–1 the rate of GDP increase was 3.3 per cent and the rate of unemployment had fallen to just over 9 per cent. The detailed study of inflation and of unemployment will be the subject

Table 2.1: GDP, inflation and unemployment

	1945–50	1951–73	1974–84	1985–89	1990–98
GDP	10.0	5.4	2.2	3.1	1.8
Inflation	36.0	5.0	10.5	3.0	2.0
Unemployment	1.2	1.8	6.2	10.0	11.3

Note: figures are for average annual percentage rate of increase.

Source: *Annuaire Statistique de la France*, Paris: INSEE, various years

of Chapter 5. Here we will focus on economic growth, investment and profits. Over the long term, the rate of economic growth diminished from 6 per cent in the 1950s to 2 per cent during the 1990s with a trough occurring roughly every 18 years. Economic growth continued until about 1974, and the fall was very brutal and deep: in 1974–5, the rate of unemployment rose from 2 per cent to 4 per cent. The break of August 1974 began a crisis that extended for a half-century, not only in France but also throughout Europe and in many other parts of the global economy. The rate of economic growth weakened through the entire world and inflation rose dramatically, particularly in France to over 10 per cent in 1974, 1975 and 1982; but then it began to disappear, giving place more recently to periods of deflation. Concomitantly, the rate of unemployment of 1 or 2 per cent before 1975 rose rather rapidly until it reached about 13 per cent in the mid-1990s. Long-term unemployment developed to an extraordinary extent and contributed to the phenomenon of exclusion (which is currently observed throughout most of the EU today) which has yet to begin to slow down.

During the period 1945–75, the economy was marked by an inflationary crisis which characterized a France in a period of strong growth; from 1975 to 1995 there were crises of stagflation (surging inflation, reduced economic growth and increased unemployment); and since 1995, growth has increased again, inflation has slowed through most of the developed world, but unemployment continued unabated until the peak of 1997. It seems today that unemployment is linked to weakness in the creation of new firms, to excesses of rigidity (regulations) and to heavy charges on employers (social and fiscal contributions), to inadequate or inappropriate training and education of the young, and to an obsolescence which affects the qualifications of older workers, rather than to globalization which many assume to be the case.

We can distinguish the two distinct periods of macro-economic performance since the Second World War, each of which is composed of sub-periods (see Table 2.2).

Table 2.2: Post-Second World War macro-economic periods of the French economy

1945-1973:	persistence of inflation, Fordist economy, colonial war, industrial changes and an opening of the economy
1945–1955:	reconstruction and establishment of the welfare state
1955–1968:	economic growth and opening of the economy
1968–1973:	stagflation
1973–1998:	persistence of unemployment; de-industrialization, the new poverty and exclusion, public sector deficits
1973–1983:	crisis, unemployment and slowing growth
1983–1998:	liberalization and profound change
1998–2001:	return of economic growth

In the section that follows we will discuss each of these periods and their principle characteristics. In Chapter 8, we will suggest what is in store for the French economy in the near future, in the context of globalization and the rapid development of new technologies of information and communication.

THE FIRST SUB-PERIOD: 1945–73

These are the years in which the French economy experienced its most impressive macroeconomic performance, in terms of economic growth, inflation and unemployment. We will examine it by treating five major elements that contributed to this remarkable achievement, which has subsequently been referred to as *les trente gloriouses*, or the 30 glorious years.

The Rise of the Power of the State as an Economic and Social Actor

The economy of France cannot be understood without an appreciation of the preponderant role of the state in the economy since 1945. The central role of the French state as the motor of the economy developed rapidly in the post-war period and continued strengthening until the reforms of the 1980s. Successive French governments (very numerous under the Fourth Republic from 1945–58) made the state the premier capitalist of Europe (after the Soviet Union), controlling around 35 per cent of French productive capital. The state determined the direction of investments and structural transformations and it also determined or influenced the primary equilibria in the economy (budgetary, external, monetary, social, geographic, and inter-occupational categories). The state continually intervened in countercyclical policy using about 30 plans of stabilization (to counter inflation and monetary

23

depreciation) and of recovery (by stimulation of aggregate demand). It used emergency measures (transfers and legislation in the face of social crises, strikes and protests) and enacted laws and ordinances included in the approximately 520,000 new legal texts each year. The French state became the most interventionist in Europe. This explains why the French spend so much of their time protesting and attempting to exert pressure on public officials with the intent of obtaining transfers and privileges.

But meanwhile, something developed which came to menace the power of the central republican government: the development of what have become the central supranational institutions of the contemporary European economic structure. The Marshall Plan (1947) furnished Europe with $12 million in reconstruction assistance, of which 23 per cent went to France, distributed by the Economic Cooperation Administration (ECA), a part of the Organization for European Economic Cooperation (OEEC). Europe began to construct itself while anticipating developments towards the twenty-first century when the state would lose some of its economic power to the benefit of pan-European and global organizations and institutions, such as the European Union and the General Agreement on Tariffs and Trade (now the World Trade Organization), and trading would evolve from national and colonial to European markets and then global markets. National firms would, of course, gradually be forced to adjust to increasing competition. The European Coal and Steel Community, the Common Market, then the European Union form the skeletal structure of such a Europe, and then the Single Market and adoption of the Euro brought Europe to its present state of integration.

The Great Economic Growth of *Les Trente Glorieuses*

From 1945 to 1975 the French economy experienced the 30 glorious years, that is to say the 30 years of almost continuous economic growth in the order of 5–7 per cent per year, thanks largely to its opening to the outside world following 1959. Unfortunately, they were 30 years that were marked by crises of resurgent inflation. Throughout this first part sub-period, the years 1945–58 showed a rate of annual growth of gross domestic product of 3–6 per cent (excluding the years 1945–9), a rate of unemployment that was continually less than 2 per cent and a rate of inflation that was rather erratic at an average of about 10 per cent per year. On the other hand, during the years 1959–73, the opening of the economy to the outside world, primarily through a reduction in tariff rates, allowed the rate of economic growth to rise to between 4 and 8 per cent per year, but with unemployment rising from 2 to 3 per cent, a reflection of the social cost of the transition. Table 2.3 indicates the extent of improvement of purchasing power of salaries that developed during the years 1960–70. In 25 years the purchasing power of salaries tripled. In fact, during the 1950s and 1960s almost all countries of the industrial world

Table 2.3: Purchasing power, salaries and prices from 1945 to 1976

	1949	1955	1967	1976
Salaries	100	200	514	1516
Retail Prices	100	143	242	474
Purchasing Power	100	141	213	320

Note: 100 = 1949.

Source: Antoine Prost, *Petite histoire de la France au XXè siècle*, Paris: Armand Colin, 1992

experienced strong economic growth until the crisis of the 1970s, as is indicated in Table 2.4.

Table 2.4: Growth and productivity in the long run %

Period	Average annual growth of GDP				Average annual growth of GDP per hour worked (2)			
	1870-1950	1950-1973	1973-1984	1973-1993	1870-1950	1950-1973	1973-1984	1973-1993
France	1.4	5.1	2.2	2.4	1.9	5.1	3.4	2.1
United States	3.5	3.7	2.3	2.4	2.3	2.6	1.0	.5
Italy	1.5	5.5	2.6	2.7	1.5	5.8	2.5	2.4
Germany	2.1	6.0	1.7	2.2	1.5	6.0	3.0	2.0
United Kingdom	1.6	3.0	1.1	1.9	1.4	3.1	2.4	1.9
Japan	2.2	9.7	3.8	3.8	1.6	8.0	3.2	2.7

Notes: a) Germany was unified by 1993, and b) Labor productivity is for the period 1973—93.

Sources: P. Maddison, *Journal of Economic Literature*, June 1987; A. Maddison, *Les phases du développement capitaliste*, Paris: Economica, 1984; A. Beitone, M. Parodi, and B.Simler, *L'économie et la société française au second XXè siècle*, Paris: Armand Colin, 1994, Table 1; OECD

The French economy recovered from its pre-war gap in performance with one of the highest rates of economic growth among the industrialized countries. After the 1970s, France surpassed the United Kingdom to become the fourth largest exporter in the world of goods and the second largest of services. The economic and social disruptions during these decades are clearly shown by an unequal expansion of activities favoring the third sector. The structure of output developed first in favor of industry with de-industrialization not really beginning until the 1970s.

Table 2.5: Primary, secondary and tertiary Sectors %

	1949	1959	1959 (1)	1973	1985
Primary agriculture	12.8	11.1	9.7	6.4	3.9
Processed agriculture	7.9	7.3	4.0	4.4	4.7
Manufacturing	44.8	48.0	41.0	37.4	31.5
Services	34.5	33.6	45.3	51.8	59.9

Note: (1) In 1959 there was a change in the definitions of sectors.

Source: Jean-François Eck, *Histoire de l'économie française depuis 1945*, Paris: Armand Colin, 1988, pp. 12, 28 and 45

Modernization and massive investments in agriculture and in industry were financed differently. Banks such as the *Credit Agricole*, which benefited from special statutes, financed agricultural investments with the assistance of government grants. The investment in industry, however, was assured by the state from the beginning, then by public organizations specially created for this purpose. The rate of investment increased until 1974 (from 22 per cent of GDP in 1950 to 32 per cent in 1974), with the proportion of productive investment being on average 70 per cent of the total, while the state share fell from 64 per cent in 1950 to 20 per cent in 1973.[7]

According to the work of Carré, Dubois and Malinvaud, technological progress explains 60 per cent of the growth of this period, during which GDP increased on average 5.4 per cent per year. They argue that this is the only period in which the rejuvenation of productive capital participated positively in growth. This growth was caused by massive investment during the years following the war, by a cost of capital that was relatively advantageous, and by the shortage of labor power. This orientation of growth represents a marked tendency for the substitution of capital for labor in the major part of economic activities. The use of capital intensified, for example in the textile industry, with the daily division of work into three shifts of eight hours each so the machines could be used 24 hours each day.

The Evolution of Sectoral Structures and Opening of the Economy

In the 1950s, the French economy was rural and protectionist. After 1960, substantial migration caused the active labor force to leave the farms to seek employment in the service sector. The initiatives of the EEC and GATT accelerated the arrival of this phase of globalization. The state as entrepreneur reindustrialized France during a period of 20 years prior to the de-industrialization that occurred during the last quarter of the century. By 1973 the proportion of the working population in agriculture had been reduced to a third of its level in 1945. This change was intensified by the decrease in real prices of agriculture products from 1949 to 1961. An index of agricultural prices fell from 180 in 1949 to 130 in 1966, to 125 in 1973, and to 100 in 1980. By 1995 it was down to 60 – it had dropped by 40 per cent in just 15 years. Stabilization of agricultural revenues was achieved only through continually increasing subsidies. Agricultural production actually increased on average by 4 per cent per year until the 1980s, after which the rate of growth decreased to about 2 per cent. But the distribution of meats, fruits, vegetables,

Table 2.6: Active population by sector of employment

	1949	1959	1973	1981	1985	1994	1997
Primary	29.2	22.1	10.9	8.6	7.5	5.1	4.0
Secondary	35.0	35.2	37.8	35.2	30.6	25.9	25.0
Tertiary	35.8	42.7	51.3	56.2	61.9	69.0	71.0

Sources: Statistique Annuaire de la France, Paris: INSEE, various issues; and Jean-François Eck, Histoire de l'économie française depuis 1945, Paris: Armand Colin, 1988, pp. 12, 28 and 45

milk and grain became very complex and to a considerable degree monopolized, due to laws controlling price and quality and the development of additional layers of intermediaries, each of which was entitled to a legal rent. These policies assured the stabilization of agricultural revenues with subsidies continually increasing. During the 1970s, French agriculture represented more than a quarter of European production.

The share of the labor force in industry remained rather constant at about 35 per cent until 1973. The rapid opening of the economy to commercial exchange with European countries, and then with the entire world, modified economic relations, and the heads of medium-sized enterprises and large firms became decreasingly protectionist. But many long-established situations were called into question, generating protests, lobbying, and strikes, which had been decreasing since 1953. Economic activity then turned toward exports, and commerce with the Franc Zone fell rapidly, by 84 per cent from 1959 to 1973, with the increase being exchange of goods and services within the European Economic Community. This explains why agriculture became very export oriented, improving from a deficit of Fr2 billion in 1959 to a surplus of Fr6 billion in 1972.

The first effect of the opening to Europe following the establishment of the European Community in 1959 was improvement of the management of firms, and therefore an increase in their productivity, in addition to the reorientation of productive activities toward new markets and new products. The state-controlled industrial enterprises increased their competitiveness, although with some difficulty. The manufacturing sector played a major role until the crisis of 1973, as it was managed and nourished by the state in the decade following the war. Indeed, it was transformed more profoundly during the 20 years following the Second World War than it was during the preceding 100 years. The production of intermediate consumption goods (semi-finished products) and industrial equipment (capital goods for firms and households) developed more rapidly than that of final consumption goods, and this difference was accentuated again in the years of the 1960s. Table 2.7 shows how industry productivity had been declining beginning in the early 1970s.

Table 2.7: Value-added per active person % annual increase

	Agriculture	Manufacturing	Market services
1951–57	5.1	4.1	3.9
1957–63	6.3	5.5	2.9
1963–69	6.5	5.6	2.6
1969–73	8.3	5.1	3.3
1973–79	4.2	4.1	1.6
1979–84	5.2	2.8	0.9

Source: A. Beitone, M. Parodi and B. Simler, *L'économie et la société française au second XXè siècle*, Paris: Armand Colin, 1994, vol. 1

French industry became more specialized after 1959, giving way in many sectors to increased imports. Imported goods amounted to only 8 per cent of consumption in 1959, but rose to 19 per cent in 1969 and to 25 per cent in 1973. By 2000 this figure had risen to about 30 per cent. Finally, it is necessary for us to note, leaving further development to a subsequent chapter, the planning and public industrial policies representing the foundation of the French economy during the 30 years. The public sector was enlarged by nationalizations (*Electricité de France, Gaz de France, Sociétés pétrolières publiques, Commissariat à l'Energie Atomique*, the Coal Industry of France, naval and aeronautic construction, Renault, banks and insurance companies, and so on) and its influence is also extended through the importance of public purchases of goods and services. The French state protected its great firms from foreign competition for as long as it could, following the model of monopolistic state capitalism.

Changes in Consumption

National income expanded significantly between 1950 and 1975 and consumers enjoyed increased quantity and variety of goods and services, as France moved into the world of mass consumption. The rate of saving increased from 12 per cent to 20 per cent of gross domestic product by 1973; however, it then declined in the ensuing years until its original 1949 level was reached in the 1990s. Households accounted for 80 per cent of national revenue in the 1950s and 1960s and this rose to 85 per cent in 1983. This latter year can be considered to be the last year in which redistribution was preferred to efficiency. By the end of the 1990s household revenue had fallen to 70 per cent of GDP. Social transfers increased annually at a pace of about 8 per cent in real value until 1983, and they accounted for 5 per cent of GDP in 1938, 15 per cent in 1949, 24 per cent in 1973, 36 per cent in 1990, and 30 per cent in 1998. An increase in the standard of living, new technologies, reduced prices for manufactured goods and a profound social evolution modified consumer behavior to a noticeable degree. In fact, French consumers devoted less of their total expenditures to food while the part devoted to housing more than doubled, as indicated in Table 2.8.

Table 2.8: Structure of household consumption, as percentage of total expense

	1949	1960	1970	1980	1990	1999
Food	60	46	36	29	26	22
Housing	12	21	26	27	27	28
Health	6	7	7	8	10	16
Transport and telecommunication	6	10	13	17	17	16
Culture and leisure	17	17	18	20	20	18

Note: The figures for 1980 do not add up to 100 per cent due to a change in definitions.

Source: *Comptes de la Nation*, Paris: INSEE

Money and Finance

The Bank of France was nationalized following the Second World War, and management of the banks and control of credit was given to it under the supervision of the Minister of Finance and the Economy. In 1948, the Fund for the Modernization of Equipment was created and it became the *Fonds de Développement Economique et Social* in 1955; this was the basic source of financing for capital until the beginning of the 1970s. A large number of bank loans were made as grants with the objective of directing investment or the construction of housing, and an extensive system of subsidies was put in place. The rediscount of commercial drafts of the *Caisse des Dépôts et Consignations* (a Public Treasury department) was facilitated. Finally, the public treasury was at the center of a financial circulation system that was very compartmentalized until 1966. It was the true banker of the economy, self-financed through the Bank of France and obligating the banks to hold in their portfolios a minimum number of short- and medium-term public obligations. Until the reforms of 1966, money and finance for France were characterized by (a) a compartmentalized system (the Public Treasury circulation); (b) no real market for either money or finance; and (c) strict control by the state.

The Vichy government (established during the German occupation in 1941) created the Association of French Banks, with obligatory membership for all banks and financial institutions, both public and private. After the war, other organs were also created such as the National Council of Credit and the Commission for Control of Banks, giving the state total control of the creation of money and intermediation between savings and investment. For 60 years, collection of savings had been a state monopoly. Furthermore, parallel to industrial nationalization (steel, coal, energy, and so on) in 1945, the four largest French banks were nationalized with approximately 55 per cent of all deposits. The compartmentalized characteristic of this system distinguished the banks of deposit, banks of business, and banks of medium- and long-term credit. All financial organs and monetary institutions belonged to a single category. Alongside the banks, there was the *Credit Agricole*, Popular Banks and the French Bank for International Trade created in 1946, all benefiting from special statutes. Finally, many public institutions directly managed by the state came to enforce the position of the state as the controller of the economy through various methods of financing. Even specialized financial institutions in consumer credit were totally under the control of the state.

After the two devaluations of the franc in 1957 and 1958 (by 20 per cent and then by an additional 17.5 per cent), the so-called 'Circle of the Treasury' was criticized by Jacques Rueff as a source of inflation. Until 1966, French inflation was greater than that of other large countries (5.6 per cent a year on average), with money creation financing more public expenditures and deficits than consumption. A true banking revolution, the first great liberalization from the control of the state, took place in 1966–7 with the opening of the banks to competition, the end of compartmentalization, the suppression of the administrative authorization of the opening of agencies, the concentrations of publicly owned financial institutions, the new merged *Banque Nationale de Paris*, and the appearance of the Visa card. Since this time, payment of interest on deposits on current account has been legally forbidden, with the objective of favoring long-term savings, and bank money (through checks on banks and through Visa and other credit cards) developed very rapidly.

In 1973, the Bank of France received a new statute that was supposed to make it a guardian of the value of money; however, it remained the lender of last resort. Rediscount was used decreasingly except for medium-term credit largely in support of exports, and even this disappeared in 1986 with a new

30

refinancing policy. Clearly monetary markets were in a period of transition. Eventually they would become both the regulator of the value of money and the means of financing consumption and producers. In this way they would be taking over from the state functions of the state that had become rather ineffectual. However, intervention by the state was not abandoned totally. In 1968, controls were established limiting loans and they continued through the 1970s. Finally, the subsequent evolution of money and financial markets and institutions shows very well the extent to which the French ideological revolution caused the state progressively to cede its place in the economy to market processes.

SECOND SUB-PERIOD: 1973-1988

The second of the two periods was marked by the introduction of two new phenomena: internationalization and stagflation. The end of the 30 glorious years was marked by a sharp decline in both economic growth and productivity gains and by steadily rising employment in all the countries of the world. France is not an exception, as indicated in Table 2.9. During the last quarter of a century, French economic growth slowed steadily, while that of the United States declined only slightly. The German Rhine model, with its excessive regulations and expensive social systems, suffered in the 1980s and then later as a consequence of reunification. Germany is no longer considered today to be the economic locomotive for Europe, and in 1999 France seemed to have taken on this role.

Stagflation (economic stagnation, unemployment and inflation) appeared at the end of the 1960s and developed into a real economic and social crisis after 1973. Increasingly apparent was the rather rapid development of economic deprivation and exclusion. Rather remarkably, given the recent history of the post-war 30 years, the idea of increased unemployment in

Table 2.9: Average annual growth rates for GDP, labor, and productivity

	1970-1980			1980-1990			1990-1996		
	GDP	Labor	Prod.	GDP	Labor	Prod.	GDP	Labor	Prod.
France	3.3	0.5	2.8	2.6	0.3	2.3	1.4	−0.1	1.5
United States	2.8	2.4	0.4	2.7	1.7	1.0	2.4	1.2	1.2
Germany	2.7	0.2	2.5	1.3	0.5	0.8	1.8	0.4	1.4

Source: 50 ans de problèmes économiques, Paris: La documentation Française, 1998

the long run came to be generally accepted in France, giving clear indication of the powerlessness of individuals in the face of deteriorating social systems and the stagnation of an economy that had been over-regulated. This will be discussed in greater detail in Chapter 5. The return to economic growth in 1997–8, and the liberalization which followed adoption of the Single European Act in 1989 permit one to hope for the disappearance of social ills such as unemployment, poverty and exclusion.

Internationalization of activities accentuated during the 1970s full economic crisis, and rather more in France than elsewhere. French financial markets were deregulated and liberalized during the 1980s following a painful loss due to the collapse of the Mitterand demand policy in 1981–2. Globalization of markets for goods and services accelerated during the 1990s, assisted by new strategies of firms and the growing importance of small and medium-sized firms in the French economy. The Single Market initiative was formally completed in 1993 and the economies of Central and Eastern Europe were opened to commerce and direct investment. Financial markets cooperated reasonably well, with the objective of becoming more attractive to foreign participants. Finally, in September 1999 the leaders of eight European stock exchanges decided to consider a single European stock exchange. State monopoly capitalism left the scene, and the state disengaged itself rapidly from the productive economy. International competition and a ceaseless flow of new opportunities replaced the state as the motor of the French economy.

The Final Economic Disengagement of the State

During the last quarter of the twentieth century state capitalism and Colbertism lost their dominant places in the French economy. The French government nationalized some enterprises again in 1982, almost 40 years after the first wave of nationalization, but after several years it decided to resell partially or totally all that it had purchased from private shareholders and to revise its approach to managing the economy. This meant the end of national planning and of dirigist industrial policies. The French state disengaged itself politically and rather clumsily under the double pressure of the European Union and the public sector budget deficits and scandals aggravated by repeated losses by stateowned firms.

Nationalizations and privatizations
In 1982, the new French socialist government nationalized or took majority control in 46 large firms for political reasons but also for strategical reasons with regards to industrial policy. Among these nationalizations were some of the largest French companies: Péchiney, CGE, Rhône-Poulenc, Saint-Gobain, Matra, Dassault, Bull and Thomson for industry and Paribas and Suez among the banks. These were added to the nationalizations of the post-war period,

which concerned principally coal, electricity, gas, railroads and banks, including the Bank of France and Credit Lyonnais. The government was forced to violate some of its original principles on occasion, for example with regard to the national railway by laying off 110,000 workers during 1948–55 and by closing secondary lines that were not profitable. In 1982, with the exception of steel (Usinor-Sacilor), the nationalizations were limited to firms that were operating profitably. State investment had been continued between 1982 and 1985 and amounted to 35 per cent of total investment in France, private investment having been considerably reduced, while operation losses, most notably in steel, Renault and chemistry, were beginning to become a very heavy burden on state finances.

In 1986, the government began to turn away from the long French tradition of Colbertism by following the example of the United Kingdom and Germany: they began to privatize the French publicly owned firms. By this time it had become the largest state owned complex of firms among the industrialized nations, double that of Germany and three times that of Sweden. The large public firms or the firms that had been nationalized were asked to become profitable. For example, they were required to gain funds from private savings so as to have a rigorous management and one that was responsible to private backers, and they were henceforth authorized to sell subsidiaries and departments free of any parliamentary intervention. In 1988, investments of large, nationalized firms represented just over 25 per cent of total productive investment in comparison with 35 per cent five years previously. Despite the position taken by President Mitterand that there would be neither nationalizations nor privatizations, the government decided to sell certain activities or terminate certain engagements (for example in ELF, Rhône-Poulenc). It also decided to modify the statute of Renault and, in 1991, the monopoly of the Post, Telephone and Telegraph which became La Poste and France Télécom and were forced for the first time to meet the challenges of competition. The new government, which came to power during 1993 to 1995, proceeded with seven new privatizations (BNP, Péchiney, Rhône-Poulenc, Elf, UAP, Usinor-Sacilor, and SEITA). Shares in Bull and Renault were sold, making the state a minority shareholder in 1996, and CGM and AGF were privatized. In 1997, the infrastructure and operations of the railroad system were separated into RFF (Réseau Ferré de France) and SNCF (Société Nationale des Chemins de Fer Français) following the influence of directives from the European Community. France Télécom was partially privatized and the market for telephone services in 2001 is totally open to competition. All this marked the intention of governments that were left-socialist to abandon the historic conception of French-style public service. It is significant that in 1998 joint operations with European firms caused the share of state capital in France Télécom to fall to 60 per cent. Also in 1998, public holdings of bank and insurance companies' shares were sold totally or partially to individual firms. In 1999, it was the turn of Credit Foncier and of La Caisse d'Epargne to be privatized and, a very special case, Credit Lyonnais as part of a rescue plan. Finally, the BNP came to acquire the majority of Paribas in August 1999. The large groups such as Thomson, Matra, Groupe Air France, as had been the case with UAP, AGF, GAN, were henceforth partially or totally owned by private capital.

By the end of the 1990s, the productive holdings of the public sector, usually with the minority participation of the state, had been reduced to: transportation (SNCF, RATP and Groupe Air France), energy (EDF theoretically no longer had a monopoly position but the state controls the firm to the extent of 100 per cent, allowing it to impose once again the nuclear choice in 1999), coal mines, communication (La Poste and France Télécom), aeronautical construction (Aérospatiale, Dassault and Snecma), automobiles (Renault), machinery and armaments (Framatone and GIAT Industries), and electronics (Thomson and Bull). Certain managers of the public or newly privatized sectors had begun to act as though they were managers of private companies, beginning to initiate takeovers and mergers and arranging transnational accords (mainly EDF and France Télécom). There is no longer a great difference between the private sector and the public sector, if we exclude from consideration the mixed capital of the public sector firms. In France as elsewhere, the ownership of a firm's capital and management of the firm are usually differentiated and separated.

In 1999, public sector activities of an industrial and commercial nature which were subject to competition represented over 900,000 salaried employees, a slight diminution since 1985. For 1997 business revenues were Fr600 billion and investment that year amounted to Fr100 billion, (primarily in Air France, Charbonnages de France, EDF, France Télécom, GDF, La Poste, RATP, SNCF). However, public sector employment as a whole increased from 3.1 million workers in 1947 to 6.6 million in 1985; by 1994 this figure had diminished by 500,000. Public sector employees represented about one quarter of the total work force of approximately 25 million, of which 3 million were unemployed. In 2001, French public services (energy, transportation, communications, and so on) have become part of the complex of French commercial enterprises selling to their clients in a competitive market, and no longer national monopolies offering service to users.

Industrial policy

At the dawn of the 1970s, the French economy was not only demonstrably modernized, but it was also integrated in global exchanges under the double influence of decolonization and the initiatives of the EEC. Public financing had permitted the establishment of a very large state-owned enterprise sector that was diversified and often utilized a high level of technology and has thus contributed to the rapid growth of productivity. At the end of the 1990s, a new need for modernization became apparent in the areas of communications and information technology as there was a lack of access to information highways, little investment by firms in new information technologies, few users of the Internet, and a high cost for telephone usage.

This system of the state as producer seemed to have reached its limits for reasons of cost and pure efficiency. On the one hand, the public sector budget exceeded 3 per cent of GDP, the national debt was greater than 50 per cent of GDP and public expenditures were in excess of 54 per cent of GDP; the global weight of fiscal pressures on the economy was the second highest in the world. It was no longer possible to ignore the social costs of using the state as both entrepreneur and dispenser of subsidies. On the other hand, the introduction of cost–benefit analysis as a component part of the rationalization of budgetary choices began in the 1970s. While this offered a technical solution to some problems, it ignored the subjective gains of individuals which, as economists know, can only be expressed as market behavior. The 'New Economists' showed this clearly: the old model of the technocracy working in the shadow of power is less socially efficient than 60 million actors working in a decentralized manner in the market. Be that as it may, the market mentality progressively invaded the bureaucratic operations of EU institutions.

Public initiative and authoritative technological choices (not for public debate) were gradually replaced by the private decisions of firms acting in markets. Many managers of companies were not accustomed to the competition and found themselves left to their own resources. Consequently, the trend toward 'voluntary' adoption of more efficient behavior became a matter of concern because it had been for too long dependent on inflation and the aid of the state. In effect, European integration offered a new chance for economic growth by generating substantial economies of scale that can be achieved in a much larger market, and, on the other hand, the dynamic interplay of the competition of prices (demand) and enhanced opportunity for innovation (supply). The devaluation of the franc, at the end of the 1960s, and the installation of the European Monetary System in the 1970s, following the collapse of the Bretton Woods system, diverted French growth towards the outside world. Today the large French firms are at least as commercially and financially aggressive and efficient as their foreign counterparts.

The opening of the French economy after 1958 was positively influenced by competition through prices and innovation and the transformation was rapid. Gross profit rates were depressed for about 20 years, at 38 per cent in 1980 down from 48 per cent in 1960 (Table 2.10). When distinguishing between the branches of activity, it can be seen that processed foods are not consistent with the profit cycle of the others. In fact, they saw increasing rates that were often the source of dissatisfaction for agricultural producers (for example at the end of 1999).   If one examines the profit rates of the various sectors of economic activity, it becomes clear that food processing did not exhibit the same pattern over time. Contrary to the other sectors the profit rate in food processing rose throughout the period. This caused considerable dissatisfaction among the growers.

Table 2.10: Profit rate for French enterprises, as a percentage of value added

	1970	1980	1990	1992
Processed food	31	33	39	40
Manufactures	28	20	32	28
Services, other than				
commerce	50	47	48	49
Commerce	35	26	28	27

Source: *Bilan économique et social de la France*, Paris: La documentation Française, 1997

Has France abandoned Colbertism? For those who answer in the affirmative, 1983 must be considered to be the revolutionary year. From 1974 to 1997, growth remained lifeless, uncertain and unequal. France 'functioned below its potential in terms of growth.'[8] The absence of strong economic development for more than two decades was one of the primary factors for justifying a slow pace of reform so action was becoming urgent. The old Colbertism–Fordism model of a mixed economy was nourished by the 30 glorious years. After 1974, a crisis situation exploded, growth disappeared and the established economic model was quickly turning out to be unacceptable and obsolete. But it was not brought into question until the middle of the 1980s. These factors, in conjunction with the political choice of the strong franc, generated the economic crisis that was born in 1974 and caused it to take on a more durable, profound and painful form.

Born at the time of the Liberation, this model in its time had assigned a key role to the large state owned enterprises (in sectors such as electrical power, railways, aviation, iron and steel industry, chemistry, oil, and nuclear power), managed by the so-called large clerks of the state. The Fifth Plan favored industrial investment by reducing uncertainty about the future, in the words of Pierre Masse, the first Commissioner of the Plan. The economy was voluntarist in the sense that with regulatory and fiscal power the state managers thought they were in a position to order the transformation to a non-existent economy or to reconstruct. Certain choices were judicious: French Colbertism was well directed toward new technologies and the development of first class French researchers and engineers. Certain large projects such as the modernization of the telephone or the TGV were brilliantly successful, even though at great expense. But these choices were too costly and too numerous and many were failures (the best known was the failure of the approach taken to Machine Bull). And while the Plan and the large projects occupied a more modest position, French Colbertism remained a major force in the economy until the 1980s. Public choices and governmental initiatives, public finances, public markets and state-client, and privileged activities and corporations were imposed upon the domestic market at great expense in efficiency. In the words of two researchers:

> this model of an administered economy issued after the war was nevertheless a good thing, with reconstruction that permitted France to become the fourth economic power in the world. From where the temptation to suspend time in order to indefinitely attempt to prolong the effects. It has now been more than twenty years that the French model of industrial state control, becoming little by little anachronistic, continues in this way to run from its launching.[9]

In the 1980s the fundamental economic principles were being steadily imposed: the corporations were not satisfied with being run without making profits, without investing and innovating; it was finally confirmed that competition was more motivating and enriching than monopolies and protectionism; the market was socially a better allocator of resources than any type of authority. The swan song in the subject of traditional industrial policy was "industrial imperative" introduced by President Pompidou (before 1973), later to be crowned as an astounding failure because it was against the norm.

Actually, the turning point of this last quarter of a century was 1983. While France was heading toward bankruptcy due to the failure of the recent nationalizations of all areas of the economy, it produced a true applied ideological revolution. The government closed Renault Billancourt submitted the grievances of the employees of the post office (PTT) and of the armaments producer GIAT to the procedures of the Commission for the Rights of Workers and Corporations. The public generosity of the 1982–3 budgets was replaced very suddenly by fiscal rigor. But new responsibilities were taken on; for example 300,000 civil servants were hired. On the other hand, the steel and iron industry (nationalized) was removed as its manpower diminished from 160,000 to 50,000 by the early 1990s, and coal miners were reduced from 240,000 to 60,000 during the same period, and to only 15,800 in 1997. In fact, these state-controlled activities only survived to the degree that they did through the generosity of public grants, principally to the coal mines.

In the preceding year (1982), the state produced more than 50 per cent of the value added of industry and insured about 75 per cent of its investments. This lack of consistency over a period of just three years showed what a difficult time the French political structure had in ridding itself of the old ideas and how sensitive it was to a little informed public that was always ready to ask for more in the way of state support.[10] This is still the same public opinion that, in the fall of 1995, accompanied the workers of public corporations in their protests in the streets against government privatization intentions. This shows that France is difficult to govern and exceedingly difficult to reform.

The 1980s can genuinely be seen as marking the beginning of the disappearance of the administered financing of the economy, of the end of state capitalism, and of the end of the traditional industrial policy of 'large projects.' Corporations learned to finance themselves in the new markets, liberalized and internationalized (especially large firms) by the end of the decade. This was also the period when the state abandoned its large projects approach and the concepts of official branches and gaps. Spontaneously, corporations found themselves exchanging and working in networks for relationships and multiple flexible sets of sub-contractors, thanks to the opportunities offered by the new technologies. The manufacturers and other CEOs took over from the public initiative in a more and more decentralized and rapidly changing world. As noted earlier by Elie Cohen in 1982, technocracy deserts the service of the state. It can be noted that this renowned economist was until recently spokesman for the French industrial model, celebrating the economic ascendancy of Japan and to a lesser degree the United States, economies that seemed to discover the virtues of 'high-tech Colbertism.'[11]

What remains of industrial politics in 1999? If one must speak of industrial politics in France in 1999, it essentially concerns the objectives of promotion of research and public–private technological transfers. As summarized by André Safir and Dominique Michel, the diffusion of technology is today one of the principal missions of new industrial politics, along the lines of what happened in the United States. The most frequent form of this kind of politics, according to the same authors, is that of a network of partnership of university, public agencies, private foundations, and private corporations. This sort of structure benefits from the fact that the spending per inhabitant on research situated France ranked second after the US. Unfortunately, according to the *Rapport Guillaume* public and industrial research relations are always rather rare in France and the small corporations are almost excluded. In the OECD countries, corporations themselves finance 67 per cent of research: in 1995, 72 per cent in the US and 62 per cent in France (or 2.8 per cent and 2.4 per cent of GDP respectively). While the trend of French productivity growth has slowed over 20 years, it should be noted that this was also the case for the other Group of Seven countries. The same general pattern is found for productivity gains for capital and for labor.

Industrial policy and planning will be discussed further in the following chapter in which we examine the role of the state in France. But to understand the past and indeed the present of France, one must always bear in mind that:

at the heart of the French exception, there is the state as actor, redistributor, producer, economic planner and social architect. A strong state, born out of the Middle Ages, consolidated under the Ancient regime, rationalized under the Republic, renowned authoritarian, bureaucratic and centralizing.[12]

Through the actions of the state during the past 50 years, France has endowed itself with luxurious infrastructures and amenities: energy and water supply, TGV transport and highways, urban development, trash collection, clean cities and rivers, works of art, and a high standard of living. This has benefitted those who live in France and has facilitated the development of

Table 2.11: Trends in total productivity, percentage gain per year

	France	US	Japan	Germany	G7
1960–1973	3.7	1.9	5.7	2.6	3.1
1973–1979	1.6	0.1	1.1	1.8	0.8
1979–1996	1.3	0.6	1.1	0.6	0.8

Source: Economic Perspectives, Paris: OECD, 1997

tourism, but it appears costly from the perspective of today. However, it must also be noted that the French suffer from a great lack of infrastructure in telecommunication and computers. Computer equipment and access to the Internet were, in 1999, the object of a new policy of liberalization especially for telephone companies and access providers. Research and development were promoted by a government that was finally conscious of what was at stake, under the aegis of relations and transfers between industry, research and teaching (laboratories and universities). In this regard, France is behind other large world economies.

To summarize, industrial policy, which traditionally had a central role in the state management of the economy, has become more modest. Once again in the words of Safir and Michel:

For forty years, the French, who never had confidence in the market, came to develop in a particular manner, an inimitable mix of devised planning, of technocratic Colbertism and of technological chauvinism to develop a facility for competitive production. But European construction, technological revolution and globalization have little by little been making this way of regulation obsolete. Industrial policy no longer works.[13]

The Economic Crisis and Growth Rediscovered

It is not unusual to read and hear these days that the economic crisis born in 1974 has ceased. Is this conclusion justified? The restoration of corporate profits toward the end of the 1980s was not followed by a net recovery and lasting investments, which actually fell from 32 per cent of GDP in 1973 to 16 per cent in 1996. Given that the new technologies were greedy in terms of investment, they are still underdeveloped in France in the beginning of the twentyfirst century. The pace of growth of GDP fell dramatically from 1989 to 1994. It is not until 1997 and 2000 that France experienced a recovery of growth to the extent of 2.5 to 3 per cent per year. Stimulated by the rise of final domestic demand and by increased exports during the previous eight years as well, investment finally began its recovery in 1997, and increased by 11 per cent in 1999. Is France adopting a new economic growth model similar to that which is attributed to the United States? Nothing can be sure as high-tech investments only represent 15 to 20 per cent of total French investment, compared to more than 50 per cent in the US. However, it hardly seems probable that the industrialized world will rediscover the solid growth of the '30 glorious years' in the near future.

The end of the thirty glorious years
Most of the world felt the hard years of the end of the 1960s: the recession of 1967, external deficits of industrialized nations, protests in May of 1968, the end of the Bretton Woods system of fixed exchanges, devaluation, increasing numbers of bankruptcies, expanding unemployment, recurrent inflation, and so on. The long economic crisis of the end of the century appeared after the first big oil shock of 1973 and, for the next three decades, a decrease in growth and an increase in unemployment.

But in France, more than elsewhere, the damage of August 1974 was clear from the statistics as GDP actually decreased by 0.2 per cent in 1975. As with every year, this summer month was marked by a strong slowdown of activity, especially in manufacturing. In this particular year, August was not, however, followed by the customary strong recovery. From 1975 to 1980, corporations strove to adapt. The government attempted to put the brakes on firings, referred them to an administrative authorization procedure and forbade them in public enterprises. The government progressively became conscious of the fact that the crisis was continuing, and that the Plan (VII) was an outdated instrument. Rigorous budgetary policies and liberalization of prices under Valéry Giscard d'Estaing and Raymond Barre replaced the voluntarist policies and stimulative expenditures of previous governments. At the same time, taxes on corporations were raised significantly. Industry redirected its efforts toward research into more profitable and exportable products. But the corporations' debts as well as those of the state resumed at the end of the 1970s and the beginning of the 1980s, feeding a new period of inflation in which prices rose by 10 to 15 per cent per year. Prices, wages, and interest rates took off.

The market economy resuscitated thanks to new monetary and financial markets, and new roles for banks

The policy of overburdening the state with debt and recourse to Keynesian demand expansion policy during 1981–3 failed and led France to the edge of an abyss. Public sector borrowing needs crowded the private sector out of capital markets and the funds that were available were costly. A new rigor was adopted in 1983 and constituted a 180-degree turn unlike anything that had been done previously. Profit was restored to its role in the allocation of capital and the direction of economic activity; increased recognition was given to the roles of both the entrepreneur and the corporation. The importance of competition and of research and development, the need to reduce the rate of increase in costs of production, restoration of corporation margins, and stabilization of public deficits were all included in the new lexicon. In essence, the French government rediscovered its interest in promoting the market economy. This meant that first inflation must be brought under control and that asset-holders regained confidence in the franc and developed a new interest and confidence in France. Central to all of this was the necessity for a stricter monetary policy and a liberalization of financial markets.

Reduction in the rate of inflation, necessary for the introduction of the European Monetary Union and a future European single currency, was extremely successful in France in comparison with other countries, as indicated in Table 2.12, even though it occurred at a slower pace. In the middle of the 1980s, due to the necessity of financing the public deficit that had been accumulating for a decade, the government liberalized financial markets. Moreover, it gave birth to a true monetary market with several new products. This brought a double benefit of alleviating the debt burdens of

Table 2.12: Inflation rates in selected economies

	1970-80	1980-85	1985-90	1990-95	1998
France	9.6	9.6	3.1	2.2	0.3
Germany	5.1	3.9	1.4	3.1	0.5
United Kingdom	13.7	7.2	5.9	3.0	2.7
United States	7.8	5.5	4.0	3.0	1.6
OECD	8.4	6.3	3.5	2.6	2.0

Source: OECD Economic Outlook, 1997 (June) and 1999 (June), Paris: Organization for Economic Cooperation and Development

corporations, households and the state, and of facilitating an industrial reconstruction that was realized throughout the 1990s. The access of the state to the Bank of France for funds was legally limited, as was its influence on the central bank's control of the money supply. This forced the state to finance itself through monetary and financial markets. Therefore, at the end of the 1980s and the beginning of the 1990s, corporations and the state progressively resorted to financial markets to obtain liquid assets in the long run. Firms pursued debt reduction and consumers stabilized their obligations. Growth increased, as did investment, although self-financing became increasing important from 1990 on.

The role of banks changed as a result of the disintermediation through which savings were borrowed directly through investors without passing through banks. New instruments on the monetary market were created by legislation and saw rapid success, growing to Fr3000 billion francs in 1999, which was more than a third of the GDP of France. The Bank of France became largely independent in 1994; its refinancing of banks foreshadowed that of the European Central Bank that was to come. Short-term interest rates

Table 2.13: Non-financial companies: investments and financing

	1970	1975	1980	1985	1990	1998	1999
Saving	16.7	12.5	12.0	12.8	16.8	18.0	15.6
Investment	22.1	19.4	19.4	16.9	18.9	15.9	15.3
Self-financing	75.5	64.5	61.7	75.7	89.4	113.3	102.0

Note: Figures are percentage of GDP.

Sources: *L'état de la France 1999-2000*, Paris: La Découverte, 1999; *Rapport préparatoire du budget*, Paris: Sénat, 1998

finally became normal in 1997–8, that is to say, lower than longer-term rates. In effect, the Bank of France no longer supported the franc, which had regained the confidence of the financial markets due to a weakening of the German Mark following reunification and an increase in German unemployment. Finally, in order not to place in jeopardy the economic recovery, the soon to be established European Central Bank was expected to adopt a policy of keeping interest rates low, and it was necessary to prepare for this during 1998 and 1999. In January 1999, the key rate was fixed by the newborn European Central Bank at 3 per cent, then it was rapidly lowered to 2.5 per cent a few weeks later.

Similarly, since the movement of capital was completely liberalized, exchange control being abolished in 1990, operations in the financial markets experienced an explosive expansion with new products, principally options. However, it must not be forgotten that 80 per cent of securities transactions in

France were public (for example T Bonds), generating an explosion of investment of loanable funds. Real long-term interest rates quickly rose in 1997 to 3.7 per cent against 2.2 per cent in the US, and again to around 5.4 per cent at the end of 1999 compared to 6 per cent in the US. This was due to two factors. First, in the long run, an interest rate is an equilibrium rate, and

Table 2.14: Real short-run interest rates

	1973	1979	1987	1992	1996	1998
France	3.3	0.4	4.8	8.0	1.5	2.8
United States	1.1	0.5	2.3	0.0	1.9	3.2
Germany	4.1	3.6	2.2	5.0	1.6	2.6
United Kingdom	3.4	-1.9	4.8	4.1	3.3	3.8

Source: OECD

loanable funds are relatively scarce and command a risk premium. Second, inflationary pressures in France were very low as we entered the year 2000. The recovery of growth in Europe and principally in France at the end of 1997 attracted assets towards stock markets, supported by the steadily rising trend of the Dow Jones in New York. It was also the case that the risk premium in capital and in revenue was noticeably reduced over six years, which reflects confidence in financial markets in the economy and in the French currency on the eve of the introduction of the Euro. Consequently, while there was a new expansion from 1997 to 1998, investment had not been very vigorous for too long in France. During these years, stocks and bonds attained values that were not realistic and attracted the interest of financial investors and savers, to the detriment of expenditure on research and development.

Evolution of the nature of domestic production: so-called deindustrialization

The evolution of the distribution of the active population among the three sectors of the economy gives clear evidence of what occurred in the last quarter of the century: the explosion of the service sector, as indicated in Table 2.15. During the last decade of the century, the large industrialized economies were clearly affected by deindustrialization, with the exception of Japan. This was manifested by a decrease on the part of manufacturing value added and employment, and increases in both of these figures for the service sector. But two factors should moderate these statistics: that relatively few people were hired in the service sector before the arrival of the new technologies, and the rapid development of outsourcing. Moreover, this concerned a reorientation of industrial activities and not actual deindustrialization. Finally, agriculture, which supported less than 4 per cent of the active population approaching the year 2000, is on the path of a necessary transformation through the long-awaited disappearance of the Common Agriculture Policy of the EU and of public interventions and subventions, and consequently a growing role of markets. The first issue we must deal with is the weakness of French employment in the service sector. The service sector is actually a heterogeneous catchall. Its recent expansion reflects not only traditional activities such as health, education, finance, culture and entertainment, tourism, and so forth, but also the arrival of new traditional

Table 2.15: Output by sector

Sector\year	1949	1959	1973	1981	1985	1994	1997
Primary	29.2	22.1	10.9	8.6	7.5	5.1	4.0
Secondary	35.0	35.2	37.8	35.9	30.6	25.9	25.0
Tertiary	35.8	42.7	51.3	56.2	61.9	69.0	71.0

Source: *Tableaux de l'économie française*, Paris: Commmissariat au Plan

activities, notably services for corporations, many of which would be classified as new information and communication technologies. In the aggregate, French employment expanded during 1974–6, while the number of jobs created each year was equivalent to those that were lost. The relationship was reversed from the end of 1997, when net employment growth became positive with 100,000 to 500,000 extra jobs being created each year. For a quarter of a century, French industry contracted more rapidly and lost more jobs than was the case in other industrialized nations. During this period, 30 per cent of all jobs disappeared in France while American industry created almost 10 per cent more jobs. As a general proposition, one would expect to see the service sector hiring workers when manufacturing reduces its employment. This has not been the case in France where a good part of service activities is mechanized. For example, during the past decade one was far more likely to see in France than in the United States robots on production lines, automated telephone systems, hotels without personnel, automatic ticket machines, bar codes, and self service pumps and checkouts. Two known causes can explain this: the higher minimum wage and the obstacles faced when creating a corporation. The relative minimum wages of France and Australia are the highest in the world at 60 per cent of average wages, while those of Mexico, the United States and Canada are among the lowest: 24, 39, 43 per cent respectively. Furthermore, France is one of five countries of the OECD that have the highest wage taxes, in excess of 60 per cent of the wage. Significant social contributions in this way add to the wage bill and raise the cost of production, although the total labor cost is higher in Germany than in France. This explains why, over the last 25 years, the size of the service sector only grew 60 per cent in France while it almost doubled in the United States.

Another statistic displays the French inelasticity to qualitative changes of productive activities. As is shown in Table 2.16, with WP being the

Table 2.16: Job Elasticities / GDP

	1987	1997	elasticities
Secondary sector value added as a percentage of GDP	29.6	26.2	
Secondary WP as a percentage of total WP	30.8	25.6	1.47
Tertiary sector value added as a percentage of GDP	66.9	71.5	
Tertiary WP as a percentage of total WP	62.2	69.2	.55

Sources: Statistiques de la population active 1977–1997, Paris: OECD, 1999

population and employment elasticity being $\varepsilon = (\Delta WP/WP) / (\Delta GDP/GDP)$ for each of the secondary and service sectors, one would find that the industrial sector with a higher elasticity is quicker to fire (or not hire) than the service sector.

The second important issue is the fact that the recent growth of outsourcing alters some of the statistics. Corporations, especially large ones, have diminished their manpower in part because they have begun outsourcing a number of services, such as computer services, maintenance, worker training, catering, transport, and so on. This costs them less in an uncertain situation and diversifies the risks they will confront in the future. As a consequence, a large number of presently recorded jobs in the category of services to corporations (over 1 million created over 25 years) were counted in the manufacturing sector about 20 years ago. The extent of the growth of the outsourcing movement in all industrialized countries makes this a problem that is realized everywhere. One can therefore say that more than half of the service sector is meeting the demands of manufacturing. In addition, a continually growing number of these services are exposed to international competition, due to the expected reduction of costs and of transport time, the programmed disappearance of boundaries, regional integration, and the instantaneousness of communications (Internet and e-mail). Finally, when one looks at services exported by the French, they are often composed of services to corporations with strong value-added, such as engineering, software, financial management, banks and insurance, distribution, and logistics.

It is within these activities that we find what one now calls the New Economy. For example, logistics in the branch of automobile production is entirely outsourced. Thanks to new technologies, a part maker can deliver the desired parts to an assembly line in less than two hours after the request was issued. The new technologies have been the origin of both low skill work, such as the so-called back office activities, or highly skilled and specialized work: computer specialists, designers, managers, and senior executives. An enormous gap or polarization exists between these two categories of work. However, improved productivity benefits everyone, according to the known principle of enrichment through exchange (or in common usage, trickledown economics), assuming that the non-qualified workers who have been hired are not discouraged by the minimum wage and other regulations. Recall that, according to Safir and Michel, 'industrial policy no longer works.'[14] The same causes explain the industrial reconversions that are always in progress, massive firings, outsourcing, mergers and acquisitions and the swarm of short-lived start-ups, of which 50 per cent on average disappear after three years.

The third, and final, issue is the reorientation or reconversion of industry. In spite of what has been written about the importance of the service sector, industry still remains one of the primary motors of economic growth. Services develop and multiply in large part to meet the demands of manufacturing. Industrial production in France grew 90 per cent over 30 years despite three periods of recession: 1974–5, 1980–5 and 1992–3. Using 1970 as the base, manufacturing output in France grew to 140 by 1980, to 160 by 1990 and to 190 by 1998. In spite of this aggregate growth, for many sub-sectors the experience was not always positive. Some industries virtually disappeared, for example the shoe industry, while others such as the frozen food industry have blossomed. The industrial reconversion in France, due in part to outsourcing, facilitated the development of agro-alimentary industries or food processing, automobiles, energy and intermediate goods. Becoming somewhat less important are house building, consumer goods in general, and machinery and equipment.

In 1998, this expansion–reconversion movement gave signs of slowing down, despite the global economic growth in France. Industrial production rose 5.2 per cent in 1997 and 4.5 per cent in 1998, and the figure continued to fall in 1999 and even in 2000 with the exception of some branches, in particular automobiles. Throughout the global economy, industrial prices were either no longer rising or actually decreased from 1997. In 1998, the industrial prices diminished 0.2 per cent in North America, 1.2 per cent in Germany, 2 per cent in Japan, and 2.5 per cent in France. World prices of the products that France exports have only risen once since 1996, 3.2 per cent in 1997. French manufacturers have seen their prices decline by 1.3 per cent during each of the years 1996–98, and this has forced them to reduce their workforce. However, the trend reversed itself in 2000 and prices began once again to increase in 2001.

Table 2.17: Industrial production for some branches of activity

Branch\year	1990	1997
Energy	100	116.6
Automobiles	100	114.0
Food processing	100	113.0
Intermediate goods	100	105.0
Consumption goods	100	98.6
Machinery and equipment	100	90.2
Construction	100	87.6

Note: The index values are for current prices.

Source: *Annuaire Statistique de la France*, Paris: INSEE, 1999

Price competition is generally less a factor than it was in 1950. At present, globalization has reduced the prices of raw materials and of intermediate goods, but also a number of finished products, most obviously to all the price of computers. More and more today, competition is achieved through innovation. This has become one of the direct engines of growth, removing the ghost of emerging deflation. The primary and pressing issue in France will be to facilitate innovation and, in particular, access to new information and communication technologies.

Changes in final consumption

Changes in final consumption consist of the trends in changes in consumption and the recent evolution of household behavior. Economic growth universally leads to a reduction in the share of income devoted to expenditures on food. On the other hand, the share of income that is spent on such household equipment as consumer electronics, appliances, telephones, and so forth has risen steadily since 1980. Services made up 48 per cent of final consumption in 1998 compared to 34 per cent in 1970. In addition, if individual public services (including education, culture, leisure activities, libraries, and social services) that are not completely commercialized are considered, which are very extensively provided in France, the proportion of services as a part of final consumption would rise by another 15 per cent. We must not forget that public budgets command 54 per cent of French GDP.

Household consumption has been stable for 10 years, at approximately 60 per cent of GDP. A new phenomenon appeared at the beginning of 1997. The demand for consumption goods increased substantially in response to a surge in the demand for durable goods: automobiles, household appliances, computers and telephones. The cause of this rise in final domestic demand is attributed to three factors: the noticeable fall in unemployment from 12.4 per cent in mid-1997 to 11.4 per cent in mid-1999; lower short- and medium-term interest rates in 1998; and the virtual disappearance of inflation in 1999. The evolution of the structure of final consumption reflects the combined influences of variations in net incomes, of relative prices and of changes in consumer preferences. In this way, consumer goods prices rose by 15.2 per cent from 1990 to 1997. In the same period, food prices rose 14.1 per cent, housing prices rose 20.8, household equipment 14.7, leisure activities 9, and restaurants 20.8 per cent. If one examines revenues, household purchasing power had declined only in 1983.

Table 2.18: Expenditures of French households

	1950	1970	1985	1990	1997
Food	42.8	26.0	20.7	19.2	17.9
Housing and equipment	16.8	25.5	26.6	27.0	29.8
Culture, leisure and restaurants	16.8	18.4	16.7	20.7	20.5

Sources: Annuaires, Paris: INSEE; D. Martina, *Précis d'économie*, Paris: Nathan, 1998

The labor participation rate of the French population fell from 56.1 to 43.9 per cent between 1970 and 1995 (Table 2.19). The participation of women in the workforce gradually approached that of men, both in rate and in duration. However, once the lengthening of the period taken by education and

Table 2.19: Disposition of the work force

	1987	1990	1995	1996	1997
Employed	75.8	78.3	77.5	77.1	77.3
Unemployed	10.5	11.3	11.6	12.3	12.4
Total workers	86.3	89.6	89.1	89.4	89.7
Active population	24.5	25.9	25.3	25.6	25.7

Note: Figures for the first three rows are as a percentage of the active population. Those for the active population are in millions.

Sources: Annuaire Statistique de la France, Paris: INSEE, 1999; *Département Emploi et revenus d'activités*, Paris: INSEE, 1999

of life expectancy are considered, the proportion of non-active people continually rose for 25 years. At the same time, social programs and income transfers were multiplied, notably in response to unemployment, exclusion and urban problems. Almost 40 per cent of the income of individuals consisted of social transfers, placing France at the head of countries in terms of the importance of redistributive measures in total GDP, with income support to workers being the primary concern.

The share of wages and salaries in the GDP has always been two points lower in France than that of the European Union (with its 15 members). This proportion has constantly decreased over the past 40 years, as it has in other countries of the European Union, making it inferior to that of the United States since 1990. In 1999, it was 66.8 per cent in France as opposed to 68.8 per cent in the United States. In reality, only 74.5 per cent of the GDP (in 1997) took the form of earned income. Furthermore, the share of social transfers (all benefits and social insurance) was 36.6 per cent of GDP in 1996, a figure that did not take into account local or para-public social services. Social transfers to households rose on average 7.5 per cent per year for 20 years until in 1999 they attained the level of 40 per cent of GDP.

The growth rate of remuneration per employee, in real terms, has weakened consistently, from 5 per cent in 1971 to no gain at all in 1995–6. Since 1997 it has recovered somewhat and has increased by 2 per cent per year on average since then. France is the only country where the minimum wage has increased more rapidly than the average salary since 1967. The minimum wage/average salary relationship was 50 per cent beginning in 1982 and was increased to 60 per cent in 1998. France and Belgium are the members of the European Union where this relationship is the highest. On the other hand, it decreased to 30 per cent in Spain and to 35 per cent in the United States. It is therefore logical that the range of French salaries was reduced, at least until 1984. In fact the relationship inter-deciles, between the top and the bottom of the income distribution, fell in France to a ratio of 3.1. To this date there has been a slight increase to 3.4, the same as that of the United Kingdom, against 4.5 in the United States and 2.2 in Germany and Belgium. In fact, it has been the change in the nature of work contracts that explains the French figures: temporary work and work of short-duration (CDD) represented 17.5 per cent of jobs in 1997, to which must be added an unknown number of part-time workers. These often consist of temporary jobs that require little qualification, for which the people are relatively interchangeable, making for low productivity, or where there is no incentive to increase productivity, and are therefore not very well paid. This explains why, when taking into account all workers, 40 per cent receive the minimum wage or less (as of March 1997), that is Fr5000 or less per month. This rate is higher in France than in many other industrialized countries, including the United States. And if the purchasing power parity (PPP) is taken into account, the standard of living of the French was fifteenth in the world in 1998.

The minimum wage especially handicaps young people, women and low-skilled workers. In France, as in Germany and elsewhere, there are more women and young people engaging in low-skilled work and thus receiving lower salaries (Table 2.20). While women were less favored in terms of

Table 2.20: Gap between men's and women's salaries, 1997

France	14
Japan	40
Canada	29
United Kingdom	26
Germany	26
United States	25
Italy	17
Sweden	17
Australia	16

Note: The figures represent the percentage by which average male pay exceeds that of females.

Source: *Statistiques de la population active*, Paris: OECD, 1999

access to higher-level jobs and while they had a higher turnover than that of men, the gap between male salaries and female salaries in France, again with Belgium, is the lowest of the OECD countries. The most significant events during the last quarter of a century, in terms of household behavior, which followed the rocketing of fiscal and social deductions from the last years of the 1970s, were the noticeable fall on the part of income earned by labor in value-added (it fell from 72 per cent in 1981 to just 59 per cent in 1990), the punishing rise in household debt during the 1980s, and the long-term decline of the rate of saving. With regard to the last, the rate of household saving fell from just over 20 per cent of disposable income in 1978 to 11 per cent a decade later; it subsequently increased slightly to 13–14 per cent during the 1990s. At the same time, liberalization of financial markets induced French households to place increased portions of their saving in shares and mutual funds. In spite of this, the individual shareholder remains underdeveloped in France in comparison with both the UK and the US. The recent fall in the savings rate to 11 per cent in January 2000, due to the increase of fiscal pressures on households as well as the failure to reduce public budgetary deficits, dried up the market of long-term loanable funds and made long-term rates rise. Investments in housing are expected to suffer, after the recovery of real estate in 1999. It is anticipated that the French standard of living will probably stagnate or increase less rapidly in the near future than it has in recent years.

CONCLUSION

In the long run, the trend of the rate of economic growth diminished from 6 per cent in the 1950s to 2 or 3 per cent by the end of the 1990s, with troughs about every 18 years. Economic growth was sustained until the middle of 1974. The fall was rather brutal and profound with unemployment doubling in just two years. The petroleum shock of this period gave birth to a crisis that lasted for a quarter of a century: economic growth rates weakened all over the world and inflation exploded to double-digit figures, particularly in France. While inflation disappeared, yielding to deflationist signs, on the other hand, unemployment, just 1 or 2 per cent before 1975, rose rapidly to almost 13 per cent 20 years later, and its duration is at the origin of the phenomenon of exclusion that was still in existence at the end of the 1990s. From 1945 to 1975, there were inflationary crises that marked a France of strong growth; from 1975 to 1995, there were stagflation crises (resurgent inflation, reduced growth and unemployment); since 1995, the growth has resumed, particularly in 1997, inflation was suppressed as in many developed economies, but emerged again in 2000, and unemployment did not begin to fall until 1998. It appears today that this is linked to a weakening in new firm creation, excessive regulation, inappropriate education for young people, and the obsolescence of the skills of older workers.

We can distinguish in this way two primary French sub-periods:

1945–1973: Persistence of inflation; Fordist economics; colonial wars;
 industrial mutations; the opening of the economy
   1945–1955: Reconstruction and introduction of the "welfare state"
   1955–1968: Economic growth and opening
   1968–1973: Stagflation

1973–2000: Persistence of unemployment; de-industrialization; new poverty
 and exclusion; public deficits
   1973–1983: Crisis; unemployment and slow growth
   1983–1998: Liberalization and profound mutations
   1999–2000: Return to lasting growth, falling unemployment

NOTES

1. By ideology we mean '(T)he assemblage of mental tools of a civilization. Essentially political, the liberal idea calls into question the foundation of policy – power' (Thierry Leterre, *La gauche et la peur libérale*, Paris: Presses de Sciences Po, 2000).
2. Henri Mendras, *L'Europe des Européenes*, Paris: Gallimard, 1997, pp. 401–402.
3. European economists generally define a liberal economy as a market economy as opposed to a planned economy (such as the USSR), centralized, or state directed (post-WWII France).
4. From 1945 to 1965 the number of US patents tripled, while French patents in the US accounted only for 9 per cent of the total. This technological advantage gives a comparative advantage to the United States in high-technology sectors. See J. H. Dunning, 'Changes in the level and structure of international production,' in Mark Casson (ed.), *Hegemony of International Business*, London: Routledge, 1983, and Routledge/Thoemmes Press, 2000.
5. François Caron, *Les deux révolutions industrielles du XXe siècle*, Paris: Albin Michel, 1997, pp. 193 and 196.
6. According to the definition offered by Gary Becker in his *Human Behavior*. Legal profit is by nature monopolistic, with scarcity being guarantied by law; competitive profit is always precarious and must continuously be re-established through innovation. It is this latter profit that is the engine of economic growth. In a Hayekian sense, a spontaneous order was taking the place of a constructed order. France was in transition between systems based on the former and the latter.
7. P. Rosenvallon, *L'Etat en France de 1789 à nos jours*, Paris: Le Seuil – collection Pointes Histoire, 1992.
8. A. Safir and D. Michel, *Avantage France*, Paris: Village Mondial, 1999, p. 46.
9. Ibid., p. 46.
10. See François de Closet, *Toujours Plus*, Paris: Grasset, 1982.
11. Elie Cohen, *Le Colbertisme high-tech: Economie des Télécom et du Grand Projet*, Paris: Hachette, 1982, p. 14.
12. 'L'exception française – L'Etat, acteur surdimensionné du nouveau jeu économique,' *Les Echos*, November 16, 1998.
13. Safir and Michel, *Avantage France*, p. 56; see also Ezra Suyleiman, *Les ressorts cachés de la réussite française*, Paris: Seuil, 1995.
14. Safir and Michel, *Avantage France*, p. 56

3 The Role of the State in the French Economy

In the 1950s, the role of the state in the French economy was profoundly changed, adopting an ideology of state intervention, planning and control, while at the same time laying the ground for initiating a modern and evolving pragmatism. It is clear, however, that France has delivered far less than was demanded by free marketers and even by EU directives. For years, the French government adhered to its original principles of flexible or indicative planning. On the supply side, the authorities utilized all the tools imaginable in a command and order economy, for the purpose of properly controlling the nature and the quantity of produced and imported goods and services. They also managed the human and financial structures of the large state owned or controlled corporations, and the means of financing and investment, of export or operating subsidies, and of qualitative and quantitative interventions in the markets, most notably that of agriculture. Industrial policy and agricultural policy would serve as the most influential instruments in the second half of the twentieth century. Especially in the first years after the Second World War, they were part of the indicative planning process that was first centralized but later decentralized. Since the crisis of 1981-3 the central planning agency has only played a rather minor role. It has been converted to an agency for statistics and for forecasting for the Minister of the Economy. Agricultural policy was delegated by the Common Market coming into effect as a result of European requests. Industrial policy, not yet fully abandoned, was transformed through the return of private capitalism as well as through the arrival of the so-called third industrial revolution, that of the new technologies of information and communication.

On the demand side, the French state remains today the most significant state redistributor of income in the world. Within the complex and continuous redistribution systems, the structure of final consumption followed governmental intentions time and again. Immediately after the war, housing became the subject of policy measures aimed at facilitating access to ownership. Other domains of consumption were the object of governmental promotion in their time, such as the consumption of milk and automobiles.

Richard Musgrave classified state interventions according to three main objectives: allocation of resources in the case of market failures; stabilization of the macro-economic situation using Keynesian counter-cyclical policy; and redistribution of income.[1] Since then, the school of Public Choice clearly demonstrated that every action of the state is of a redistributive nature. Regulatory functions partly make up the first category. Stabilizing and redistributive interventions appeared after 1945. These are the new roles that the state took on. In reality, in France, allocative actions were originally justified through the desire to direct economic activity and that later became distinctly redistributive in nature. As a matter of fact, the former regulatory roles of the state absorbed 42 per cent of the state budget in 1938 and 26 per cent in 1994, while the share of the new roles of the state went from 44 per cent to 63 per cent. Concurrently, expenditures of the local public budgets and so-called para-fiscal budgets (for example, social security) saw great growth after the 1960s and the first decentralizations. Finally, since its creation, the EEC, then the EU, has also appeared to be of an interventionist nature, especially in the subject of regulation.

To simplify, it can be said that the state as a regulator, producer and planner plays a well-accepted role in the reallocation of resources, in the market or private and in the public sector. The state function as stabilizer of the macro-economic situation is the subject of another chapter. The redistributive role of the state, when it is possible to clearly isolate it, possesses a political foundation and nature. It does this simultaneously in the determination of a social function of preferences and in the equilibrium of forces that are exerted on it in the political market.

It is habitual in France for one to turn to the state when something is not going well. The French state, the largest per capita redistributor of income in the world, has inculcated in the citizenry the expectation of always receiving more, while at the same time expecting always to pay less. This runs the gamut from repetitive strikes and the claims of public and private sector workers to the petitions of small firm entrepreneurs and the protectionist demands of larger firms. In the words of Claude Imbert: 'risk exists in the very nature of the firm. Thus the French handicap comes exactly from the fact that we tend to depreciate this risk in favor of a cult of intervention and of an ideology of compassion: it makes the state the guarantor against failure and places the citizen in a protective enclosure.'[2]

The history of the Common Agricultural Policy (CAP) illustrates how the French state serves as both a reallocator of resources and a redistributor of income. The economic disengagement of the state during the past 20 years is notable not only in terms of agricultural policy but also in the disappearance of 5-year planning and in the privatizations that mark the end of French Colbertism. The evolution of French and then EU agricultural policy provides us with a mapping of the evolution of the initiatives of the French state over a 50 year period. The primary original challenge of the French government was to guarantee income and stability to farmers. However, the means of intervention and transfers that were chosen created a trap for later governments. Since the 1980s, the problem has become that of disengagement of the state and the EU from the agricultural sector.

Agriculture has always held a place in the EU for two reasons: first, because of the electoral power of farmers, especially in France and Germany; and second, agriculture consumes half of the budget of the European Union or approximately Fr290 million per year. Therefore, it easy to understand that reforming agriculture is both politically significant and risky for governments, and they must form a compromise between the response of negatively affected farmers and the necessity of reform. In addition, it is clear that as many as seven reforms of the CAP have had the objective of diminishing aid to agriculture. Moreover, French agriculture faces a new problem, that of the aging population. The number of farms is at a rapidly declining, 4 per cent a year was the average in the 1990s, while the wives of retired farmers have replaced their husbands on the land. This decrease in the number of farms is due to 40 per cent of farmers being older than 50 years of age and the fact that young people rarely choose to follow in their farming parent's footsteps.[3] It is estimated that there was a decline by 21 per cent in farms in France and 15 per cent in the EU between 1993 and 2003. Agricultural work dropped 50 per cent in France between 1975 and 1995, while production rose more than 25 per cent in the same period. In 2000, farmers counted for less than 3.5 per cent of the active population in France.

THE ORIGIN OF AGRICULTURAL POLICY

How was governmental intervention born? After the war, the French government was forced to respond to the protests of irate farmers. In the mid 1950s, European governments took part in marathon discussions leading to the inclusion of ten articles in the Treaty of Rome that dealt with agriculture. European agriculture, principally German and French at the time, took precedence over coal and steel in the constitution that initiated the early stages of the single market; a central role was given to the CAP. Beginning it operation in 1960, the CAP was intended to serve three main objectives: (a) to obtain single agricultural prices in the Common Market with the free circulation of products; (b) to put into play the community preference by taxing imports and subsidizing exports; and (c) to maintain a financial solidarity between member-states through national and regional compensatory transfers. Intervention prices were fixed as floor prices and were designed to be 90 per cent of the objective prices, which were superior to the world price. The FEOGA (European Fund for Agricultural Orientation and Warranty) and the FORMA (Fonds d'Orientation et de Régulation des Marchés Agricoles) in France, as well as specialized agencies for governmental intervention and commercialization, were established to insure the stocking of goods, export restitution, and compensatory aid payments to producers. Restitution for exports paid to exporters permitted the sale of grain at the global price, including when this price is lower than domestic prices, while community prices were aligned to higher national European prices.

The overall objective of stabilizing revenues for French farmers was achieved. From 1962 to 1972, their annual income growth was 5 per cent (in constant francs), but average productivity growth in agriculture was 8 per cent per year. Since 1970, the external agricultural commercial balance has been positive. Each year on average, exports increased 5.2 per cent while imports declined by 1.2 per cent. Overproduction forced public agencies to stock more and more of the surplus product. A natural consequence was a sharpening of trade conflict between Europe and the United States and other agricultural exporting nations.

The cost of the CAP was supported by higher charges on consumers and taxpayers. The CAP, at the beginning of the 1990s, represented about half of the EU budget. However, after 1970-2, farmers' incomes ceased increasing and the overall effectiveness of the CAP was brought into question. The Uruguay Round of GATT and the enlargement of the EEC to 12 members with the inclusion of three large agricultural producing economies, Spain, Greece and Portugal, triggered an urgent need for profound reform of the CAP. The final accord of the Uruguay Round in 1993 called for the gradual disappearance of subsidies, which were to be reduced 36 per cent in 15 years, and domestic financial aids as well as free entry of global agricultural commodities into the European market. This agreement did not pertain to agricultural production for non-alimentary purposes, such as the industrial use of seeds, corn and beans.

The Reform of 1992 and the 2000 Agenda

The reform of 1992 substituted direct aids (transfers) to farmers in place of price intervention. Direct aid, proportional at the surface, was by an obligation to withdraw from production 15 per cent of farmland, decreasing to 10 per cent in 1995. Intervention initiated by prices declines were to be reduced by 15–35 per cent, depending on the product, by 1995. New measures were introduced that favored the protection of the environment, for example regulations on the usage of nitrates in fertilizers. Giving increased attention to world prices, the new version of the CAP compensated the losses of farmers by establishing a system similar to the deficiency payments program of the United States which offers subsidies to farmers when changes in free market prices greatly reduce their income.

The disappointing harvests of 1996, notably in the United States, raised the global price of many products to the level of that of Community prices, and the land set-asides could be partially reduced. The increase in sick animals, the most dramatic of which was mad cow disease, the accentuated competition resulting from the acceleration of globalization of pork and chicken production and distribution, new behaviors associated with the consumption of previously exotic fruits, wines, and other products all disturbed the operations of the 1992 version of the CAP. In the words of Pascal Fontaine:

> European agriculture must continue to adapt to face capital payments: the enlargement of the European Union to the countries of Central and Eastern Europe, largely rural, the opening of a new door of multilateral negotiations on Jan 1, 2000 and the adoption of a new communal financial framework. In the directions that it fixed for the common agricultural policy in the 2000 Agenda, the European Commission proposed to deepen the 1992 reform in establishing a new decrease in prices of agricultural products in primary sectors of agriculture, such as beef and milk, accompanied by compensations to producers under the form of direct payments. [4]

In the year 2000, it was finally admitted that the CAP had to be abolished. The share of agriculture in the total value-added in France fell to less than 3 per cent in 2000 against 12 per cent in 1960, but continued to represent 22 per cent of the agricultural production of the EU. Reform of the CAP would therefore have to base its initiatives on recognition of the necessity of free exchange of agricultural products, the wisdom of no longer penalizing European consumers, and the necessity of reducing barriers against developing countries or former communist countries and their agricultural exports. Unfortunately, the governments of the 15 did not establish a very innovative common approach due to uncontrolled political tensions and divergent estimates of the extent to which there was an actual crisis of agricultural prices. France, the most-favored and also the most conservative country involved in the CAP, was under pressure by farmers over the 2000 Agenda negotiations. Moreover, with the 1996 reforms of agriculture in the United States, a political decision conceived as a modern reform of the agricultural sectorand the liberalization of markets did not provide shelter from a price crisis. Therefore, the principles of the CAP were left the same and the difficult choices were postponed to a date not yet determined. The modifications that were introduced concerned only the levels of European prices and the setting of the intervention price. Again in the words of Pascal Fontaine: 'in setting the objectives for agricultural policy in Agenda 2000 the Commission of the EU proposed that the 1992 reforms be deepened by programming a new price floor for the products of large scale agriculture, of beef and of milk and a variety of payments to producers in the form of direct payments.'[5]

The story of the CAP and its reforms can be told by relating the experience with beef, which in the end became the story of mad cow disease. A new regulation establishing a unique organization of the beef and veal market defines the structure and the role of EU financing and the CAP until 2006. Further reforms are expected to be initiated within this new structure of regulation.

The Story of a Mad Cow

In the beginning, European production of beef was insufficient given the stated objective of European self–sufficiency, and production had been encouraged by PAC subsidies and floor prices as was the case with the other farm productions. The introduction of milk quotas after 1984 left many dairy farmers close to bankruptcy because they were not prepared to switch to breeding meat cattle. Furthermore, pork and chicken production had been improving because of a sharp decrease in the prices of animal feed. Since that time, pork and beef have been competitors on European markets. The FEOGA bought up to 780,000 metric tonnes of beef in 1985, a substantial increase from 260,000 tonnes in 1980, but this could neither prevent the fall of the beef prices nor compensate the farmers totally for their losses.

By 1987, new subsidies were paid to farmers as but this time as social transfers. In 1989, the buying-in principle of intervention on meat prices was replaced by a tender principle restrained within upper limits. This was not enough. The situation of cattle–breeding farmers worsened. The various EU policies have succeeded in increasing European production, but this resulted in an excess of supply in the late 1980s, deepening the decrease in farmers' incomes when cattle prices continued to fall. Five years later, when the PAC was reformed, the EU had been enlarged and the single market process was completed. It was then decided that market support would be no longer primarily based on the price of meat. The end of price intervention was to be offset by an increase in the subsidies and the premiums paid directly to producers. Fortunately the price of beef was stabilized but this was not to last long. The British mad cow crisis in 1996 (bovine spongiform encephalopathy, known as the BSE virus) made both the consumption of beef and beef prices fall sharply all over Europe. In

1999, the European Council decided once again to reform the CAP over the next two years by gradually reducing market supports, including a cut in the intervention price and changes in buying-in arrangements, and offsetting this by restructuring the direct aid paid to producers. Public intervention would not disappear entirely, an additional cut of 20 per cent in the intervention price being decided, but it will essentially be replaced by programs such as aid for private storage and slaughter premiums. In November 2000, French beef producers were powerfully hurt by a new and unexpected French mad cow crisis, which required thousands of French cows to be killed, followed by a collapse of French consumption of beef by 60 per cent, and bans on French meat imports imposed by Spain, Italy, Hungary, Poland, Russia and, later, on the entire EU. The impact was magnified since this excess supply came on top of the CAP policy changes.

THE STATE AS PLANNER

At the very beginning of the post-Second World War reconstruction period the idea was to make the Republican State the sort of commander-in-chief of the national economy. The Commissariat Général du Plan (CGP), the general planning agency, was created in 1946 by General de Gaulle and Jean Monnet, who took it in charge of it, and placed it under the direct control of the Ministry of Finance (1954) and later of the Prime Minister (1962). Its roles were defined as those of clarifying choices and strengthening the role and the power of the state, preparing planning laws and norms so as to assure the consistency of decisions that were made, promoting policy discussion among agencies, forecasting, and assessment of CGP activities. The CGP was supported by a dozen or more agencies with responsibility for specific areas of policy and policy research; they are too numerous to be listed here.

The mission and the nature of the CGP in France changed enormously from one plan to another. The first five-year plan focused on the reconstruction of destroyed buildings, machines, infrastructure and factories after the war. A reform profoundly modified the role of the CGP in 1982, and the most recent plan was reduced to an indicative strategic plan. Central French planning operated its mutation towards a contractual planning, then towards a decentralized planning, and finally regional planning. The last plan was no longer called a plan but a contract. The dates of the various plans are given below with the primary objective of each briefly indicated:

1947–1953 : First plan of modernization and equipment, birth of CGP
1954–1957 : Second plan of modernization and equipment

1958–1961 : Third plan of modernization and equipment
1960–1961 : Intermediate plan
1962–1965 : Fouth plan of economic and social development
1966–1970 : Fifth plan of economic and social development
1971–1975 : Sixth plan of economic and social development
1976–1980 : Seventh plan of economic and social development
1980 : The project of the eighth plan was not submitted to Parliament
1982-1983 : Intermediate plan. The plan became a law (voted by
   Parliament).
1984–1988 : Ninth plan of economic, social and cultural development
1989–1992 : Tenth plan
1992–1993 : Preparation of the Eleventh plan
1993–1995 : Eleventh plan
1994–1998 : Contracts of Plan

The plans can be regrouped into four categories: (a) the reconstruction plans: 1946-1961, (b) the growth and development plans: 1962-1975, (c) the crisis plans: 1976-1988, and (d) the strategic plan: 1989-1995.

The Reconstruction Plans

All of the early plans were adopted in a context of considerable urgency, with primary attention being paid to coal mining, electricity, iron and steel, cement, agricultural machinery and transport. They sought to assure adequate supplies of food for the population, to modernize agriculture, to reconstruct industry while attaching priority to activities such as those of construction and public works, to modernize the economy, and to develop the exporting industries so as to achieve equilibrium in the external balance. Then in 1958, the Third Plan took a new direction with the opening of the national economy to imports, French entry into the EEC, the Algerian War and the inflationary tensions that resulted, and the next arrivals in the market – the baby-boomers born after the war. In addition, General de Gaulle, coming to power in 1958, imposed his wish to make France an exemplary economy. A new instrument was introduced in the service of planning: the National French Accounts Department, with an explicitly long-term view of economic development.

Planning for Growth in an Open Economy

The plans pertaining to growth and development marked the period of 1962–75. Since the advent of the Common Market, it appeared that growth must continue to be supported. The French went from a situation of scarcity to one of abundance and of mass consumption. From this moment, the French plan took on new style and speed and began to develop in a less dirigist manner. The plan no longer selected priority branches, but now its planning became indicative and flexible and it facilitated economic and social development in a very broad sense. Beginning with 1962, the five-year plan was subject to a parliamentary vote. This was the first symbolic step in the direction of state disengagement. The economic and social context was newly modified by the political unrest of May 1968. Economic growth seemed to be affected only to a minor degree, but inflation exploded and the pace of investment in public infrastructure slowed. It was discovered that there was an unequal balance between supply and demand for specific skills in the workforce, and laws were passed that developed programs of professional training. The last plan of this period, which had been implemented by President Georges Pompidou in the de Gaullian spirit of an industrial imperative, was also disrupted by a crisis, that of the first oil shock.

Global competition intensified during the 1970s because countries began to specialize in their production, in large part as a result of the impact of technological progress. Consequently the French government adopted a set of prioritized objectives and indicators referred to as social collective preference. Industrial policies and the plan continued to respond to the new challenges of open-market competition, while French corporations were urged to reconstruct themselves, farmers were offered assistance to become competitive, and housing construction was supported. With regard to this last point, France was the last country in Europe to have resolved the housing shortage caused by the war. After 1971, the French state once again became the economic commander-in-chief that it had been following the war.

Unfortunately, the achievement of the Sixth Plan was brutally compromised by the oil price shock. The two oil shocks of 1973–4 and 1979 made the price of oil soar from \$3 to \$33 in just six years. With these erratic changes, and despite its flexibility, the objectives of the plan could not be sustained – it was as though the economy had once again been closed.

The Crisis Plans

In the Seventh Plan a list of programs of public infrastructure investments was compiled called the PAP (Priority Programs of Action). At the same time other initiatives, such as the RCB (Rational Budget Choices), were designed to improve the effectiveness and selectivity of public expenditures. The major event of the end of the 1970s involved the French political leaders and their understanding that economic management was more than just a question of will. As Hubert Prévot said: 'we have learned two lessons,…,France cannot permit itself to go against the grain of general movement of the western economy. The planner must no longer fix objectives in absolute value.'⁶ Despite this, the new Socialist government of François Mitterand (1981) drove France to the edge of bankruptcy in two years while acting against the grain and doing the opposite of what the other countries were doing in the same context of international crisis.

In 1981, the government wished to restore the plan with new methods. The failure of the intermediate plan (1982–3), an economic recovery plan based on stimulation of consumption, renewed their desire to reinforce planning in France. They therefore concocted an extraordinarily complex and sophisticated reform of the CGP, its agencies, and its methods, in providing it with new institutions. For example, the National Commission of Planning was introduced, Priority Programs of Implementation replaced the PAP, and plan-related contracts were signed between the state and the regions and between the state and the large state-controlled corporations. On the other hand, as will be discussed in Chapter 7, a new sign of decentralization appeared, with an increased role being given to administrative regions and local governments in the management of territory. Decisions gained credibility in the opinion of both the government and public decision-makers, with adoption of a new instrument, a macro-economic model with multiple scenarios, implemented with the help of Vassili Leontief and Andrew Shonfield.⁷

The Ninth Plan, which was adopted in 1984, was entirely different from its precedents. It established a concrete, contractual relationship of decentralization between the state and the regions. These were the first contracts of the state–region plan, which established a contractual base for the sharing of finance and operations. Objectives pertaining to the struggle against inflation and to employment were accompanied by reductions in the total of wages and salaries and in labor costs, thanks to a rate of increase in wages that was less than that of productivity. Emphasis was placed on technological deficiencies (for example, modernization of telecommunications), assisting corporations and households reduce their indebtedness, opening borders to movements of goods and services, the strong value of the franc, and increasing French engagement in Europe. The funds were distributed as follows: Fr44.7 billion to the state and Fr28.8 billion for the regions; 38 per cent was allocated to transport, 17 per cent to economic policies, 11 per cent to waste treatment and social actions, and 10 per cent to education and training.

The coherence and coordination of the decentralized pieces of the plan, at the level of the regions, departments and communes, was assured by the CIAT (Inter-ministerial Committee for the Management of Territory) in collaboration with non-governmental organizations such as the Chambers of Commerce. The different laws of decentralization required the local governments to finance a number of initiatives and infrastructure projects through their own taxes in the name of decentralization of planning and public expenditure, including education and public transportation.

The Strategic Plans

With the Tenth Plan (1989), the nature and the significance of what was left of the planning structure was once again transformed. A second form of state–region contracts was introduced, based on three principles: selectivity; simplification of the execution of procedures; and realization of the decentralization through an enhancement of the role of the prefect of the region. Plans of regional development were established in each region utilizing research aimed at long-term development. Another very important component was access to the structural funds of the EU. The state provided Fr52 billion and the regions Fr46 billion. Priority was given to the regions that were experiencing problems with industrial conversion and to rural regions. Again, this will be discussed further in Chapter 7. The strategic phase of planning returned, in 1989, to the task of identifying specific actions to initiate, and to determine the direction of structural and qualitative policies, but the earlier notions of quantitative objectives and of specific programs had been abandoned. Economic policy assessment finally arrived in France in 1990, while a number of countries in Europe and America had already been practicing it.[8] A twin objective was sought: of informing the people and of effectively executing decisions.

With the Eleventh Plan, planning *per se* disappeared and was replaced by the five-year laws covering 1993–7. These laws can be qualified as the third version of the contracts of the state–region plan. Regional elected officials prepared regional plans in collaboration with corporations, professional bodies, non-governmental organizations, and local labor unions. Priorities were given to rural development, teaching and research, transportation infrastructure and economic competitiveness. One of these laws, titled University 2000, contractually reunited all the levels of the government and the budget for universities – city, department, region, and state. Dialogue and cooperation became the practice. In 2001, the future of regional planning itself seems uncertain.

THE STATE AS PRODUCER AND ITS INDUSTRIAL POLICY

The twin goals of competitiveness and maintenance of a benevolent social policy lie at the heart of the challenge facing France. Competitiveness ultimately means trimming back the role of the government, the overall tax burden and the size of the public sector. In short, it means that France must become more Anglo-Saxon or more liberal, as the French put it. Almost no French politician on the left or right will openly endorse such free-market policies. But in fact, the logic of liberalism is built into the Euro, the European single market and the free-trade global economy that France has embraced. France is indeed moving in a liberal direction, but you mustn't say it.

These are the words of Antoine Garapon, an expert on the French justice system, who concludes: 'what distinguishes France today is a republican hypocrisy.'[9]

The author of these lines says it all and leaves nothing to be added. However, to establish more precisely the truth in regard to the role of the state in France in the year 2000, one must investigate within the quantitative and qualitative evidence scattered through the dark landscape of economic data. Much of public discourse, above all that of the political sector, is marked by hypocrisy. But we must also admit that the French leaders and bureaucrats have little preference for transparency, something that seems to contrast with the relative transparency that generally reigns in the United States. In this section, we will examine the evolution of the interventionist ideology in France and the specific means of governmental intervention in domestic industrial production. Planning *à la française* is only briefly discussed. The structures and restructuring of the French economy are examined in greater detail in Chapter 6.

The State as the Producer

The errors of public decision in France were most costly to those whom they were supposed to help. In other words, this country characterized itself by the preeminence of the public sector or, more generally, by the political sphere. The characteristic of market policy, according to the analysis of James Buchanan and Gordon Tullock,[10] was precisely not to be a market: the rule of law was vague, not truly reinforced and unstable. On the other hand, the decisions taken in the context of civil law engaged the participants. For example, a contract between the two parties has the force of law.

When a new enterprise fails, this can be due to a poorly defined product, poor management, lack of leadership, instability in the legal context, or barriers of entry that were underestimated. It can also consist of a harmful effect from governmental industrial policies imposed upon hypothetical choices rather than on realities, as was sometimes the case in the France of the twentieth century.[11] Independent of the weight and impact of the planning, these wrong choices were in part explicable through the importance of the public sector in the large firms and in the mass production of goods and services. In addition, before they were to be completely privatized, the nomination by the state of senior executives of the large state-controlled firms was done with political rather than professional criteria in mind.[12] However, some observers argue that the conservative attitude of national pressure groups, producers and organized workers were against the liberalization objectives of Brussels.[13]

More often, the history of an industrialization process begins with local endeavors. These are the craftsmen who work as an alternative to mass production, and are primarily organized in networks or in cooperatives. Corporations here are small and are managed by extremely well-qualified people. Rather than producing the same thing as the rest of the economy, such as products and standardized services, these new enterprises gave birth to narrow and highly flexible markets. These markets, like the individuals who created them and made them successful, are extremely flexible tools. Innovation, market development, and expansion continued to grant them this chance to succeed even with mass production already in place. Moreover, we must not forget that the creation rate of enterprises determines a large part of the employment rate. What was true in the nineteenth century is also true for today where industry explodes in the new economy and its services (information technology, electronics, telephone, Internet, and so forth), causing mutations as radical as those inflicted by the first two industrial revolutions.[14] What is true for the twentieth century that is different than in the previous century is the fact the new enterprises were created by the state from existing firms and parts of firms and operated under its protection, as was the case with Credit Lyonnais, Charbonnages de France, and Bull, among others.

Brief History of Industrial Policy in France

Can any one guideline or a clear coherence in the complex of French industrial policy over the past 50 years be distinguished? Their diversity would suggest that these policies should be classified into two categories: structural policies and international competitiveness policies. The behavior of leaders and the elite remained essentially interventionist until quite recently. Each of the post-Second World War periods we will examine offered a mixture of the two categories of policies, sometimes one of them unfolding more clearly than the other; sometimes neither was dominant. What is most evident is a profound change in the nature of industrial policies on three occasions: after the opening of the Common Market; after the economic crisis of 1974; and after the economic policy failures of 1981–3. The de-nationalization of the 1990s should not properly be considered as industrial policy.

In the second half of the twentieth century, France represented a realized example of a mixed economy: private enterprises composed essentially of small and medium corporations, and a public sector consisting of large corporations and their subsidiaries, with the state contributing all or part of their capital. In acquiring control of economic activity, French governments pursued the chosen objective, whatever the cost. The economic leaders thought that human will could lead the economy, an idea that was popular at the time in Europe. For some the USSR provided a model that had some attractions. In order to finance such an economy, taxes were raised at first and then, later, recourse was taken to financial markets. Today public expenses account for 54 per cent of the GDP and the tax burden 45 per cent. From the beginning of the 1990s, public investment has represented more than a third of total investment in France.

The years 1945–58

During the years from 1945 to 1958, French leaders and intellectuals vigorously rejected private capitalism and the market economy. The state was seen to function as the only leader in the economy as well as in the area of social policy. It seemed that governments after the war had adopted the same ideology as the authoritarian government of Vichy (1939–44):[15] they pursued great projects and conserved the existing large state firms, including Credit National, Banque Française for the Commerce Exterieur, the railroad, Compagnie Générale Transatlantique, Compagnie Nationale de Rhône, Régie Autonome des Petroles, and many others. Their intention was to do battle with private trusts. Economic intervention took three directions: planning, public appropriation of the means of production for activities judged to be strategic, and extensive investments for infrastructure, supervised by a new minister, the Minister of the National Economy.

So that these activities could be financed, the circulation of the public treasury was established, capital and loanable funds having failed to materialize and aid from the Marshall Plan having proven to be insufficient. During a period of 30 years, public investments in infrastructure initiatives and large enterprises and the participation of the state in private investments were the source of budget deficits. The Caisse de Dépots et Consignation (a department of the Treasury), the Fonds de Modernisation et d'Equipment, then the FDES (Fonds de Développement Economique et Social) intermediated between private savings and budget allocations, and investments. The new Institut National de la Statistique et d'Etudes Economiques (INSEE) and its publication *Statistiques et Etudes Financières* brought their logistic support, and the Ecole Nationale d'Administration provided the future elite and leaders of industry and finance. Nationalized firms served as instruments for the restructuring of industry, transport and the banking sector. The steel industry was not nationalized until later. Large firms such as Les Charbonnages de France, EDF, GDF, and Le Commissariat a l'Energie Atomique were created.

The years 1958–81

At the beginning of the second half of the twentieth century, industrial policy was a synonym for nationalizations, restructuring of the nationalized firms, and the creation of additional public firms. Eventually, towards 1960, there occurred a complete change of nature, and policy became applied to the development of manufacturing beyond the state sector. De Gaulle wanted an industrial France that was self-sufficient. New industrial policy took the name of industrial redeployment. At this time, in addition to the new agency for the management of territory (DATAR), the Gaullian concept of an industrial imperative, later taken on by Pompidou, presided over the great projects initiative. The primary participants were the technocrats of prominent schools (ENA, Ecole des Mines, Inspection des Finances, Ecole Polytechnique). The venues were the great public monopolies like the EDF (Electricité de France), SNCF, PTT (Postal), and CEA (Commission d'Energie atomique). During the same period, the banking and financial sector took its first steps towards liberalization. The aim was directed toward the compartmentalization of banks and they were granted the right to accept private savings. Fiscal advantages were granted to shareholders and bond holders. The savings rate for households grew from 11 per cent of their income after taxes in 1959 to 17.5 per cent in 1978. Moreover, an ample movement of de-budgetization made certain public financial institutions (CDC, Credit National, Credit Foncier, eand so on) become independent of the scrutiny of the public treasury and, after that, of parliamentary control. We should recall that this was also the time of the adoption of the first planning contracts.

The start of the Fifth Republic was marked by a rather original approach to industrial policy. General de Gaulle had directed policy towards one of prestige and independence. Concentrations and large infrastructure and institutional projects such as La Villette, Le Concorde, Les Halles, the nuclear program and the atomic bomb, the plan for Calcul and Bull, and naval construction were put into play. Unfortunately, many saw failure.

Industrial policy, until the 1970s, consisted in aiding corporations experiencing difficulty or in the process of going into bankruptcy: Lipp, Manufrance, Le Creusot, textiles, and so on. The last major case was Unisor and Sacilor, taken over by the state in 1978, regrouped, and then nationalized in 1981 – later to become denationalized. The case of the automobile manufacturer Renault was different. To penalize the Renault family, accused of collaborating with the German occupation, the corporation was placed under state control. It continued to serve French leaders and the dominant labor union in accordance with the social model, granting social benefits and generous working conditions to its employees, occasionally receiving aid from the state, and moving many of its operations outside the Paris region and even outside France, for example to Vilvoorde in Belgium.

The presidency of Charles de Gaulle made a lasting impression on French society, industrial policy choices, and the means used to implement that policy. After de Gaulle's conservative administration, state ownership was left strengthened. However, state intervention grew in two directions at the same time: an orientation toward the outside world in which Europe was to replace the African colonies, and an orientation toward dialogue between the social partners (syndicates, workers and employers). It was at this time (between 1960 and 1970) that the planners searched for a contractual route with economic actors, the so-called middle route. Such a reform was possible because the French economy was still rather closed to the outside world. Regional development policy also took a fresh turn with the new strategy of poles of development. But the decentralization wished for by de Gaulle, which actually was only a regionalization of state intervention, cost him failure in a national referendum.

The establishment of a new role for the state became an evident necessity but was only actually reached after the crisis of the 1970s. As Jean-François Eck writes:

> the functions of the public sector...quickly appeared to be too numerous, if not contradictory: for example what of models that ignore profitability in the name of the national imperative? [And after the nationalizations of 1982] wanting to be at the same time industrialist and banker, producer and transporter, supplier of both electricity and gas, protector of coal and refiner of petroleum, the state mixed up things. It confronted contradictions and ignored what was essential – the clear determination of objectives in the service of a coherent economic policy. [16]

It was only around the mid-1980s that the foundations of the state roles of producer and leader became the subject of discussion among the political leadership.

What is called industrial policy is therefore actually a grouping of several types of interventions. The most constant was the restructuring of the industrial sector over a lengthy period of time but with expected goals differing according to the periods. Following the strategic nationalizations after the war, industry as a whole was showered with aid and diverse objectives, many which were included in the five-year plans. After Europe opened its economies, some corporations were split into smaller entities while others disappeared.

1981 and beyond

Awareness of the phenomenon of deindustrialization was a consequence of the first great oil shock. It became necessary to determine a new industrial policy in the 1980s at the same time that the government was initiating its series of nationalizations. Instead of a policy of self-sufficiency, a selective policy centered on certain activities was chosen. It was thought necessary to limit the competition between corporations in the same industry, as the underlying notions were that competition would not serve the governments objectives, it results in duplicative investments that just increase costs, only some ofwhich will ever be profitable, and it is socially useless.[17] The government favored some regroupings, such as the aluminum producer Pechiney, and it asked nationalized banks to make credit easier for the smaller firms.

A second major turn in was taken by the state in the matter of industrial policy after the unfortunate failure of the Socialist policy of 1981–2. At this time, the divorce between discourse and reality began. Contrary to the message of the new government, industrial voluntarism lost its integrity. It is significant that the term industrial policy disappeared, to be replaced by modernization policy and industrial strategy. It consisted of a mix of policies focusing on the industrial environment and policies of recovery for large state-owned enterprises. The key industries, principally steel and coal, were accorded reconversion assistance. The restructuring and cooperation of exporting industries such as automobiles, telecoms, and aeronautics, with their European partners, were favored. Plans concerned cutting-edge activities (the plan for electronic goods, for example, was accelerated). The recovery of certain firms soon appeared impossible, including the pulp and paper company La Chapelle-Darblay, and the automotive firm Chausson, despite substantial subsidies from the state. Policies of social action regarding unemployment were put into effect. As for the large nationalized enterprises, a good majority were incapable of becoming profitable in the long run, their difficulties being aggravated by the rapid decrease in state aid and by the opening up to competition, to which their leaders were not capable of responding.

The years from 1984–6 marked the appearance of a new type of industrial redeployment. This was the opening of Europe and the imminent advent of the Single Market, which was implemented by the Single European Act. The state mandated, often at great costs, the downsizing of the coal, metal and naval construction industries. Creusot-Loire (coal) lost 37,000 employees, Boussac (traditional textiles) fired 17,000 workers, and so on. Economic free areas were invented, where tax laws were reduced and labor market flexibility was introduced. What remained of this rather revolutionary period was a drastic reduction of state aid as well as the creation of true monetary and international financial markets that drove the large private and public corporations to turn towards private financing. The time had passed when the state would help every large corporation in difficulty. From then on, it would only intervene in leading and advanced activities, such as aerospace, or in buoyant and exporting branches, such as automobiles. The Fonds Industrial de Modernisation loaned savings at a low interest rate that had been collected through the new Comptes pour le Développement de l'Industrie, or CODEVI. The true hexagonal revolution began to take place in 1983 when the newspaper *Le Monde* ran for two days on the front page an unexpected laudatory article praising the roles of profit, corporations and the market. This was an ideological revolution. It especially justified the change in the direction of governmental policy. Public opinion in 2000 was not yet totally convinced, and that can be explained by the fact that politicians continued to hold the same anti-market, anti-profit and anti-capitalist positions as they had done before the accession of the Mitterand government to power in 1981. It is what Elie Cohen refers to as economic or industrial rhetoric, where the words do not reflect the acts.

Contemporary Industrial Policies

'Today France must respond to a major challenge, that of the dislocation of its system of production.'[18] This was the defeatist evaluation of the old agency for planning. According to it, in the period of transition of the late 1990s, French industry suffered from three handicaps: (a) competitiveness that strategically reduces some activities and not well differentiated between specific activities; (b) insufficient cooperation and coordination through networks of firms; and (c) extreme regional gaps in performance. The cause of this situation was specified as being the conservatism of many French firms that are often more focused on restructuring by retrenchment and reduction of the workforce than on restructuring through innovation and risk-taking. It has been said that France lacks entrepreneurs because the cost of establishing a new firm is higher in France than it is in other industrialized countries.[19] This situation appears to have been reversed after 1998. One of the factors that were favorable to this improvement was the financial market: the prospects for growth of value added were realized in the market price of shares. Both the creation of new firms and economic growth benefited from this.

Accompanying this contemporary transformation of the economy, the appropriate industrial policy, in our opinion, should be modest and broadly focused on facilitation of the development of economic activities. The following would appear to be desirable elements in such a policy:

1. Promotion of networking and cooperation among firms that reveals their common interests and assists in the development of network infrastructures.
2. Fiscal assistance in the development of competitiveness for all activities without privileging any specific areas, to support the diffusion of research and innovation, and to recognize that investment in human capital has been proven to have the highest return.
3. Stimulation of regional dynamics so as to realize the potential of the regions, to train and educate workers with the skill needs of the future in mind, to establish linkages between universities, research institutes and companies.
4. To expose the current and future labor force to other cultures through student exchanges, foreign study and internships abroad, and to think in terms of cultures of entrepreneurs, innovators and creators.

The traditional industrial policy of France is outmoded and is on the verge of disappearing; the above represents what we are convinced is an industrial policy that is appropriate to the present and the foreseeable future.

The truth of Colbertism and Saint-Simonism: no one is responsible

If high-tech Colbertism was a success with the French telephone system, but then the success story of the TGV in large part unfolded without the participation of political decision-makers. Beyond these two examples, other large corporations under state control which were not doing innovative things and were just engaging in costly projects simply failed. When an entrepreneurial activity disregards the consumers, the shareholders, and the competition, its survival can only lie in the hands of the tax collector. For de Gaulle, the primary consideration was the prestige of France. In the end, the absence of considerations of efficiency and competitiveness had its impact on the values of shares on the stock exchange.

Financial Times writer Andrew Jack wrote:

> [T]he most extreme example of France's most expensive exceptions: the state's approach to managing and restructuring public enterprises. [Credit Lyonnais loss] was a sum unprecedented around the world...[These losses] were the result of...structural failures that reflected problems across much of the state-controlled corporate sector, and involved connivance and incompetence among many of the country's elites...[and that this] had little effect on their later careers. [20]

Jean-François Revel recalls, in his analysis of enduring state control of the economy, that all that is collective is considered as irresponsible because it is so by nature, even in partially state-controlled societies.[21] Elie Cohen named this mix of private and public, economic and political, favoritism and incompetence an 'imbroglio politico-industrialo-technologique,'[22] and it is what Maurice Parodi prefers to call 'Colbertism and Saint-Simonism.'[23]

Currently we see the French public sector and its exceptionalism subjected to a fundamental reconsideration, although rather belatedly. It was with great insight that Andrew Jack examined not only the anti-economic, centralized and political nature of public enterprises, but also the rapid transformation of the benign neglect approach to the negative consequences of heavy-handed state control:

> In the second half of the 1990s, many aspects of old-style French capitalism were being called into question. Pressure from domestic and international competitors, top management changes, the demands from more aggressive investors (pension funds mainly) and from customers all conspired to bring about change. The transformations taking place in the public sector played an essential role. A mixture of ideological evolutions and a simple desire to be rid of loss-making companies motivated governments of left and right alike to continue to sell off the rump of state-owned businesses,...By the end of the decade, just a handful of companies remained in state hands.[24]

The privatizations that were planned in 1993 have basically been achieved at the end of 2000.[25] More than 1100 corporations were partially or totally privatized. The number of employees in the public sector, 1,102,500 in 1999, represented a reduction of 40 per cent since 1995.

Traditional *capitalisme à la française* no longer exists as we begin twenty-first century. The causes of its demise can be summarized as incompetence, political and economic scandal, European competition, globalization, economic liberalism as pursued by Brussels, the accumulation of public deficits during a period of over 25 years, an increasing tax burden and, to a lesser degree, the change of a developing party still weak in public opinion. Despite the ideological campaigns of some in the press and some political leaders, French consumers aspired to more freedom of choice, to access to new technologies and to lower prices rather than the CAP, customs tariffs, indirect taxes, and state monopolies such as EDF and France Télécom. The ordinary citizen was tired of the scandals and wheeling and dealing of all kinds across the spectrum of state activities. This was also one of the causes of low participation in elections. A half-century of state management of the economy led to a deterioration of the popular image of democracy. But it is never too late to undo the damage. The disengagement of the state from the economy towards the end of the 1990s indicated 'the beginning of the end for French-style capitalism,...,[and] by the late 1990s, the era during which the state could dictate events, control companies and use them as instruments of its own policies was finished.'[26] From now on, the French were part of a world economy based on knowledge, with technology sweeping away the hierarchies and upsetting established institutions and traditional values.[27]

Not all French newspapers give recognition to the fact that France has made its way to the second millennium in an almost revolutionary manner – *Le Monde Diplomatique* is just one example. Much of the press continues to give credence to the opinion of a political leadership that must be considered reactionary. As André Safir and Dominique Michel wrote: 'France, a country of exception, if not exceptional, is the only nation that tried to make the globalization of the economy a scapegoat, an excuse for all the insufficiencies.'[28] They argued that 'this attitude is the most comfortable for us, because it makes us innocent. It equally makes our leaders, elected officials and leaders of corporations innocent, those who for twenty years have been incapable of reducing unemployment, because they are incapable of comprehending (or admitting) the reasons.' However, the gains of the internationalization of the exchange of goods and services plus the gains of privatization far surpass the costs of the transition, and these gains are here to stay in the long run.

THE STATE AS PRODUCER OF PUBLIC SERVICES

Without a doubt public services constitute one of the major French exceptions. After the war, de Gaulle and successive governments that followed him nationalized the large corporations, they established a five-year planning process and consequently defined the field and nature of public services. At the time, the plan was implemented to achieve the goal of asserting priorities for investment decisions, subsidies and legal reforms. Among the planning instruments, nationalization was to realize the strategic objectives of reconstruction and modernization of the principal productive activities, and then the orientation and specialization of these activities. Deciding which of these public services to produce raised another more subjective question. It was decided that the government, rather than the citizens, must make the decisions, according to the widespread idea of the time that the people were incapable of expressing their needs effectively and coherently in the market and that the supply of goods and services would be inappropriate. There were two other notions that were at the origin of the expansion of public services: (a) the public sector was more social than the market in that it did not make profit at the expense of consumers and it was in theory more egalitarian; and (b) consumers did not know what was good for them.

Demand-side economic theories were in style and Keynesianism had arrived in France. This approach to the economy ignored the key role of the innovator, who was soon to be recognized as being so crucial. It did not envision that the market should be seen to be a process whose equilibrium is continually in adjustment. Most importantly, it gave the state the role of directing economic activity, on the assumption that it was in control of its expenses and would use them in the interest of Keynesian counter-cyclical fiscal policy and the orientation of investments. Public services, in the same way as industrial or agricultural policy and planning, revealed a desire to construct an authoritarian system. It was never a question of democracy, but rather of equitable representation of employers, employees and corporate bodies in the institutions and processes of administration.

All the service activities in which the state and/or the local communities financed all or part of the capital and operation were seen essentially as public services. Such an objective, less clear for insurance or banking, was clearly relevant for transport, teaching, postal services and communications. In addition, there were a variety of services provided through institutions and public agencies that were not usually counted as public services. These agencies were extensions of the government ministries. For example, when the government decided to introduce a regional development policy, the Département d'Aménagement du Territoire et à l'Action Régionale was established and given authority in 1963 and shortly thereafter worked with the Conseil National d'Aménagement du Territoire (CNAT). The restructuring of agricultural land was then seen as a public service – even though a number of farmers complained of both the methods employed and the results. The Comité Interministériel de l'Aménagement et du Développement du Territoire (CIADT) supervises the allocation of land, with job creation being one of its primary objectives.

French public services are part of the much-vaunted French exception. Their management entails a mixture of monopolies, political direction, acquired privileges, the perceived need to introduce technology, and the wish to redistribute income.[29] It is also true that this rather jumbled mixture proved to be acceptable in certain cases, but rather costly in others. The state was supposed to cut back non-profitable public services, for example, secondary railroad lines. It was supposed to keep afloat year after year public service corporations such as the SNCF or budgets like the Caisse de Retraite des Cheminots or the postal and telephone system. At certain periods, it refocused its firms' activities and restructured them organizationally.

The national education system has rapidly become uncontrollable and apparently not amenable to reform.[30] In addition, the monopolistic centralization of schooling caused it to deteriorate in quality. Its mission to educate students in culture as well as the world of work was sacrificed in deference to the concerns about inequality of access and national standards regarding levels of instruction, quality of programs and recognition of diplomas. The century-long concerns of some nourished the resurgence of the ideas of decentralization and of introducing competition among educational institutions. In this way, the world of schooling opened itself up to globalization. Interest in foreign languages was reaffirmed, students increasingly began to take up internships abroad, the new technologies of information and communication entered the schools, albeit belatedly, curricula were for the most part updated, universities were assured continuous training, and so forth.

Finally, the failure to achieve the objectives of the public services are due primarily to the fact that the absence of the market and market prices distorts the signals coming from consumers. Supply determination, its nature and its quantity are thus arbitrary. This is what principally explains the return to the private sector – and to the market – of several of the individual public services in various countries of Europe. Even justice, too slow and costly, was deprived of one part of its activities through the growing recourse to private sector mediation and arbitrage mechanisms.

At the onset of the third millennium, Jean-Marie Chevalier asks: 'the idea of public service,…,is it still supportable?'[31] Public service as a whole is judged as well by the ordinary Frenchman as it is by the academic social scientist as being 'routine, corporatist, not very efficient, administratively intrusive and habitually generating a budget deficit.' Under pressure from the state and European directives, monopolies that are or were public services, such as funeral and burial services, municipal trash collection, certain health services, and so on, have had to modify their style of management, and certain public service missions have been delegated and transferred to the private sector, as with the Law of 1993. France Télécom has been privatized recently, but had previously out-sourced several of its services. The postal service no longer retains its local monopoly. Water services were often leased out. Electricité de France outsourced certain services, and its monopoly was recently partially opened to competition, although in an extremely limited manner. It is probable that, one day, utilities will be offered in a competitive manner by private entrepreneurs – even if the state or the local governments continue to impose on them a schedule of requirements.

France trailed other EU members in this process. It often did not apply European directives, using as justification one of the traditionalist and cultural exceptions where public service has benefited from a regime that stalled for time. The legal principle presently implemented in the EU opens all activities to competition and free exchange. All the member states of the EU signed the following articles of law in the Treaty of Rome:

> States and corporations are not to decree nor maintain any measure against the rules of the treaty...Corporations charged with service management of general economic interest or presenting characteristics of a fiscal monopoly are to be

submitted to the rules…of competition, in the limits where application of these rules does not lead to the failure of the accomplishment in law or in fact of the mission with which they were charged. The development of exchanges must not be affected…Member states must respect prohibitions against agreements, understandings, abuse of dominant positions, to limit their subsidies, and must respect the free movement of merchandise, services and people.

Public service corporations were to oblige to adhere to these same rules. It is therefore not surprising that the French state has occasionally been condemned by the European Court of Justice.

FINAL THOUGHTS ON THE EVOLUTION OF INTERVENTIONISM IN FRANCE

The undeniable benefit of what is often referred to as the European construction is to have opened up all branches of the economy to competition, and not solely those that comprise the former state-run firms. It was unfortunately in exactly these activities that the French economy excelled. According to Gary Becker, it is the profit to be attained in a competitive market that facilitates the creation of value-added, new activities and employment.[32] This is because they are short-lived and they feed a complex and unforeseeable process of innovations, gains in productivity, new ways of organization, and new contracts.[33] In this way, they provide work for the entire economy, as well as extra tax revenues to the state. In their defense, the French have rediscovered the virtues of the market. It is clear that this revolution in thinking is far from being fully achieved.   More so than for just ideological reasons or because of conservative-protectionist convictions on the part of many individuals, numerous voices preach fear and reactionism:

> For forty years, the French, who do not have confidence in the market, knew how to develop a certain manner, an inimitable mix of devised planning, of technocratic Colbertism and technological chauvinism to develop a system of competitive production. But the European construction, technological revolution and globalization, little by little, have made this method of regulation obsolete.[34]

France turned, slowly but surely, towards the economic liberalism that was so discredited in the past. Within the hexagon, as much as in the countries participating in international exchange, the advent of a free market progressively eliminated the distortions resulting from the actions of the governmental interventionists.   The allocation of factors of production among activities, in actuality forced by the actions of consumer demands

among activities, in actuality forced by the actions of consumer demands and innovation, brought market-based economies continually into a Pareto-optimal situation.[35]

One of the other beneficial consequences of the global opening of European economies, and of the French economy in particular, is often omitted. Until 1994, the Bank of France was under the direct control of the government and it had the monopoly on the production of money. One of its mandates was that of assuring that the economy would be provided with the credit it required. Elsewhere, the structure of domestic production was to a large extent monopolistic and oligopolistic, which favored a succession of salary increases, generally in excess of that justified by gains in productivity. Today, the productive system as a whole is completely exposed to competition, first from firms throughout Europe, but also from all reaches of the globe. Corporations can no longer respond to salary demands by ignoring either the prices charged by foreign firms and or the innovations of their competitors – thus removing one of the primary sources of inflation.

But the weakening of the Euro made an imported inflation reappear in terms of intermediate goods as well as generating inflation through marked-up prices on domestic products. In reality, in France the state remains the primary employer, consumer, investor, borrower and, as always, the primary producer. It is therefore obligated to master its costs and to utilize its power to influence prices and domestic salaries. Actually, the French government and private actors in the economy cannot hope for the return of a closed economy, with stable activities and occupations and a steady-state growth. The French economy finds itself in the middle 'of a definitely uncertain world. It's the price of the regaining of dynamism that it fully knew how to take advantage since December 1958; in opening itself to the rest of the world, it gave up the framework in which it had known all along how to operate its reconstruction and accomplish its modernization.'[36]

We present in Figure 3.1 a representation, taken from the work of Yves Crozet, of the nature of the interventionist French state at the end of the 1990s.[37] State economic action is dominated by the three solidly established preferences indicated in the center of the figure. It is a real concern how a role so solidly anchored in tradition will be able to evolve. The economic situation in the middle of the 1990s was one of high unemployment, a slow rate of economic growth, high interest rates and substantial public sector deficits and debts. Several solutions were advanced, including: (a) introducing more flexibility in the labor market; (b) reducing government deficits, expenditures and taxes; (c) abandoning the policy of the strong franc, prior to 1999 and participation in the Euro, after 1999; and (d) liberalizing all aspects of the French economy and giving

Figure 3.1 The Interventionist State

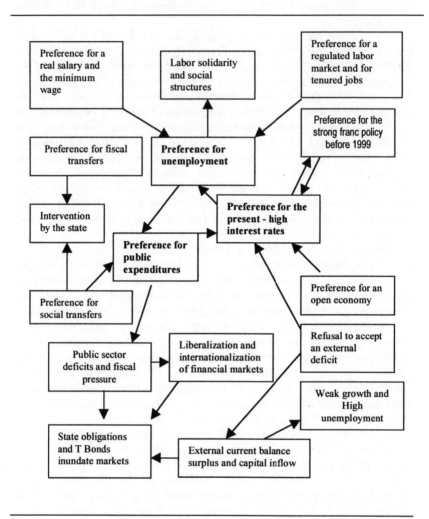

more power to market forces in accordance with the pressure from Brussels. A writer for *The Financial Times* stated, while reporting at the end of 2000 on several reports of major global economic organizations, that:

> economists in the main multilateral organizations from the OECD and the IMF to the European Central Bank have warned of the dangers ahead if public spending is not cut further, investment encouraged and labor rigidities removed. Only in

this way can France build on the past three years' average annual growth of 3 per cent and achieve a medium-term sustainable target slightly below this level.'[38]

Why has the evolution of French economic policy been so retarded? Crozet comments that 'the flexibility in this structure is probably going to be rather marginal,…,since the abandonment of one or the other of the three key preferences will impose a substantial cost.'[39] But, according to Elie Cohen, in the French tradition, it is perhaps tempting to believe that the solution may be found in a certain withdrawal.[40] Some of the more recent governments have timidly begun to adopt an attitude that is somewhat more liberal, in the classic sense of the term, than has been the case in the past. But French ministers are no more disposed to more liberty than are their counterparts in Britain or Germany. The electorate, the political parties and French labor unions are essentially conservative in the sense of defending their privileges and their complex social benefits. The ordinary French citizen is comfortable with the status quo. According to the Friedman notion of the 'iron triangle,' nothing moves when everything moves. This explains the dominating role of ideology in France.

The result is the rejection of the liberalization of the economy and the disappearance of protected professions and of the opening to the world in conformity with globalization.[41] The protests against the WTO and the EU indicate the presence of organized constituencies and interests, a short-term vision that focuses only on the costs of the transition, and the complete absence of a basic economic culture, and a preference for faith in the humanity of the state, its bureaucrats and its politicians.

NOTES

1. Richard Musgrave, *The Theory of Public Finance*, New York: McGraw-Hill, 1959.
2. Claude Imbert, 'La leçon de choses,' *Le Point*, no. 1462, September 15, 2000, p. 5.
3. *Cahiers Agreste*, Paris: Ministère de l'Agriculture et de la Pêche, October 1996, no. 6-7.
4. Pascal Fontaine, *Dix leçons sur l'Europe*, Luxembourg: Eurostat, 2000, p. 20.
5. Ibid.
6. B. Cazes, and P. Mioche, *Modernisation ou décadence: Contribution à l'histoire du Plan Monnet et de la planification en France*, Aix-en-Provence: Publications de l'Université de Provence, 1990.
7. 'Les mathématiques au service de la démocratie,' in the words of Pierre Massé, former Commissaire au Plan.
8. According to the decree of 22 January 1990: 'evaluation consists of determining whether judicial, administrative or financial means adopted ensure that the expected effects of a policy and its objectives will be achieved.' An

interministerial body and the *Conseil Scientifique d'évaluaton* with 11 members are to perform this evaluation.

9. Thomas Sancton, 'The French are on the roll,' *Time Magazine*, July 17, 2000.
10. James Buchanan and Gordon Tulock, *The Calculus of Consent*, Ann Arbor: University of Michigan Press, 1971; and James Buchanan and R.D. Tollison (eds.), *The Theory of Public Choice–II*, Ann Arbor: University of Michigan Press, 1984.
11. Charles Sabel and Jonathan Zeitlin, 'Historical alternatives to mass production: politics, markets and technology in nineteenth-century industrialization,' *Past and Present*, August 1985, 108, pp. 133-176.
12. Several examples are given in: Andrew Jack, *The French Exception*, London: Profile Books, 2000.
13. The forceful statements of Minister Claude Allègre are only truths recognized by many others.
14. François Caron, *Histoire économique de la France, XIX–Xxe siècles*, Paris: Armand Colin, 1997.
15. Richard Kuisel, *Le Capitalisme et l'Etat en France: Modernisation et dirigisme au XXème siècle*, Paris: Gallimard, 1984.
16. Jean-François Eck, *La France dans la nouvelle économie mondiale*, Paris: Presses Universitaires de France, 1994, p. 53.
17. For a fuller discussion of these costs see Fred Hirsch, *Social Limits to Growth*, Cambridge, MA: Harvard University Press, 1976.
18. Commissariat au Plan, ' Quelles politiques pour l'industrie française? Dynamiques du système productif: analyses, débats, propositions,' Paris: La documentation Française, September 1997.
19. 'Les obstacles à la création d'entreprises,' *Les Echos*, January 30 and 31, 1994, p. 4; "Trop d'administratifs, pas assez d'entrepreneurs – l'école en retard d'une révolution," *Challenges*, May 1998, p. 86.
20. Jack, *The French Exception*, pp. 168–169.
21. Jean-François Revel, *La grande parade – Essai sur la survie de l'utopie socialiste*, Paris: Plon, 2000, p. 265.
22. Elie Cohen, *Le Colbertisme hi-tech: Economie du grand projet des Télécom*, Paris: Hachette, 1992.
23. Alain Beitone, Maurice Parodi and Bernard Simler, *L'économie et la société française au second XXème siècle*, Paris: Armand Colin, 1994, Ch. III.
24. Andrew Jack, p. 192.
25. *Répertoire des entreprises contrôlées majoritairement par l'Etat*, Paris: INSEE, November 2000.
26. Jack, *The French Exception*, p. 194.
27. Jonas Ridderstrale and Kjell Nordstrom, *Funky Business: Le talent fait danser le capital*, Paris: Les Echos Editions, 2000.
28. André Safir and Dominique Michel, *Avantage France – France S.A. contre World Corp.*, Paris: Editions Village Mondial, 1999, pp. 12 and 24.
29. Elie Cohen, 'Ne pas confondre service public avec service du public,' *Chroniques Economiques DEDEIS*, no. 3, March 15, 1996.
30. Claude Allègre, *Toute vérité est bonne â dire*, Paris: Fayard Robert Laffont, 2000. Claude Allègre was Minister of National Education for three years during a recent socialist government.

31. Jean-Marie Chevalier (ed.), *L'Idée de service public: Est-elle encore soutenable?*, Paris: Presses Universitaires de France, 1999.
32. Gary Becker, *The Economic Approach to Human Behavior*, Chicago: University of Chicago Press, 1978.
33. Pure surprise and unforeseeable innovation are defined by Israel Kirzner in *Discovery and the Capitalist Process*, London: Routledge, 1986, and *Discovery, Capitalism and Distributive Justice,* Oxford: Basil Blackwell, 1989.
34. Safir and Michel, *Avantage France*, p. 56
35. Israel Kirzner, *The Meaning of Market Process*, London: Routledge, 1992.
36. Eck, *La France dans la nouvelle économie mondiale*, p. 43.
37. Yves Crozet, *et al., Les Grandes questions de l'économie française*, Paris: Nathan, 1997.
38. Robert Graham, 'Economy, France survey,' *The Financial Times*, November 10, 2000.
39. Crozet, *Les Grandes questions*, p. 8
40. Elie Cohen, *La Tentation hexagonale: la souveraineté à l'épreuve de la mondialisation*, Paris: Julliard, 1994.
41. Jean-Yves Naudet, *Economie politique*, Aix-en-Provence: Presses Universitaires d'Aix-Marseille, 1999.

4 France's External Economic Relations

The primary effect of globalization is to link more directly and extensively one national economy to potentially all others. It is through this linkage that both the positive consequences, such as efficiency, specialization and higher incomes, and the negative consequences, such as (short-term transitory) unemployment, dislocation and uncertainty, are forced upon a nation. Thus, it is appropriate that discussion of France's trade and financial relations with the external economy should be examined at an early stage in this book.

Of all the countries of the European Union France is the most interesting to study from the standpoint of the debate between proponents of protectionism and those of freer trade. More than is the case in the other member countries, French businessmen and political leaders have traditionally endorsed the policy of self-sufficiency. The reasons for this are somewhat complex but include an attachment to traditional colonial trading partners, a belief that France was not prepared in the post-Second World War period to meet competition from Germany and the United States, and a Gaullist notion of France's national interest.

This chapter begins with two sections in which we examine the dynamic between protectionism and free trade in France prior to and following 1945. Trade data since that date will focus on both the composition of goods and services traded and the geographic aspect of France's trading partners. Financial flows are presented in the fourth section, at which point we will then be prepared to examine the impacts of liberalization of trade and finance on the French economy. The sixth and final substantive section treats France's economic relationships with other regions of the world, with a special emphasis on those with the European Union and its various deepening and broadening initiatives.

TARIFF AND TRADE HISTORY UP TO 1945

While it must be accepted that during the nineteenth century the French state did not have the institutional structure and the financial weight to plan or direct the economy that it was to gain in the years following the First World War, one policy tool it was able to use to further the interests of French producers was trade protectionism. In 1860 the Cobden–Chevalier (Anglo-French) free trade treaty started Europe toward a network of free trade agreements, each of which included a most-favored-nation clause, that within a decade brought Europe as close to complete free trade as it would ever get prior to the Treaty of Rome in 1958.[1] Then, in a series of three steps, in 1884–5, 1892–7 and 1910, the French government significantly increased tariffs, in a direct reversal of the policies of the Second Republic (1851–70). This resort to protectionism is referred to as *mélinisme*, in reference to one of its most enthusiastic promoters, Jules Méline, after whom the tariff of 1892 was named and who headed the government during 1896–8.[2] The fundamental thrust of state policy was to develop the market of greater France, France plus its colonies, for domestic producers. Prior to the Great War, however, actual policy initiatives were limited to a collaboration begun in 1842 between the state and the railroad companies and support of French agriculture.

The rail project involved loan guarantees by the state, assistance in the construction of infrastructure, and purchase or support of lines in difficulty. The persuasiveness of the railroad lobby was matched by that of the highway lobby, notably that of Michelin. The result was an argument in favor of a state policy that would unify the national territory and make more efficient domestic exchange. Agriculture benefited from assistance to cooperatives and support of financial institutions such as Caisses de Crédit Agricole and Casses d'Assurances. The traditional conservatism of the rural population was thought to make the small-scale family farm a bulwark of democracy. André Gueslin has commented that: 'in 1913, the state is present in the economy but in a limited way, without sufficient means and above all without a clear design.'[3] In none of these policies were the efficiency concerns and the welfare of consumers of traditional liberal free trade theory present. While the thinking of French policy-makers did not evolve noticeably, their capacity to engage the state in the economic life of France was greatly enhanced by the exigencies of the First World War.

The war itself gave the state a commanding position in the economy that it was hard to reduce during the peace. First, there was the need to provide assistance to the areas that had suffered destruction and damage during the conflict. Second, the state found itself burdened with the need to give maintenance payments to wounded soldiers and to the families of those who had been killed in action. Third, in order to put people back to work the state had to spend funds on various work and income support initiatives. The result was increased expenditures in a context in which tax revenues had been greatly reduced. It was thought that France could make up the budget deficit from German war reparations, but these never amounted to what had been agreed at Versailles. This situation put the French government clearly in a defensive and isolationist mentality – this was no time for a free trade initiative.

Paul Hohenberg has written: 'tariffs were the first instruments of a more active economic policy, as well as the weapons on a rear-guard action against social and economic change.'[4] In France during the inter-war period the basic policy objective was that of trying to recapture the pre-1913 economic structures and performance which had taken on the aura of a golden period. This required an effort to regain pre-war levels of consumption; but, given the rigidity of French production, the result was an increase in imports, weakness in external accounts and, in 1926, devaluation of the franc. This was a pattern that was to mark French economic performance well into the post-Second World War period, with subsequent devaluations in 1936 and several times during the post-war period. Douglas Ashford notes that: 'André Siegfried wrote, in 1931, of the superiority of a self-sufficient agrarian economy and of the damaging effects of imposing a world economic order on France.'[5] This is in conformity with Charles Kindleberger's conclusion that for France tariff protection did not lead to an opportunity for industry to regain the home market and to restructure itself, perhaps along infant industry lines. Rather it served to dampen the stimulus to change provided by the competition of initiating industries and tariffs caused France to isolate itself from progressive and competitive tendencies abroad. This policy allowed continuation of a situation in which 'coalitions of interests maintain production at relatively low levels and high prices.'[6] The lack of recognition of the beneficial consequences of free trade, although a British-developed doctrine had been imported to France by Frédéric Bastiat in 1824, is shown by the fact that protectionism in the inter-war period started out as an effort to ensure the viability of Siegfried's self-sufficient agrarian economy and then, due to pressure from various lobbies close to the government, became generalized as protection for everyone.[7]

During the 1930s France was slower than other countries to suffer the effects of the prolonged depression, although analysis of this period is open to dispute.[8] The external account was in deficit and at first it was thought that devaluation should be avoided and that a combination of reduced production (to allow prices to reverse their decline), budgetary tightness, and tariff increases, on top of the existing quotas, would be sufficient to bring the account back into balance. However, it was impossible for any industrial economy to escape the depression for long. Trade data in Table 4.1 shows how dramatically France's exports and imports plummeted between 1926 and 1934. Exports of finished manufactures were especially hard hit, as were imports of industrial inputs. Devaluation could not be avoided and in 1936

*Table 4.1: The composition of French exports and imports, selected inter-
war years (million francs)*

	1926	1930	1934	1938
Exports	59,678	42,835	17,850	30,590
Food	5,079	5,886	2,584	4,393
Industrial inputs	16,784	9,992	5,160	9,843
Finished manufactures	37,815	26,957	10,106	16,354
Imports	59,598	52,511	23,097	46,065
Food	11,595	11,822	7,484	12,429
Industrial inputs	40,435	29,325	11,371	26,864
Finished manufactures	7,568	11,364	4,242	6,708
As Percentages				
Exports				
Food	8.5	13.7	14.5	14.4
Industrial inputs	28.0	23.3	28.9	32.2
Finished manufactures	63.4	62.9	56.6	53.5
Imports				
Food	19.5	22.5	32.4	27.0
Industrial inputs	67.8	55.8	49.2	58.3
Finished manufactures	12.7	21.6	18.4	14.6

Source: *Annuaire Statistique de la France*, Paris: INSEE, 1961

the value of the franc was reduced by about 30 per cent. By 1938 the effects of the depression were moderated as Europe began to arm itself in preparation for war, and both exports and imports of industrial inputs rose significantly as shares of goods traded.

One of the primary multilateral institutions of this period for France was the Franc Zone, a currency area based on the French franc. Established in 1930, the Franc Zone was designed to maintain fixed exchange rates between the French franc and the currencies of France's overseas Departments and several countries of the Communauté financière africaine. Its objective was that of ensuring stable economic conditions throughout the zone and of encouraging the trade flows of primary goods to France and of French manufactures to the lesser-developed countries, primarily in Africa and Asia. This initiative was terminated in 1994 after repeated requests from the World Bank and the International Monetary Fund, who saw it as a distortive and inefficient intervention.[9]

While the Franc Zone never came to dominate France's trade, during the period 1926–38 its importance did grow considerably, as is shown in Table 4.2. French imports from this area rose during the four years in the table from 15.6 per cent (1926) to 26.4 per cent (1938), while exports grew from 11.6 per cent (1926) to 26.5 per cent (1938). This is the result of a decline in trade of finished manufactures in general and the relatively strong impact of the depression on aggregate demand, and therefore on imports, in industrialized economies, as much as it is of the wish of the government to pursue a policy of semi-self-sufficiency and to concentrate on just the domestic and colonial markets. Trade with the Franc Zone was disproportionately dominated by imports of industrial inputs required in the military build-up.

On the eve of the Second World War, France was an economy that had shielded its agriculture and manufacturing industries behind a wall of tariffs, subsidies and quotas. These guaranteed a stable and predictable market but shielded both sectors from more efficient production abroad and from a need to specialize in lines of production for which France had a true comparative advantage. Whether by confluence of events or by policy initiative, the importance of Franc Zone trade was growing. All of this was pastbinding and it would be necessary for France to move away from each aspect of this situation in the context of the more open economy, beginning with the late 1950s.

FREE TRADE AND PROTECTIONISM IN FRENCH THINKING SINCE 1945

France's external relations in the post-Second World War period cannot be studied without making specific reference to the consequences of war. War destroys productive capacity and human and material resources, creates shortages of goods, causes savings to disappear and saving to plummet, usually generates inflationary pressures and unemployment, and leads to a deterioration in the external balance. In the brief span of 15 years France experienced recovery from the devastation of the Second World War, the inflationary pressures of the Korean War, a humiliating defeat in Viet Nam, and the profoundly disruptive conflict in Algeria.[10] While hardly the most important consequence of these events, trade and foreign investment policies and relations were powerfully affected. Data on these flows will be presented in the next two sections of this chapter; for now we will concern ourselves with the policies and events of a period that is marked by France's final opening to global markets and to the abandonment of the protectionist thinking that was dominant for more than half of the twentieth century.

Table 4.2: France's trading partners, selected inter-war years
   (million francs)

	1926	1930	1934	1938
Exports				
Great Britain	10,594	6,894	1,565	3,559
Germany	4,384	4,155	1,989	1,851
Belgium	9,525	5,442	1,978	4,181
United States	3,673	2,435	836	1,683
Spain	1,456	1,129	396	389
Italy	2,225	1,681	552	485
Switzerland	3,642	3,095	1,266	1,930
Netherlands	1,785	1,225	548	1,345
Franc zone	9,314	8,766	5,356	8,071
Other	13,080	7,995	3,364	7,096
Imports				
Great Britain	6,142	5,298	1,649	3,239
Germany	4,925	7,937	2,226	3,153
Belgium	4,876	4,199	1,469	3,160
United States	7,820	6,148	2,190	5,277
Spain	877	1,508	498	192
Italy	771	1,527	484	578
Switzerland	1,008	1,133	524	994
Netherlands	1,776	1,756	627	1,187
Franc zone	6,920	6,571	5,749	12,214
Other	24,483	16,424	7,681	16,649

Source: *Annuaire Statistique de la France*, Paris: INSEE, 1961

   The basic question confronting France in this regard was whether the geographic pattern and composition of exports and imports that had been developed during the pre-war years would be suitable for the years following 1945. As we have just seen, French trade was heavily concentrated on its colonies and the exchange was a typical imperial one of exports of manufactured goods from the center and imports of industrial inputs from the colonies. This pattern was marked by two features that would cause problems in the years to follow: (a) it was dependent upon continued privileged access to colonial markets; and (b) because that access was privileged French industry was under no competitive pressure to make efficiency-enhancing investments. Events of the first 15 years would show how powerful the effects of these structural problems could be.

   Following the conclusion of the war the French tendency to revert to its condition of quasi- self-sufficiency was predicated on the notion that France could at last, in the 1950s, realize the as yet unachieved potential inherent in mutually beneficial exchange between the imperial center and its colonial partners. To this was added the consequence of inflows of Marshall Plan aid, which allowed France to cover its chronic external deficit and, thus, to reduce the pressure to confront competition from producers in other industrialized economies.[11] Throughout this period French decision-makers were troubled by the lingering question as to whether French industry would be able to compete with firms in the United States and, most anxiously, with those in Germany.

Following the Second World War France introduced a series of economic plans through which the state sought to guide the economy to a successful recovery. The First Plan was designed by Jean Monnet (1947) and its primary focus was on reconstruction and modernization of production. Within two years the trade account was close to balance and by 1950–1 France's exports had regained their 1929 level, in contrast with a steady decline during the intervening years.[12] At this time, however, trade with industrialized countries accounted for only 47 per cent of total trade and the rest was with colonies (the Franc Zone) and other less developed countries.[13] Modernization was tried through a strategy of giving an industry adequate protection to ensure it captured the domestic market and then urging the firms in that industry to achieve efficiencies through specialization, increased use of technological advances, and economies of scale. This was backed up with financial assistance. John Sheahan concluded that in one sector studied, equipment manufacturers, while a few firms responded positively, the great majority of firms did little if anything positive.[14] As a result, by 1955 the share of manufactures in France's exports was lower than it had been in 1929 or 1913.[15] Thus, while the economy entered the period known as *les trente glorieuses*, marked by full employment, rapid growth, and increasing incomes, France's trade position was slow to transform itself and industry remained, at least psychologically, attached to the domestic and Franc Zone markets.

For the steel industry the situation was quite different since the Schuman Plan (1951) forced the coal and steel industries into a competitive structure with their counterparts in the countries that would a few years later form the membership of the European Economic Community (EEC). With some exceptions, French steel was deprived of its tariff protection, it was confronted with the need to restructure its production and was forced to prepare itself to meet foreign competition. The path toward modernization was not a smooth one, however, as many subsidies were allowed to continue and the French government itself was criticized by the High Commission of the European Coal and Steel Community (ECSC) for its interference with price movements that the government considered to be inflationary.[16]   While some major adjustments were made in French steel production, the unfortunate context has been that of a global shift of traditional production to low-cost locations in the developing world.   Therefore, steel has remained a troubled industry for France throughout the entire post–war period.

Establishment of the ECSC put the six countries firmly on the path of economic integration. When the EEC was created by the Treaty of Rome in 1957, France finally committed itself to its *grande ouverture* to the markets of other industrialized economies. This also involved explicitly a gradual transition from protectionism and a desire to be self-sufficient within the domestic and Franc Zone markets toward acceptance of its place in the new international division of labor. Unfortunately, development of a satisfactory position in the relatively open global economy was not quickly realized.[17] As was the case in the 1930s when trade policy was determined by policy objectives that had nothing to do with efficiency gains and benefit to the consumer, France's decision to pursue the economic integration of the major European economies was dominated by the need 'to achieve the greatest possible interdependence between Germany and its neighbors.'[18]

The Third Plan was adopted just prior to the decision to participate in the EEC. In it were emphasized continued regulation and control of trade within the Franc Zone. J.R. Hough comments that, in a wonderful recapitulation of mercantilist thought, 'external trade was seen almost as an undesirable necessity, with imports being needed to provide those goods which could not be provided,…,by domestic suppliers and exports being required to procure the foreign exchange to pay for the imports.'[19] Thus, although Gérard Marcy argues that there was an erratic trend toward liberalization within the continued policy of protectionism throughout the 1950s, one can wonder how long significant liberalization would have taken without the EEC initiative.[20]

Upon the return of Charles de Gaulle to power in 1958 all of this was to change. In part this was due to the vision of de Gaulle, but one must also recognize that by this time France's position in the world had changed dramatically. Of primary importance was the fact that having as a central focus of external economic relations the colonies and the Franc Zone was no longer an option. The defeat at Dien Bien Phu in 1954 sounded the death knell for France's colonial empire. Soon after, independence was negotiated for Morocco and Tunisia and, after a bloody conflict and an attempted coup against his government, de Gaulle recognized the independence of Algeria. A self-governing status for African territories within a French Community of States was introduced and five smaller colonies were integrated into France as overseas territories.[21]   One of the first actions of the ex-colonies was to diversify their trade and investment relations to the detriment of France.

France had no choice toward the end of the 1950s but to abandon the notion of Franc Zone self-sufficiency and to adopt a more open position *vis-à-vis* other industrialized economies.

More in conformity with the opening of the domestic market to foreign competition was the set of reforms introduced by a committee appointed by the de Gaulle government that was headed by Jacques Rueff. In 1958 the French economy was suffering from inflation that was in part due to the budgetary demands of the Korean War and colonial conflicts, a persistent current account deficit, and an outflow of capital. The Rueff committee made a dramatic break with the past by recommending tax increases, government expenditure cuts, including many subsidies, and stopping the price indexation of wages. The franc was devalued by 17.55 per cent and two zeros were removed from it and from all prices. Most of the import quotas were removed and France moved to compliance with the Code of Liberalization and the Common Market Treaty.[22]

France's experience with European economic integration will be discussed in some detail later in this chapter. For now it is sufficient to note that with France's participation in the EEC and with the reforms introduced by the Rueff committee in 1958, one can legitimately argue that France crossed 'the threshold of irreversible opening.'[23] The statistics that are most indicative of the impacts of the 1958 initiatives are those that show the shares of French exports and imports with the Franc Zone and the EEC (of the nine). Between 1959 and 1973, France's exports to the Franc Zone declined from 32 per cent to 5 per cent (by 84 per cent) while those to the EEC increased from 33 per cent to 56 per cent (by 70 per cent); imports from the Franc Zone fell from 24 per cent to 3 per cent (by 87 per cent) and those from the EEC rose from 31 per cent to 55 per cent (by 77 per cent).[24] Franc Zone trade grew, but by about half of the rate by which total French trade grew. This shift in trade partners, more than anything else, indicates the degree to which the opening was in fact a real transformation. From this time on the Franc Zone ceased to the main arena for French producers. Beyond this share shift, there remains the question of trade creation at the cost of trade diversion with the cost being borne by other industrialized countries whose goods would be competitive with those of the EEC. Research indicates that trade with industrialized economies other than the EEC grew during the EEC's first decade roughly at the rate that would have been expected in the absence of the Treaty of Rome. Hence, French trade with the other members of the EEC was the result of 'the creation of truly new trade flows.'[25]

An opening to foreign competition will result in some industries being exposed to imported goods with which they cannot compete while others find they are able to make inroads into foreign markets. Thus some firms will fail and others will expand. The broad array of goods produced in a hitherto protected economy will be reduced and production will be concentrated in fewer lines of output where the surviving firms will be able to take advantage of economies of large-scale production. In addition to a restructured geographic pattern of trade an economy should also move toward a higher degree of specialization. This too has been borne out in studies of both the EU and France, in particular. The first response one would expect to see following an opening to foreign competition is an increase in inter-industry trade, as each economy finds its comparative advantage and increases production of those goods. Concomitant with this is an increase in imports of goods from other industries. As integration progresses in the context of an economy based on large multinational firms, specialization is developed within an industry, in part as a consequence of cross-border investment, mergers, and acquisitions. Intra-industry trade can be either of similar goods, such as mid-price automobiles, where consumer tastes are important, or of dissimilar goods, where one country specializes in, for example, expensive designer clothing and the other in lower-priced mass market clothing. Since the early 1980s inter-industry trade within the EU has declined (albeit from a high level) and intra-industry trade, especially of dissimilar goods, has increased significantly. This pattern is particularly true for France, Germany and the United Kingdom.[26]

A different approach to the question of specialization was taken by Carré, Dubois and Malinvaud. They found that France's imports were depressed during the 1950s because of the stabilization program of 1952 and the devaluation of 1958. During the next decade, however, imports experienced two jumps of about 25 per cent each in 1963 and 1968–9. Conversely, exports were slowed in the early 1950s due to rapidly growing domestic demand and prices but the devaluation gave them a powerful boost and they continued to grow throughout the 1960s. What Carré, Dubois and Malinvaud find important is the fact that, after the creation of the EEC, both exports and imports grew substantially more rapidly than did French production. The opening of markets of the six members of the EEC meant that the goods France could produce competitively gained market share throughout the area and the converse was true for goods that France had been producing inefficiently. They also concluded that it was not changes in the structure of foreign demand that caused this increase in specialization but rather that 'the widening of the market in which activity of French firms takes place, and the increased specialization that [French firms] can and must adopt, are thus very largely the result of the political choice made by the six European countries in the middle of the 1950s.'[27]

Data that support the conclusion that French manufacturing was increasingly exposed to foreign competition following membership of the EEC is given by Adams in his examination of the relationship between imports and consumption, and exports and production, for the years 1959–80. The import ratio increased from 8 per cent to 25 per cent during this period for manufacturing and from 13 per cent to 20 per cent for non-manufacturing. For exports of non-manufactured goods there is no growth at all as the ratio remained between 8 and 9 per cent, but manufactured goods doubled to 27 per cent. Adams also concludes that trade liberalization is the causal factor.[28]

Thus far we have examined the positive aspects of market liberalization, but there is also a less attractive side that cannot be ignored. During the 1970s and 1980s France was subjected to a series of external shocks that transmitted disrupting forces across all national borders: the two OPEC price hikes in 1973 and 1979, the increase in raw material prices in 1976 and 1977, and the rise in the price of the dollar during the first half of the 1980s.[29] For France the consequences were inflation, reduction in real wages, recession, and a large deficit on the trade account. During 1976–8, Prime Minister Raymond Barre introduced his counter-inflationary program which rejected the traditional French approach of budgetary deficits and devaluation and then a liberal program in which price controls were lifted and the value of the franc was fixed in the newly introduced European Monetary System (EMS). More will be said about the EMS later, but, in the context of two treblings of the price of petroleum products in the course of six years, any economic plan was bound to fail.

Unemployment rose dramatically during this period and the voters rejected the Barre liberal approach in 1981 and the Left under François Mitterand was given the mandate to govern. A combination of redistributive Keynesianism, renewed protectionism against non-EU trading partners, and borrowing to cover the budgetary and external deficits was introduced. This approach also failed due to the inability of French industry to produce the goods that were demanded, to the depression of world demand, and to the substantial rise in the dollar. The external account deteriorated from a slight surplus in 1978 to a deficit of almost Fr100 billion in 1982. The departure from liberal policy was brief and Mitterand was forced to reverse his initial policies and to focus on 'competitiveness, a strong franc and the search for growth through exports, investment and greater liberalization.'[30]

France of the 1990s was quite different from that of 1938, which we dealt with at the end of the previous section of this chapter. It is now generally accepted that French industry must adapt to the demands and challenges of global competition. No longer can the world of self-sufficiency, protectionism, subsidies and *l'état providence* be considered a viable option. French manufacturers and providers of services have accepted internationalization of economic activity within the context of the European economic integration process and global trade liberalization. While agriculture has been far more resistant to this change, it is clear that French farmers must accept equally dramatic change in the near future. However, from the discussion in Chapter 1, it is also clear that the French way, indeed the continental way, of adapting to globalization is quite different than it is in the Anglo-Saxon world.[31] The role of the state in French economic activity has diminished but it has not been Thatcherized. It would take us too far afield to detail at this point all of the various manifestations of the French approach to opening the country to international competition; much of this will be discussed in other chapters. But it is a sign of the new spirit that so many French economists note, with Alain Henriot, that France is the world's fourth largest exporter of goods and the second exporter of services, and that France is an actor of the highest level in international trade.[32]

TRADE DATA SINCE 1945

Three aspects of France's trade performance since 1945 are of interest to us:

1. the balance of trade;
2. the product composition of exports and imports; and
3. the geographic pattern of exports and imports.

The preceding discussion has emphasized the shift in French thinking from self-sufficiency and the Franc Zone to an opening to foreign competition and to finding a place in the global division of labor. The crucial period for this transition was 1958 and the five years that followed.

With regard to the balance of merchandise trade, Table 4.3 indicates deficits in every year except 1950, 1955, 1978 and 1986, and two multi-year periods, during 1959–61 and again during 1992–8. It is of interest to note that both of these periods of trade surplus were years immediately following a major initiative of deepening the degree of integration in the EU: the Treaty of Rome (1957) and the Maastricht Treaty on European Union (1992). These turn-arounds from years of substantial trade deficits offer evidence for the argument that France has supported the deepening of European economic integration in part as a response to the lack of competitiveness of French manufacturing. However, the two most severe periods of deficit were in the 1970s and the early 1980s, following OPEC price hikes in 1973 and 1979 respectively.

With regard to the composition of France's exports and imports, we note in Table 4.4 the very contemporary pattern of rough balance in total trade for most of the categories. This is indicative of intra-industry rather than inter-industry specialization, especially in the sectors of processed foods, metal products, chemicals, industrial equipment and consumer goods. The old

Table 4.3: France's merchandise trade balance, 1946–97.

	1946	1947	1948	1949	1950	1951	1952	1953	1954
Exports	1.0	2.2	4.3	7.8	10.8	14.8	14.2	14.1	15.1
Imports	2.6	4.0	6.7	9.3	10.7	16.2	15.9	14.6	15.2
Balance	−1.6	−1.8	−2.4	−1.5	0.1	−1.4	−1.7	−0.5	−0.1

	1955	1956	1957	1958	1959	1960	1961	1962	1963
Exports	17.4	16.2	18.9	21.5	10.8	33.9	35.7	36.4	39.9
Imports	16.7	19.8	22.7	23.6	10.7	31.0	33.0	37.1	43.1
Balance	0.7	−3.6	−3.8	−2.1	0.1	2.9	2.7	−0.7	−3.2

	1964	1965	1966	1967	1968	1969	1970	1971	1972
Exports	44.4	49.6	53.8	56.2	62.6	77.0	98.5	113.0	130.4
Imports	49.7	51.0	58.6	61.1	68.8	89.1	105.1	117.0	134.7
Balance	−5.3	−1.4	−4.8	−4.9	−6.2	−12.1	−6.6	−4.0	−4.3

	1973	1974	1975	1976	1977	1978	1979	1980	1981
Exports	158.1	217.2	220.8	272.7	319.4	357.1	426.7	489.8	575.8
Imports	164.2	250.2	229.6	293.6	330.9	354.9	440.3	551.8	635.2
Balance	−6.1	−33.0	−28.8	−20.9	−11.5	2.2	−13.6	−62.0	−59.4

	1982	1983	1984	1985	1986	1987	1988	1989	1990
Exports	632.2	722.7	850.	906	864	889	998	1,143	1,177
Imports	725.7	726.3	870.4	931	863	921	1,030	1,188	1,227
Balance	−93.5	−43.6	−20.3	−25	1	−32	−32	−45	−49

	1991	1992	1993	1994	1995	1996	1997
Exports	1,221	1,249	1,122	1,241	1,360	1,395	1,551
Imports	1,251	1,218	1,136	1,249	1,363	1,366	1,456
Balance	−30	31	−14	−8	−3	31	95

Note: Military goods are not included. Figures are in millions of francs.

Sources: *Annuaire Statistique de la France*, and *Comptes Nationaux*, Paris: INSEE, various years

colonial system pattern of exports of French manufactured goods in exchange for imports of raw materials from colonial countries no longer holds. This overall pattern holds for trade with the EU and the US, it breaks down for the four other areas. Japan tends to export industrial equipment to France and import processed foods and consumer goods; Africa exchanges energy for

Table 4.4: Composition of France's trade, by major trading partners, 1994

Good category	EU	US	Japan	Other OECD	Africa	Asia	Total
I. France's imports							
Agriculture	3.5	2.0	...	5.3	16.7	3.4	4.3
Processed foods	10.2	2.3	...	4.8	6.5	3.6	8.1
Energy	3.3	1.6	...	17.3	35.1	0.4	7.6
Minerals	0.2	...	...	2.3	2.5	0.1	0.5
Metal products	10.1	5.6	3.4	9.7	5.8	3.4	8.8
Chemicals	18.9	13.0	8.5	21.3	3.3	6.6	15.9
Industrial equip.	19.3	62.0	55.3	15.2	4.6	35.7	23.8
Electrical goods	2.4	0.8	8.3	2.7	...	9.4	2.6
Automobiles	8.8	0.9	10.2	1.7	...	0.9	6.2
Auto. parts	7.7	1.6	4.7	4.7	0.3	1.1	5.4
Consumer goods	15.3	10.2	10.2	13.9	26.3	35.7	16.5
Others	0.5	0.1	...	0.4	0.3	...	0.3
II. France's exports							
Agriculture	7.2	2.2	0.4	2.9	5.4	1.0	5.5
Processed foods	11.1	5.3	13.2	5.6	9.2	8.4	10.0
Energy	2.4	2.1	0.2	1.0	1.7	0.6	2.4
Minerals	0.1	...	...	0.1	0.1	0.1	0.1
Metal products	9.1	9.5	7.6	10.0	6.8	5.4	8.4
Chemicals	17.0	12.1	15.2	19.4	10.6	11.3	15.4
Industrial equip.	19.3	49.4	24.0	29.0	33.8	53.0	26.3
Electrical goods	2.2	0.3	0.3	2.4	0.7	0.9	1.8
Automobiles	8.2	...	1.6	6.8	3.0	1.6	6.6
Auto. parts	8.7	5.9	1.2	6.1	6.6	2.2	7.2
Consumer goods	13.6	12.1	34.4	16.0	21.8	15.7	15.6
Others	0.8	0.1	0.2	0.2	0.1	0.1	0.5

Notes:
1. All figures are percentage by partner. Thus each column sums, vertically, to 100.0, with minor exceptions due to rounding of figures.
2. Asia refers to rapidly developing countries.
3. ... indicates a number less than 0.1.
4. Omitted are figures for Middle Eastern countries, Eastern Europe, Switzerland and other countries.

Source: *Annuaire Statistique de la France*, Paris: INSEE, 1996

industrial equipment; and Asia and other OECD countries export consumer goods in exchange for French industrial equipment.

Trade by major trading partners and regions, shown in Tables 4.5 through 4.7, makes it clear why the composition of trade with the EU and US are so

Table 4.5: France's merchandise trade with global regions

	1950	1960	1970	1980	1990	1994
France's exports to:						
Region						
European Union	3.7	14.5	49.5	272.3	745.6	795.7
Other Europe	0.8	2.9	20.3	50.3	86.7	95.3
NAFTA	0.5	2.4	6.7	26.0	84.4	107.4
Rest of Americas	0.6	0.9	2.5	15.7	37.4	24.6
Asia	0.2	1.9	4.9	39.3	100.8	161.5
Africa	4.0	10.1	12.1	62.3	84.7	78.9
World total	9.9	23.7	98.5	469.7	1,142.2	1,290.7
France's Imports from:						
Region						
European Union	2.6	11.3	50.4	296.6	795.6	789.1
Other Europe	0.4	1.6	17.7	42.9	92.6	91.5
NAFTA	1.3	4.3	11.8	51.6	115.6	119.6
Rest of Americas	0.7	1.1	2.9	13.7	40.9	24.3
Asia	0.8	4.2	7.3	108.4	144.5	157.7
Africa	2.9	7.0	12.6	49.9	84.7	78.9
World total	8.8	24.0	105.1	570.8	1,266.6	1,263.6
France's merchandise trade balance with:						
Region						
European Union	1.1	2.2	−0.9	−24.3	−40.1	26.6
Other Europe	0.4	1.3	2.6	7.4	−5.9	3.8
NAFTA	0.9	−1.9	−5.1	−25.6	−31.2	−12.2
Rest of Americas	−0.1	−0.2	−0.4	2.0	−3.5	0.3
Asia	−0.6	−2.3	−2.4	-68.7	-43.7	3.8
Africa	1.1	3.1	-0.5	22.4	18.6	21.3
World total	*	-0.3	−6.6	−101.1	−124.4	27.1

Notes:
1.   Figures are in billions of francs.
2.   European Union consists of the 15 members of today at the time of writing.
3.   NAFTA refers to the United States, Canada and Mexico.
Data that are available by country for 1950 are incomplete in the 1966 issue of *Annuaire Statistique de la France*. Data for the countries given accounts for 91 per cent of Exports and 82 per cent of imports. Thus the regional totals may not be accurate.

Source: *Annuaire Statistique de la France*, Paris: INSEE, various issues

similar to the overall pattern – about 70 per cent of France's trade is with these two partners. The EU dominates French trade, but Table 4.7 indicates that the Americas and Asia are virtually tied for place as France's number two partner. We also note the fact that trade with the Franc Zone countries, primarily in Africa, has dwindled from over 25 per cent in 1938 (see above) to 5 or 6 per cent in 1994 – it is now less than is that with Other Europe, the Americas or Asia. While trade with Africa between the wars was always below that with the countries of the EU (see Table 4.2), this was not true in the years of European reconstruction, as is indicated by 1950. It is also true that France has maintained a sizeable trade surplus with Africa throughout this period, with the exception of 1970.

The last two tables in this section, 4.6 and 4.7, show the changes in the flows of goods and services between France and its major trading partners.

Table 4.6: France's trade with major partners

	France's exports to:		Imports from:		Balance	
	1990	1994	1990	1994	1990	1994
Belgium	107.3	113.0	111.8	115.1	−4.5	−2.1
Germany	196.8	221.2	238.7	225.0	−41.9	−3.8
Italy	129.9	121.3	146.5	122.2	−16.6	−0.9
United Kingdom	108.1	127.9	91.8	100.8	16.3	27.1
United States	69.6	90.8	103.2	107.7	−43.6	−16.9
Canada and Mexico	14.8	16.6	12.4	11.9	2.4	4.7
China	7.7	12.0	12.0	22.7	−4.3	−12.7
Hong Kong	6.4	12.9	4.0	9.9	2.4	3.0
Japan	21.9	25.4	50.9	47.1	−29.0	−21.7
Saudi Arabia	7.1	7.3	15.6	15,4	−8.5	−8.1
Algeria	14.8	13.4	10.6	8.3	4.2	5.1
Morocco	10.7	12.0	10.3	11.9	−0.4	0.1
Nigeria	2.9	2.5	3.5	6.0	−1.6	−3.5
South Africa	2.8	4.6	4.2	3.0	−1.4	1.6
Tunisia	8.5	9.8	5.3	6.7	3.2	3.1

Note: Figures are in billions of francs.

Source: *Annuaire Statistique de la France*, Paris: INSEE, various issues

We have already noted that the EU is by far France's largest trading partner. That relationship held rather constant during the first years of the 1990s. Of the major trading partners the United States surpasses the UK as a source of imports although the failure of French manufacturers to succeed in the US market continues. The UK continues as France's largest single source of a trade surplus. The trade balance with Asia has improved (due to a strong export growth), Africa (and the Franc Zone) continue to decline in importance

Table 4.7: France's trade: shares by partner

	France's exports to		Imports from:	
	1990	1994	1990	1994
Percentage share by region				
European Union	61.6	63.2	62.8	62.4
Other Europe	7.6	7.4	7.3	11.6
NAFTA	7.4	8.3	9.1	9.5
Rest of Americas	2.7	1.9	3.2	1.9
Asia	8.8	12.5	11.4	12.5
Africa	7.4	6.1	6.7	4.6
Percentage share by region ex EU				
Other Europe	22.0	20.1	19.4	30.9
NAFTA	21.4	22.6	24.2	25.3
Rest of Americas	9.5	5.2	8.6	5.1
Asia	25.6	34.0	30.2	33.2
Africa	21.5	16.6	17.7	12.2

Source: *Annuaire Statistique de la France*, Paris: INSEE, various issues

and low-cost imports from Other, that is Eastern Europe, have demonstrated the strongest growth. The performance of French manufacturers will be discussed in Chapter 6, but we can see a general evolution that is in conformity with the exigencies of trade liberalization and globalization. The increase in imports from low-cost Eastern Europe, the dominance of the relationship with the EU, and the loss of advantage on both sides in the Franc Zone and African trade are all examples of this.

LIBERALIZATION OF FINANCIAL RELATIONS

The impact of globalization on financial flows has been at least as important as it has been on flows of goods and services. The reduction of restraints on the movements of capital has led to a dramatic growth in the interdependence of all national economies. Economic theory informs us that this leads to an improved allocation of capital on a global basis and to gains in the efficient utilization of labor and other resources everywhere. In this section of the chapter we will examine: (a) how financial liberalization has affected France's balance of payments situation; (b) how the franc has performed during the various post-1945 exchange rate regimes; and (c) the degree to which France has participated in a more open and efficient allocation of direct investment.

Prior to the Second World War, France's balance of payments situation can be divided into two periods – before and after 1931. During the immediate pre-First World War years through the onslaught of the depression the current account was in surplus, except for the war years through 1920. These surpluses were usually between Fr5 and 10 billion and were largely the result of receipts from services exports that were large enough [Fr8–14 billion] to offset sizeable deficits on the trade account. From 1931 through 1937 the current account deteriorated to a series of deficits as large as Fr6.3 billion (1932), as services exports fell to around Fr6 billion and the trade account continued in deficit [Fr5–12 billion].[33] The last year of peace, 1938, saw the current account in balance with the trade deficit equaled by a surplus in services.

The 1920s were perhaps the highpoint of France's economic relationship with its colonies. In addition to the comfortable exchange of manufactured goods for raw materials, the colonial lobby encouraged a project of infrastructure or public works, especially in North Africa (in particular Morocco) and Indochina. These projects were financed by loans raised in metropolitan France. While the formal plan proposed by the Minister of Colonies in 1921 was quickly abandoned it did stimulate private sector pressures for such a program. These expectations could not be sustained during the following decade as the effects of the depression on colonial markets and demands for manufactured goods reduced the attractiveness of investments there.

After 1945 the colonial option was no longer viable for France. The immediate concern was with reconstruction and applying scarce capital to the requirements of domestic industry. For the longer run, it soon became clear that the major focal point for France's external relations would have to be Western Europe. As has already been noted, it was not until the Treaty of Rome was adopted that France began to act on this awareness.

The Franc in the Context of Financial Market Liberalization

From 1947 to 1971 the international monetary regime was the Bretton Woods system. Administered by the International Monetary Fund, Bretton Woods was a system of fixed exchange rates, with participating countries gaining access to IMF loans for short–term financing of short-term balance of payments deficits in exchange for giving up the right to devalue their currency by more than 10 per cent. National governments were expected to use monetary and fiscal policy to bring the domestic economy in line with what was required by external balance. Since the value of a nation's currency is inversely related to its rate of price inflation, price stability, often at the expense of domestic employment, was the key to a stable exchange rate. This proved to be a trade-off that most French governments were not willing to make.[34] The following is a brief examination of the impact of domestic inflation on the value of the franc; the details of macroeconomic policy are treated more fully in Chapter 5.

France participated in the initial round of currency alignments in 1947 and 1948; the program of René Mayer (1948) took steps to liberalize the economy and for a while it appeared that inflation would be reduced. However, raw material prices rose sharply as a response to the demands of the Korean War (1950–4) and the balance of payments was soon in deficit. This inflationary situation was exacerbated by the war in Indochina, for which defense goods had to be imported due to domestic supply shortages. The roller-coaster ride continued when the policies of Antoine Pinay and Edgar Faure managed to bring inflation down again during the mid 1950s, but inflation returned again concurrent with the military conflict in Algeria. As a consequence of this price behavior the franc was intermittently under pressure and the government found it necessary to resort to a *de facto* devaluation of up to 20 per cent in 1957 and a formal devaluation of 17.4 per cent in December 1958. As was noted earlier in this chapter, concurrent with this devaluation was adoption of the Rueff Plan of economic liberalization. For the next decade domestic inflationary pressures were countered by enforced austerity plans introduced by the government. It was only in the turmoil following the conflict of May 1968 that price pressures got out of hand and it was necessary, in August 1969, to resort once again to devaluation.

This Bretton Woods system was brought to an end in 1971 when the United States devalued the dollar and then cut the link to gold. In essence currency rates from that time on were flexible and largely determined by market forces. The major European countries chose not to float their currencies individually but rather established a joint float in relation to the dollar, with a band for each participating currency of 2.25 per cent above or below that central rate. This system was referred to as the snake in the tunnel. Unfortunately, one year after this initiative OPEC effected its first oil price increase. This led to a round of price inflation and economic recession that affected the entire global economy. France was forced to borrow heavily abroad and decided to let the franc float freely in 1974; this of course resulted in another devaluation. Then in 1979 OPEC once again tripled the price of petroleum introducing yet another round of inflation and economic stagnation. Europe's response was the creation of the European Monetary System (EMS) that same year in an effort to establish a condition of monetary stability, at the instigation of Valéry Giscard-d'Estaing and Germany's Helmut Schmidt. Similar to the 1972 system, the EMS did introduce the European Currency Unit (ECU) as a unit of account, a fund for loans to countries in balance of payments difficulties, and a structure in which the adjustment to an external deficit, and the downward pressure on that currency, would be shared by surplus countries as well. For France this was a period of difficulty in its external accounts. It was weak in particular in comparison with the other key currency in the system, the Deutsch mark. As a consequence, the franc was devalued in 1981 (8.5 per cent), 1982 (10 per cent), 1983 (8 per cent), and 1986 (6 per cent). According to Jean-François Eck, the current account required four years to regain balance after the first oil shock, and then seven years to recover after the second.[35] What may well be the final resolution of Europe's monetary ambiguity was adoption of the European Monetary Union (EMU) in the Maastricht Treaty of European Union in 1991.[36] Within a decade, the EMU would establish the ECU as a single currency for Europe and would replace the national central banks by one institution, the European Central Bank.

The only point it is necessary to make here about European monetary integration is to note that throughout this process of institution building France has been one of the key and most committed supporters and initiators. Several reasons account for this strong involvement. First, France was always interested in furthering the European integration process as a means of enmeshing Germany in a structure of conflict-reducing relationships. Monetary accommodation and integration is the final stage in this process. Second, France's history of inflation and devaluation, especially after the justification provided by the successes of the period from 1945 to the first OPEC shock, came to be seen as an indication of weakness and failure. Again, this was especially true when France's performance was compared with that of Germany. Removing the option of currency devaluation also removed the option of domestic inflation and, as we will argue elsewhere in this book, one of the primary causes of the loss of competitiveness of French manufacturing. Third, the evolving process of globalization meant that inward-focused economic policy based on the impermeability of national borders was decreasingly tenable. The opening of national goods and service markets, the liberalization of financial relations, dramatic advances in production, communication and transportation technologies, and the rise of information-technology sectors of the global economy all meant that traditional French policy no longer met the country's needs.

This history and France's balance of payments experience have had their impacts on each other, as is made clear by Table 4.8. France's post-war trade weakness dominated the first decade, although the policies of Pinay and Faure brought some improvement in the mid-1950s. A decade of improvement began with the Treaty of Rome and the devaluations of 1957 and 1958 but was ended by the turmoil of 1968 and then the end of the Bretton Woods system. A brief period of recovery was ended by the actions of OPEC that marked the death of *les trentes glorieuses*. Devaluations of the franc stimulated French exports in the mid-1980s but a generalized European stagnation caused the current account to become negative until the Maastricht Treaty and the promise of exchange rate and price stability moved the trade account sharply into surplus during the most recent decade.

Foreign Direct Investment

Direct investment involves the purchase of shares in a firm producing or distributing goods or services with the intent of exercising control over decision-making in that entity or the construction of an entirely new facility. This is in contrast with portfolio investment, which entails the purchase of assets merely for the return (interest, dividends or profits) that investment will bring. Thus direct investment is a phenomenon that has in the first instance more significant impacts on production, employment and other economic variables than does portfolio investment, and in the second instance is far more politically charged. During the 1960s and 1970s direct investment was seen to be one form of the extension of imperialist control over a host national economy. Jean-Jacques Servan-Schreiber's book *Le Défi américain* (1967)[37] raised the issue in a very public way and was influential in confirming the reservations of many in France about the Americanization of their economy and society and about the perceived or anticipated loss of control over their economic lives. As a consequence of the intense scrutiny that has been given to the activities of foreign-owned multinational corporations, the actions of governments to regulate some of their activities and, perhaps most importantly, increased awareness of the positive link between investment and employment, almost all nations have become far more accepting of foreign investment. Indeed, governments in general go to great lengths to encourage and to facilitate foreign direct investment.

Three tables help to give us an understanding of France's experience with direct investment in recent years. Table 4.10 shows that the direct investment account was basically in balance for the years 1975, 1980 and 1985, that there was a virtual explosion of FDI abroad in the early 1990s that quickly subsided

Table 4.8: Balance of payments, France, 1946–74

	1946	1947	1948	1949	1950	1951	1952	1953	1954	1955	1956	1957	1958	1959	1960
Current account	-2.0	-1.6	-1.5	-0.6	-0.1	-1.0	-0.6	-0.1	0.3	0.6	-0.7	-1.2	-0.2	0.7	0.6
Goods	-1.5	-1.5	-1.4	-0.5	-0.1	-0.8	-0.6	-0.3	-0.2	0.1	-0.8	-0.9	-0.3	0.7	0.6
Services & transfers	-0.2	-0.1	-0.1	-0.1	...	-0.2	...	0.2	0.4	0.5	0.1	-0.3	...	...	...
Capital account	0.9	1.3	0.6	...	...	...	0.1	...	-0.2	-0.2	-0.1	0.3	0.2		
Long term capital														-0.7	-0.6
Short term capital														0.3	...
Errors & omissions	1.1	0.3	0.9	0.6	0.1	1.0	0.5	0.1	-0.1	-0.4	0.8	0.9	...	-1.0	-0.6

	1961	1962	1963	1964	1965	1966	1967	1968	1969	1970	1971	1972	1973	1974
Current account	0.9	0.9	0.5	0.1	0.8	0.2	1.0	-6.8	-7.6	1.4	8.5	1.5	5.0	-16.8
Goods & services	0.8	0.8	0.4	...	0.6	0.2	3.3	-2.2	2.5	5.6	-6.1	8.9	12.1	-7.1
Transfers & other	0.1	0.1	0.1	0.1	0.2	...	-2.3	-4.6	5.1	-4.2	2.4	-7.4	-7.1	-10.2
Capital account	-1.1	-1.0	-0.6	0.5	0.3	2.2	-1.4	4.4	8.2	-3.7	0.5	0.5	-6.9	0.7
Long term capital	-0.1	-0.3	0.1	0.4	0.1	0.1	0.1	-5.9	-1.4	2.0	1.8	...	-7.2	1.6
Short term capital	-1.0	-0.7	-0.7	-0.9	-0.4	-2.3	-1.5	10.3	9.6	-5.7	-1.3	0.5	0.3	-1.0
Errors & omssions												-2.0	1.9	16.1

Note: The categories of data are different for the periods up to 1958 and from 1959 on. Short term and long term capital and erroros and omissions are not reported for all years.

Source: Annuaires statistiques de la France, Paris: INSEE, various issues

Table 4.9:   Balance of payments, France, 1974–97

	1974	1975	1976	1977	1978	1979	1980	1981
Current account	−16.8	9.4	−28.5	−16.3	31.6	22.1	−17.6	−25.8
Goods & services	−7.1	19.9	−17.5	−3.4		39.2	...	−2.7
Transfers & other	−10.2	−10.5	−11.0	−12.9	−14.8	−17.1	−17.6	−23.1
Capital account	0.7	6.0	23.5	−1.5	−31.3	−24.4	8.0	37.9
Long term capital	1.6	5.5	−7.6	2.9	−15.1	−21.4	−35.8	−49.7
Short term capital	−1.0	0.5	31.1	−4.4	−16.2	−3.0	43.8	87.6
Errors & omssions	15.1	5.0	17.8	−0.3	2.3	9.6	−12.1	−6.6

	1982	1983	1984	1985	1986	1987	1988	1989
Current account	−79.3	−35.7	−7.3	−3.1	12.7	−30.0	−28.8	−29.8
Goods & services	−49.0	−6.5	17.9		23.4	−20.5	−14.4	−16.1
Transfers & other	−30.3	−29.2	−25.2	−23.6	−10.7	−9.5	−14.4	−13.7
Capital account	85.9	31.9	.8	1.2	−18.3	24.8	24.7	70.5
Long term capital	8.0	68.9	44.1	29.4	−54.0	13.1	−3.8	73.3
Short term capital	77.9	−37.0	−43.3	−28.2	35.7	11.7	28.5	−2.8
Errors & omissions	−15.4	3.8	6.5	−1.9	5.6	26.6	22.1	13.1

	1990	1991	1992	1993	1994	1995	1996	1997
Current account	−53.6	−34.5	20.5	52.4	44.7	54.5	105.0	230.1
Goods & services	−25.9	.4	75.8	118.5	131.0	70.6	119.5	200.2
Transfers & other	−27.7	−34.9	−55.3	−66.1	−86.3	−16.1	−14.5	29.9
Capital account	80.2	12.4	−33.6	−66.9	−42.5	−40.4	−115.9	−264.0
Long term capital	89.4	12.4	117.9	−23.7	−255.9	70.7	−352.3	−221.5
Short term capital	−9.2	...	−151.5	−43.2	213.4	−111.1	236.4	−42.9
Errors & omissions	14.5	−2.2	−14.1	10.9	33.9	−16.7	4.6	25.7

Source: *Annuaires statistiques de la France*, Paris: INSEE, various issues

for a short period, and that FDI in France expanded so that the initial deficit in the decade was followed briefly by a surplus in 1995. FDI in both directions expanded in the second half of the decade with flows abroad maintaining a substantial advantage. Thus, the direct investment balance during the 1990s has been one of a large deficit with the exception of a couple of years. According to analysis done by the US Department of the Treasury, the formal French investment regime is among the world's least restrictive; however, inward direct investment is constrained by a number of negative factors.[38] These include: relatively high payroll and income taxes; pervasive regulation of labor and products markets; and sometimes negative attitudes toward foreign investors; as well as some formal sectorally-based FDI restrictions that tend to favor intra-EU investments. This is in spite of the considerable efforts at liberalization that have been pursued by the French government for over a decade. France is third, behind the United States and the United Kingdom, as a recipient of FDI (Table 4.11), although closer to the United States, Italy and Germany in the importance of FDI to the domestic economy than to either the United Kingdom or the smaller open EU countries.

Table 4.10: Foreign direct investment flows, France, selected years

	1975	1980	1985	1990	1991	1992	1993
French FDI abroad	6.1	13.3	20.0	146.6	115.6	101.1	68.9
FDI in France	6.2	14.1	19.9	49.2	62.5	84.4	68.8
FDI balance	0.1	0.8	−0.1	−97.6	−53.1	−16.7	−0.1
	1994	1995	1996	1997	1998		
French FDI abroad	60.5	78.6	148.6	196.8	239.4		
FDI in France	60.8	118.7	117.7	135.3	165.4		
FDI Balance	0.3	40.1	−30.9	−61.5	−74.0		

Note: Data are in billion francs.

Sources: *Annuaire Statistique de la France*, Paris: INSEE, various issues, and Banque de France

Table 4.11: Major countries as host to foreign direct investment, 1996

Country	Stock of FDI	FDI/GDP
United States	3,300	8.4
United Kingdom	1,371	23.1
France	754	9.6
Belgium	690	50.3
Canada	690	22.4
Netherlands	652	32.4
Spain	516	17.4
Germany	425	3.5
Italy	391	6.3
Japan	157	0.7

Note: Data are in billions of francs.

Source: Banque de France

It is clear from Table 4.12 that the United States is the single largest FDI partner for France. However, the figures for the US are dwarfed by those for all EU countries combined, by a factor of about 4 to 1. Given the 40-year-long effort to integrate the EU economies this should not be at all surprising. Trade and FDI figures are usually complementary and, as was shown above in Table 4.5, the preponderance of the EU linkage is also found in trade relations, to an even larger degree.

Movements of FDI should result in a more rational allocation of capital, should have an impact on labor and capital productivity, incomes and total output, and should alter the structure of production toward one which is in conformity with the economy's comparative advantage. The extent to which this has been true for France is taken up in the section that follows.

Table 4.12: Source and destination country of direct investment, France, 1996

	Stock of FDI in France	Stock of French DI Abroad
In billion francs		
United States	144.7	176.5
The Netherlands	121.1	135.6
Belgium/Luxembourg	62.2	107.8
United Kingdom	90.0	85.9
Germany	80.7	49.7
Switzerland	69.8	53.3
Italy	49.9	40.1
Sweden	24.3	...a
Japan	14.7	...a
Spain	9.8	51.7
Brazil	...a	18.7
Others	47.6	184.2
Total	714.8	903.5
Percentage share		
United States	20.2	19.5
The Netherlands	17.4	15.0
Belgium/Luxembourg	9.0	11.9
United Kingdom	13.4	9.6
Germany	10.9	5.5
Switzerland	9.3	5.9
Italy	6.7	4.4
Sweden	3.0	...a
Japan	2.0	...a
Spain	1.3	5.7
Brazil	...a	2.1
Others	6.9	20.4

Note: a Data for these countries are included in Others.

Source: Banque de France

THE IMPACT OF LIBERALIZED TRADE AND FOREIGN
INVESTMENT ON THE FRENCH ECONOMY

The opening of a nation's factor and goods markets is designed to have
significant impacts on all aspects of the national economy, including but not
limited to those that have just been mentioned. Economic theory tells us that
the employment and earnings of scarce factors of production will rise, while
those of abundant factors will decline. These changes in relative earnings will
cause labor and capital to be reallocated among the various sectors and
industries of the economy. As increased exports and imports force a
restructuring of output and production in traded goods industries rises and
falls, some regional economies will similarly rise and fall. To the extent that
the state is responsive to these changes, tax-transfer schemes will work to
compensate the losers in the process of liberalization at the expense of the
winners. These changes and responses are both interesting and important and
most of them will be discussed in subsequent chapters. In this section we will
limit our discussion to the impacts of liberalized trade and foreign investment
on French economic performance, using research conducted by specialists in
this area of economic analysis.

One of the first important examinations of the performance of the French
economy was done in 1975 by Carré, Dubois and Malinvaud. They looked
specifically at the relationship between trade and productivity during the
1950s and 1960s. Their analysis of the rapid growth of output during this
period showed that it could not be explained as a return to the situation prior
to the disruption of the Great Depression and the Second World War. Neither
could it be attributed to rapid growth of France's traditional markets: this was
a factor only during the pre-1958 years and even then accounted for only half
of the growth that occurred. Rather it was the creation of the EEC that led to
increased international trade which in turn brought economies of scale, access
to new technologies, and increased specialization.[39] They argued that, for at
least the three decades leading up to 1958, French industry had sought almost
entirely to produce goods that would meet the demands of the internal French
market and some foreign markets to which it had privileged access, and that
this was facilitated by maintenance of a wall of tariffs and quotas. Each
producer in this situation offers a wide range of products produced with short
production lines and at high cost. Starting from this position, the lowering of
barriers following the Treaty of Rome had powerful effects on French
productive efficiency. Fewer product lines were offered, economies of scale
were achieved and France specialized in the products in which it had an
international advantage. This also led to a competitive climate.[40]

By the middle of the 1980s the stimulus from the creation of the EEC had weakened considerably. As a 1989 report by the French government demonstrated, while import growth continued its expansion between 1970 and 1989 from 16 per cent of GDP to over 34 per cent, exports peaked in 1984 at 33 per cent of GDP and declined for the next five years to about 30 per cent.[41] While it was argued that one-third of this deterioration in the trade balance was due to relative strength in France's macroeconomic situation and weakness in that of the major trading partners, the rest of the deterioration was caused by a loss of price-competitiveness of French goods. In another report issued one year later, four elements in this weak price-competitiveness were specified:

1. a system of mandatory fiscal charges that were excessive in the context of the EEC;
2. a public sector of high quality that was burdened by monopoly;
3. decision-making in France remained highly centralized; and
4. the educational system was not well suited to the needs of a modern, open and competitive economy.[42]

One of the consequences of this weakness is the lack of an international orientation and presence of France's small and medium-sized firms, which have been responsible for so much of the recent growth in industrialized economies – the rate of export for large firms was 33.6 per cent in 1986 while that for small firms was only 17.4 per cent. Finally, the 1989 report noted the lack of inter-industry specialization of French producers and suggested this might be indicative of a French inability to realize its true comparative advantages. However, in the environment in which intra-industry specialization within a steadily integrating European economy is increasingly important and in which intra-firm trade is significant and growing one would not necessarily expect marked specialization by sector rather than specialization within sectors. The latter appears to have been the condition of the French economy and need not in itself indicate inflexibility or an inability to adapt to changing market conditions.

As has been noted above, the decade of the 1970s was one of stagnation that extended into the next decade. The policy response to this deterioration in the economic situation of France and the EU was adoption of the Single European Act (SEA) in 1986. Also referred to as the completion of the internal market, the SEA sought to realize the unachieved potential of the creation of the EEC. A decade following its adoption has allowed sufficient time for its impacts to be evaluated and it is to two studies done in the late 1990s that we now turn our attention.

One factor that has been especially important during this period has been the liberalization of financial markets and the increased flows of direct investment. This process has been implemented on a global basis; thus France's experience will not be all that different from that of other advanced industrialized economies. Recent research on the consequences of French direct investment abroad and of foreign FDI in France by Fontagné and Pajot gives a rather positive view of this financial liberalization. They demonstrate, first of all, that there is a positive relationship between FDI and both exports and imports. For the period 1984–95 French-owned firms abroad increased both imports to and exports from France, with the net impact being about Fr70 billion of exports annually. The net annual trade impact of foreign firms located in France was Fr40–50 billion of imports.[43] Thus, firms operating abroad have a positive impact on the trade balance of the parent country, and for France the net effect of these two flows is positive for the balance of trade. Second, they found that while this impact was positive for France's goods trade, the impact of FDI in the services sector on international trade was negligible or non-existent. Finally, Fontagné and Pajot conclude that the increased international trade generated by FDI flows in and out of France has been disproportionate with other EU members but not at the expense of trade with non-members. That is, in the terminology of the customs union literature, trade creation has dwarfed trade diversion. This latter conclusion of little or no trade diversion is confirmed by work done by the EU Commission and reported by Buigues and Sapir.[44]

From this research it is clear that liberalization of capital markets and increased FDI has created new trade; but what has been the impact of that new trade on employment and production? Claude Vimont has examined this question, using data for 1991.[45] His basic findings are reproduced in Table 4.13. There are three very interesting and important findings that can be gained from Vimont's work. First, there was a net positive impact on employment in France of over 100,000 jobs for this year. Second, while job losses in manufacturing were over 200,000 they were more than offset by gains in the services sector. Third, there was a net shift in employment away from unskilled employment toward managerial and skilled jobs. The latter two findings indicate the changes in France's structure of output that have occurred as the economy responds to its revealed comparative advantage, as would be predicted by economic theory. In manufacturing, the lowest-skilled jobs have been lost to production facilities in low-cost, Third World economies – often to foreign subsidiaries of French firms, as France has in effect moved toward specialization in managerial and technical work. Unskilled work has been transferred from manufacturing to tourism and overall gains in both of the higher-skill categories have been realized. In general, then, freer trade has delivered what has always been promised for an advanced industrialized economy by those who promote this policy – net

Table 4.13:   Jobs created and destroyed by international trade, France,
1991

Category	Industrial products	Tourism	Other services	Total services	Total
Managers and technicians	−15	34	21	55	40
Supervisors, and skilled labor	−85	134	14	148	63
Unskilled labor	−107	106	4	110	3
Total	−207	274	39	313	106

Note: Data are in thousands of full-time jobs.

Source: Claude Vimont, *Le Commerce extérieure français: créateur or destructeur d'emplois?*, Paris: Economica, 1993, p. 24

employment has been created and skilled jobs have replaced unskilled jobs. Of course, other structural and macroeconomic factors have also been at work, so unemployment in France has not in fact been reduced. This will be examined in greater detail in Chapters 5 and 6.

FRANCE IN THE WORLD ECONOMY

After the Second World War, liberalization of output and factors of production dramatically altered France's relations with the rest of the world. Liberalization on the global level has gradually reduced the importance of privileged access to markets of ex-colonies and of their access to the French market.

Any examination of the relationship between France and the rest of the world must recognize that it is composed of bilateral linkages between France and the other areas and of initiatives of the EU in which France participates. In this section we will treat first the linkages of primary economic importance, those with the EU and the United States, only perfunctorily since they receive attention throughout the book and would take us far afield to do them justice here. Then linkages with the Third World will be explored more fully, both bilaterally and through EU relations with the Third World. Each of these relationships is rich in history and quite complex so we will give only a brief examination of each. Non-economic aspects of these relationships, such as defense and security, will be left for others to examine.

France has been one of the strongest proponents of the European integration process since its beginning just after the Second World War. Since one of the stated objectives of the institutions of the European

Community was the creation of a structure or relationships that would preclude another war on European soil, France's enthusiasm is not difficult to understand. Beyond this fundamental concern for security, acceptance of the Treaty of Rome put France on an entirely new trajectory regarding its economic development and policy. As we show in this book, prior to 1958 France was characterized by a weak manufacturing sector, highly protected and unproductive agriculture, commitment to a set of colonies that were a drain, and an aversion to investment. As Frances Lynch put it:

> When the Treaty of Rome setting up the European Economic Community entered into force, many of these blockages had either been overcome or were being addressed within the new structures of the EEC. Thus the period 1944–58 marked in France a transition from a highly protected and controlled imperial economy, which was dependent on the United States for national security and financial assistance, towards a more independent state which was linked to neighboring states at similar levels of economic development in a set of legally binding arrangements.[46]

The other chapters in this book detail the extent to which French productive agents and regions have benefited from transfers and other expenditures emanating from Brussels and the extent to which the French policy-making procedures have been altered. Agriculture has been almost entirely subsumed in the Common Agricultural Policy, and infrastructure improvements are heavily dependent upon EU participation. Macroeconomic policy has virtually disappeared as a national responsibility with adoption of the single currency. This will bring its own tensions but the arena in which these policy battles will be fought has clearly been relocated to Brussels.

The relationship with the United States has evolved from one of post-war dependence to increasing independence within the structures of the EU. The trade and investment relations have been examined earlier in this chapter so what remains to be examined is a rather fundamental conflict that has developed concurrently with the emergence of globalization. As was noted in Chapter 1, the United States has been seen as the prime mover behind both trade liberalization and market deregulation, and the rapid pace of technological and institutional change – and even the rapid pace of life.[47] Thus economic change is often linked with Americanization and cultural imperialism. Among Europeans the French feel this the strongest and have been leaders in EU policy to ensure cultural autonomy. This is an important economic matter, not just because of the revenues and employment that are involved but also because this understanding of the essential character of the relationship between Europe and the US can spill over into trade and investment relations. One of the factors that exacerbates this situation is the apparent inability of consecutive US administrations to comprehend how others can see, in the words of one former US official, that television is anything more than a toaster with a picture. The French would see this as one of the most powerful transmitters of cultural values. This one example of cultural policy can serve to demonstrate that, in spite of shared cultural values such as democracy, individualism, Christianity and capitalism, the two entities often have dramatically different perceptions of the same issue or policy question.

As Lynch noted, the Treaty of Rome had a powerful impact on French policy and institutions, and on the way France related to other parts of the world. The second event was the end of the Cold War. Ultimately this led to the current situation in which enlargement of EU membership to include Central European countries is being negotiated and to a shift in the center of the European economy, noticeably toward the East. This has drawn attention away from the US and from recently signed agreements such as the Transatlantic Partnership.[48] With the threat of Soviet expansion removed as a French and European concern, the necessity of a continual focus on strong multifactoral relations with the US is simply not there. The entire architecture of global economic relations has been altered, and Walter Lippman's notion of an Atlantic Community seems less and less compelling. Indeed the New Transatlantic Agenda called for a transatlantic market place rather than for a free trade agreement. Many of the other initiatives have not amounted to much or were stillborn. France's trade and investment relations with the US are pocked with important problems – from genetically modified grains to hormone-fed beef to the influence in France of US multinational corporations. And one can wonder, as Keynes did in 1933, whether increases in GDP are more likely to come from freer trade with the US or from improving intra-European relations or relations with the Third World. This is particularly the case now that global trade liberalization has brought tariff barriers down to being insignificant for most trade.

France's relationship with the Third World is primarily focused on Africa. This relationship is composed of two elements: those within *la Francophonie* and those that are not part of it. The former relationships are based primarily on culture and language, including education, research, and communication. They are also multilateral in nature and are nested in a complex of North–North (France, Belgium, Canada, and Switzerland), North–South and South–South (for example, scholarships for African students in educational institutions in Morocco) ties.[49] The initiative implemented by France has, as would be expected, become more structured and influential than the somewhat analogous British Commonwealth. *La Francophonie* is essentially a relationship between France and Africa; in the Western hemisphere only Canada and Haiti are members and in Asia only Laos, Cambodia and Vietnam. In each of these countries the percentage of the population that functions in the French language is a minor fraction of the whole, except for Haiti and, in Canada, Quebec and New Brunswick. It is in

Africa that large populations of francophones outside Europe are to be found and where the institutional structure is the densest and most extensive.

In contrast with the British Commonwealth, *la Francophonie* is explicitly based on use and preservation of the common language and its primary activities are cultural in nature. Established in 1969 at a conference held in Niamey (Niger), the formal organization of *la Francophonie*, the Agence de coopération culturelle et technique (ACCT), has as its objectives multinational cooperation in the areas of education, training, culture, science and technology, and the rapprochement of the peoples of member nations. In contrast to the scores of official and unofficial entities listed by the Commonwealth Secretariat, *la Francophonie* comprises just 19 organizations and associations, half of which are concerned with language and literature written in French.[50]

As was noted above, *la Francophonie* preceeded by the Franc Zone in 1930 in an effort to manage the fixed exchange rate that had been established between the French currency and those other countries that used the france in their monetary systems. This currency system was abolished in the early 1990s under pressure from the World Bank and the IMF, but by the time Charles de Gaulle returned to the presidency in 1958, France's trade with these countries had declined to about 6 per cent of the total and the Franc Zone accounted for less than 2 per cent of France's direct investment abroad. Thus the only linkage that was sustainable in the post-Second World War years was the linguistic and cultural one.

While the relationships between the colonial powers of the nineteenth century, Britain, France and Spain, and the countries over which they held dominance have had a real presence and value to many of the participants during the past few decades, one must wonder how important these cultural and institutional structures will be in the years to come. Market-based economic relations with primacy given to efficiency and material gain are demonstrating that previously beneficial preferential relationships are in the end costly affairs which neither partner in the exchange may wish to continue. As English becomes the functional universal language of scientific enquiry, of business and of mass culture, and as the old imperial powers no longer hold any advantage in the development of knowledge, other countries such as the United States, Japan, Canada or, indeed, countries in the developing world may come to be seen as more important contributors to progress and development. Thus, the evaluation of Jean-Louis Roy a decade ago that 'the Francophonie has become a work of our time,....,it is revealed capable of thinking and of acting as a single entity, devoted to vitality and growth'[51] may be an expression of enthusiasm rather than of cold perspicacity.

In describing the cultural relations between France and the Third World the concept of cultural imperialism is often used. By this is meant that one culture is dominant, either through the compelling nature of its elements or due to the market-size dominated economics of culture goods production, and that this culture crowds out those of, perhaps, smaller nations. Among industrial countries Canada and France have pressed this argument most consistently, but the concept also fits well into the received experience of most ex-colonial societies. It would take more space than is available here to discuss this adequately. While it may strike some as imperialist to argue Domingo Sarmiento's point about the superiority and civilizing influence of European and US science and rationality,[52] a less arrogant position can be put that suggests that the values of personal liberty and participatory democracy, espoused by both Europe and North America, do have positive benefit for citizens of Latin America and Africa. If this point is accepted, then Americanization, Europeanization and, indeed, Francization should properly be seen as modernization, a concept that is far less charged with notions of manipulation and exploitation.

To turn to the EU and the ACP Countries: the European Economic Community negotiated the Lomé Conventions, in the mid-1970s, with 70 African, Caribbean and Pacific (ACP) countries that were members of imperial or colonial preferential trading arrangements with individual European countries. The primary powers were, of course, Britain and France. The objective was to protect these developing nations from being excluded from their major industrialized market by the common external tariff of the EEC, as well as to ensure that Europe would have privileged access to raw materials from ACP countries. Trade liberalization on both global and regional levels has cast a less favorable light on arrangements such as this which fall short of full compliance with the principle of non-discrimination of the General Agreement on Tariffs and Trade (GATT), enforced now by the World Trade Organization (WTO). Preferential trade arrangements are generally allowed only if it is understood that they will be instrumental in moving all participants in the direction of the WTO's ultimate objective, global free trade. The EU obtained a waver for the Lomé Convention until the year 2000, but understands that any successor agreement must be fully WTO-compliant.

In recent years the EU preferential treatment of bananas from ACP countries, especially from the Caribbean, has developed into one of the most heated trade conflicts with the United States, acting on behalf of large US-based multinational companies with plantations in Central America. The WTO has acted favorably on a complaint presented by the US but the EU has spent years slowly exhausting all avenues of appeal and delay in implementation. The US limited access to its market for a variety of non-related EU goods, and the cost to European companies and workers was far out of proportion to the benefits received. Only in 2001 was the issue resolved, and it was done in a spirit that led some observers to hope that other more substantial US–EU trade conflicts could also be resolved.[53] Quite apart from the banana issue, economists would argue that, given the growing openness of markets around the world and the facility with which capital moves, ACP countries would gain from free trade that was global rather than preferential in nature and that EU consumers should be free to choose which goods, imported or not, they wish to consume. In a simulation of the effects of continued EU–ACP preferential free trade, Matthew McQueen has shown that while the EU gains in export sales the results for ACP countries would be a loss of welfare, pressure toward balance of payments deficit, slower growth, and a loss of import duty revenue.[54] Finally, the fact that the individual ACP countries are so dramatically different in their levels of development, industrialization, and income suggests that no single blanket structure, such as Lomé Convention, could be appropriate for all of them. It also suggests that both France and its ex-colonies would be best served by such a multilateral structure.

The relationship between the EU and Latin America has developed considerable interest during the 1990s. As the EU seeks to expand its presence out of its immediate region, Latin America is one of the most promising potential partners. The development of a more open, and less ideological, focus throughout Latin America has increased its attractiveness. From the standpoint of Latin America, the EU provides a much-desired alternative to the US as a linkage with an industrialized region with a large market for its goods and services. The economy of Central America is not large enough to capture much attention from European nations but the combination of Argentina, Brazil, Chile and some of the other South American nations presents Europe with a market that is worth cultivating. Here we will examine the roles of history and language, on the one hand, and, on the other, trade and investment in the development of this relationship.

While the US congress has stalled progress toward the sort of Western Hemispheric trade agreement sought by proponents of free trade, the EU has been engaged in discussions with Mercosur, the regional trade grouping of Argentina, Brazil, Paraguay and Uruguay. The first agreement was signed in 1992, after a meeting in the Portuguese city of Guimaraes, and a commitment to seek closer ties was made by both parties at a Heads of State and Government meeting in 1994, in Corfu.[55] For its part Mercosur has achieved agreements of association with other Latin American countries, such as Bolivia, Mexico, Chile, and the members of the Andean trade agreement. Trade between the EU and Mercosur plus Chile amounts to $6.2 billion in EU exports and $5.1 in EU imports. Frustrated by lack of progress with the US, but encouraged by developments elsewhere, Argentine President Menem was quoted to the effect that if it wished to do so the US could apply for membership in Mercosur! It is also noteworthy that Argentina is currently considering pegging its currency to the dollar and the Euro rather than just the dollar. Recent trade and exchange rate conflict between Mercosur's two largest members, Argentina and Brazil, suggest that future progress may be slow in coming; the EU is also concerned that the lack of an institutional structure may put the entire initiative in jeopardy. As is generally the case, one of the chief stumbling blocks to future progress remains EU agricultural interests as such an agreement is seen as a threat to the Common Agricultural Policy. This should, of course, be considered a diminishing force as changes occur in the CAP if only because of the financial implications of enlargement of EU membership unless such changes are introduced.

Nonetheless, both sides see advantages to pursuing a closer relationship. The EU is anxious that South America should not come explicitly within the orbit of the US through a formal Western Hemispheric trade agreement, from which the EU would be excluded. Mercosur and its associate members see in the EU a successful initiative to forge a close relationship in all aspects – economic, cultural, political and security – among nations that are certainly as heterogeneous in their languages, institutions, and cultures as are the South American nations. Surely something could be learned from this experience. Finally, both the EU and Mercosur find comfort in agreements that are purely economic in nature and devoid of the implicit political and security agendas that invariably accompany an agreement with the US.

Progress on closer relations between these two parties will also be difficult in the context of the EU's concentration on expansion of its membership and the enormous concentration of attention and resources that this will require. In a report on the subject for the French Assemblée Nationale, deputy Alain Barrau noted that, while the EU was the primary trading partner of Mercosur and the EU would be the primary beneficiary of an opening of Latin American markets, the protectionist position of the French government was one of the major stumbling blocks.[56]

NOTES

1. Rondo Cameron, *A Concise Economic History of the World*, Oxford: Oxford University Press, 1997, pp. 298–301.
2. André Gueslin, 'Les politiques économiques au XXe siècle,' *Cahiers français*, no. 255, March–April 1992, pp. 47–8.
3. Ibid., p. 50.
4. Paul Hohenberg, *A Primer on the Economic History of Europe*, New York: Random House, 1968, p. 161.
5. Douglas H. Ashford, *Policy and Politics in France: Living with Uncertainty*, Philadelphia: Temple University Press, 1982, p. 147.
6. Charles P. Kindleberger, *Economic growth in France and Britain: 1851–1950*, New York: Simon and Schuster, 1964, pp. 278 and 279.
7. Ibid., p., 286.
8. Michel Zylbererg, 'De la guerre à la depression (1914–1939),' *Cahiers français*, no. 255, March–April 1992, pp. 16–17.

9. François-Pierre Le Scouarnec, *La Francophonie*, Canada: Boréal, 1997, p. 46.
10. This is stressed in Jean-François Eck, *Histoire de l'économie française depuis 1945*, Paris: Arman Colin, 1996, pp. 18–22.
11. François Cochet, *Histoire économique de la France depuis 1945*, Paris: Dunod, 1997, p. 67.
12. Jean-Charles Asselain, 'L'ouverture à la concurrence internationale,' *Cahiers français*, no. 255, March–April 1992, p. 60.
13. Roger Frydman, *L'économie française: croissance et crise*, La Garenne-Colombes: Éditions de l'Espace Européen, 1992, p. 51.
14. John Sheahan, *Promotion and Control of Industry in Post-war France*, Cambridge, MA: Harvard University Press, 1963, p. 235.
15. Asselain, 'L'ouverture', p. 60.
16. William James Adams, *Restructuring the French Economy*, Washington, DC: Brookings Institution, 1989, pp. 123–128.
17. Frydman, *L'économie française*, pp. 51–56
18. Adams, *Restructuring the French Economy*, p. 122.
19. J.R. Hough, *The French Economy*, New York: Holmes and Meier, 1982, p. 197.
20. Marcy's argument is referred to in Sheahan, *Promotion and Control*, p. 234.
21. Alfred Cobban, *A History of Modern France, vol. 3: 1871–1962*, Hammondsworth, Middlesex: Penguin Books, 1965, p. 241.
22. Leland B. Yeager, *International Monetary Relations*, New York: Harper and Row, 1966, pp. 398–400.
23. Asselain, 'L'ouverture,' p. 59.
24. Eck, *Histoire de l'économie française*, p. 27.
25. J.-J.Carré, P. Dubois and E. Malinvaud, *French Economic Growth*, Palo Alto, CA: Stanford University Press, 1975, p. 406.
26. Pierre-André Buigues and André Sapir, 'L'impact du marché unique sur les grands pays européenes,' *Revue d'économie politique*, vol. 109, no. 2, March–April 1999, pp. 182–186.
27. Carré, *French Economic Growth*, pp. 398–407.
28. Adams, *Restructuring the French Economy*, pp. 155–161.
29. Christopher Flockton and Eleonore Kofman, *France*, London: Paul Chapman, 1989, pp. 63–64.
30. Ibid., p. 70.
31. The French and other variations of capitalism are contrasted in Pierre Conso, 'L'apparition de nouveaux modes d'organisation industrielle et de management.' in Christian de Boissiue (ed.), *Les mutations de l'économie française*, Paris: Economica, 1997, pp. 112–118.
32. Alain Henriot, 'Quelle place pour la France dans la novelle géographie des échanges internationaux?,' in Christian de Boissiue (ed.), *Les mutations de l'économie française*, Paris: Economica, 1997, p. 222.
33. *Annuaire statistique de la France*, 1961, Paris: INSEE.
34. This is reviewed succinctly in Eck, *Histoire de l'économie française*, ch. 1.
35. Ibid., p. 172.
36. For a review and analysis of this initiative and the events leading up to it, see Peter B. Kenen, *Economic and Monetary Union in Europe*, Cambridge: Cambridge University Press, 1995.
37. Jean-Jacques Servan-Schreiber, *Le Défi américain*, Paris: Editions Denoel, 1967.

38. United States, Department of the Treasury, *1998 Investment Climate Statement: France*, Washington, D.C: US Government, 1999.
39. Carré, *French Economic Growth*, pp. 404–407.
40. Ibid., pp. 416.
41. Ministère de l'Économie, des Finances et du Budget and Ministère du Commerce Exterieur, *Où en est la compétitivité française?*, Paris: La documentation Française, 1989, p. 22.
42. Ministère du Commerce Exterieur, *La competitivité de l'économie française dan la perspective du marché unique*, Paris: La Documentation Française, 1990, pp. 35–50 and 62.
43. Lionel Fontagné and Michaël Pajot, 'Investissement direct a l'étranger et commerce international,' *Revue économique*, vol. 49, no. 3, May 1998, p. 604.
44. Pierre-André Buigues and André Sapir, 'L'impact du marché unique sur les grandes pays européens,' *Revue économique et politique*, vol. 109, no. 2, March– April 1999, p. 181.
45. Claude Vimont, *Le Commerce extérieure français: créateur ou destructeur d'emplois?*, Paris: Economica, 1993.
46. Frances M.B. Lynch, *France and the International Economy: From Vichy to the Treaty of Rome*, London: Routledge, 1997, p. 211.
47. This is examined in Kristen Ross, *Fast Cars and Clean Bodies*, Cambridge, MA: MIT Press, 1996.
48. Excellent coverage of this is given in David C. Gompert and F. Stephen Larrabee (eds.) *America and Europe: A Partnership for a New Era*, Cambridge: Cambridge University Press, 1996.
49. Jean-Louis Roy, *La Francophonie: L'émergence d'une alliance?*, Lasalle (Québec): Hurtubise, 1989, ch. II.
50. Jean-Marc Léger, *La Francophonie: grand dessein, grande ambiguïté*, Lasalle (Québec): Hurtubise, 1987, pp. 200–204.
51. Le Scouarnec, *La Francophonie*, p. 46.
52. Roy, *La Francophonie*, p. 111.
53. Referred to in Ofelia Schutte, 'Cultural identity: the aesthetic dimension,' in Marina Pérez de Mendiola (ed.), *Bridging the Atlantic: Toward a Reassessment of Iberian and Latin American Cultural Ties*, Albany, NY: SUNY Press, 1996, ch. 12.
54. Anthony DePalma, 'US and Europeans agree on deal to end banana trade war,' *New York Times*, 12 April 2001, p. C1.
55. Matthew McQueen, 'ACP–EU trade cooperation after 2000: an assessment of reciprocal trade preferences,' *Journal of Modern African Studies*, vol. 36 no. 4, 1996, pp. 669–692.
56. Franck Petiteville, 'Europe/Amérique latine: La synergie des logiques d'integration?,' *Revue politique et parlementaire*, vol. 98, no. 983, May–June 1996, p. 47.
57. Alain Barrau, *Union européenne et Mercosur: mariage ou union libre?*, Paris: Assemblée Nationale, 1999, p. 7.

5 Employment and Incomes

Concurrent with the liberalization of movements of goods, services, capital and labor during the latter half of the twentieth century, France has experienced a substantial change in the employment and incomes of its citizens. There is a natural tendency to want to link the two phenomena causally but, as is generally the case, other things were taking place concurrently so causality cannot be assigned without a more thorough study. Changes in technology, in demography, in political processes and in social behavior may have only a tenuous connection to liberalization of product and factor markets or to the development of integration within the European Union. Furthermore, while some of these changes have been experienced by other EU members, not all of the latter have been so affected. In this chapter we will examine the experience of France, at times in contrast with other major industrialized economies, with rising unemployment and with growing inequality in the distribution of income.

INTRODUCTION: DOMESTIC ECONOMIC POLICY IN THE CONTEXT OF GLOBALIZATION

During the inter-war years and during the first couple of decades following the Second World War, the larger industrialized nations could be described as closed economies. That is, movement of products and factors was highly constrained by tariffs, migration quotas, currency restrictions and a host of other measures. France could certainly be categorized in this way. In a world of closed economies, each nation could manage its domestic economic policy without regard for two-way linkages with other economies. For example, John Maynard Keynes argued in 1933 that in the midst of macroeconomic collapse each nation would do well to close its borders so that a policy of stimulating aggregate demand could have its full impact on domestic employment without the leakage that foreign trade with open borders represented.[1] In a situation with high unemployment, the benefits of full employment would dwarf those of freer trade. When economies are open this policy option is not available and the determination of the optimal employment and income policy becomes a far more complex matter. In this section we will examine the consequences of an open economy for domestic employment and incomes and for the policy options of the national government. This will be applied to the situation of France, especially during the years following the OPEC price hikes in the 1970s. Finally, we will discuss the consequences for French policy-makers of membership in the European Union.

Full-employment Policy and the Change from a Closed to an Open Economy

The impact on policy formation of a transition from a closed to an open economy is dramatic and in some ways it becomes an issue of increased complexity. To take just one example, while the optimal use of monetary and fiscal policy in both situations has been determined in economic theory, the exchange rate and the degree of its flexibility is one of the crucial factors in policy formulation. With fixed exchange rates a nation's fiscal policy can work well to stimulate or restrain output and employment, whereas with exchange rate flexibility fiscal policy in ineffective. This is because fiscal policy works through parallel chains of impacts on aggregate demand and on money demand and interest rates. With flexibility these two chains work at cross-purposes, one negating the effectiveness of the other, while under fixed rates they work toward the same objective. The reverse is true for monetary policy, with it being effective under flexible rates but ineffective when exchange rates are fixed. Monetary policy works through impacts on the interest rate and this has impacts on both aggregate demand and on capital in/outflows; in the latter exchange rate regime the two impacts work together whereas in the former they conflict with each other. There is no need to explore this further here, and the reader is referred to any textbook on international economics or finance for a fuller explication of this aspect of economic theory. The only point to be made here is that under different exchange rate regimes, different policy initiatives will be called for to achieve the same policy objective, in this case the reduction of unemployment.

During the first three decades of the post-Second World War period France, and the rest of the industrial countries, functioned in the Bretton Woods system of fixed but adjustable exchange rates. When this system collapsed in the early 1970s, France participated with other EEC members in experiments with the snake in the tunnel (1972), the European Monetary System (1979), and finally the European Monetary Union (1999).[2] The first two initiatives involved a joint float of participating currencies against the dollar and other non-participating currencies. Each participating currency was allowed to fluctuate within a band of 2.25 per cent above or below its central rate. The French franc was therefore constrained in its movement *vis–à–vis* its major trading partners in the EEC, but the bloc of EEC currencies could move without limit against other currencies. When some member currencies came under speculative attack in 1992 and 1993 the bands were widened to 15 per cent, thus avoiding formal abandonment of the system but allowing individual currencies virtually unrestricted freedom to fluctuate against each other. Adoption of the Maastricht Treaty on European Union (1992) committed member countries to achieve economic and monetary union, including a common currency, a single monetary authority and integration of financial markets. With nothing more than just a sincere commitment to adopt a single currency France would no longer even have an exchange rate to manage.

Throughout this period of experimentation following the end of the Bretton Woods system the exchange rate mechanism in which France was situated changed from fixed but adjustable, to fixed within the European float, to almost freely floating within the European Monetary System, back to fixed within the EMS, and finally toward a single currency with monetary union projected for completion on January 1, 2002. For this reason alone formulation of an effective policy to stimulate output and to reduce unemployment was rather more uncertain and unpredictable than was the case prior to the abandonment of Bretton Woods.

The essential point to be made in regard to acceptance of monetary union is that in doing so France and the other nations of Euroland (the 11 countries that are participating in the monetary union) have lost one policy instrument for affecting domestic economic performance and conditions. The loss of the exchange rate is only the most dramatic development in what had historically been taken to be the primary economic functions of a national government – managing the domestic economy and redressing the economic grievances of its citizens. This process of self-emasculation by national governments is generally taken to be one of the central consequences of the process of globalization. This has occurred on both the global and the regional level. For France, as well as other nations, the post-war structure of global economic institutions did impose constraints on government action. The International Monetary Fund made it more difficult to use currency devaluation or revaluation as a policy tool. The General Agreement on Tariffs and Trade disallowed some behaviors and sanctioned others regarding the resort to tariff and non-tariff barriers as means of constraining the international movement of goods. Combined with a series of tariff-reducing rounds under GATT sponsorship it became increasingly difficult for the government to resort to protectionist measures in case of economic distress.

It is at the regional level, however, that the structure of constraints on national policy options has been most extensively developed through France's participation in the European integration process. Full treatment of this development would go far beyond what is required for the objectives of this study, so a great deal of material will be examined only for its impacts ofnFrench employment and incomes policy formulation. We have just noted the role European monetary integration has played in the loss of the exchange rate as a policy option. Similarly, acceptance of the Treaty of Rome and membership in the European Economic Community committed France to a customs union in which it would be able to participate in the GATT process only as a member of the EEC. Thus loss of control over its external tariff and non-tariff barriers meant that commercial policy was no longer a policy option for having an impact on domestic economic conditions.

Monetary union has explicitly removed monetary policy from EU national governments, but of equal importance is the fact that in order for this to be implemented thenational economies of the participants were required to conform to a set of convergence criteria. This was necessary because, if several national economies were to accept a single currency and exchange rate, the national economic conditions that would normally generate an exchange rate would have to be brought within rather narrow limits. Thus, the national government budget deficit would have to be no greater than 3 per cent of GDP, the national government debt would have to be no more than 60 per cent of GDP, inflation could not be higher than 1.5 per cent above the average rate of the three countries with the lowest rates, long-term interest rates would have to be kept to within 2 per cent of the average of the three countries with the lowest rates, and the currency could not have been devalued within two years of entry to the union.[3] It is clear from this that the French government also gave up its capacity to use fiscal policy as a means of affecting domestic economic performance.

Fully two-thirds of the budget of the EC/EU has gone to two areas that have traditionally been major expenditure items of national governments: support schemes for agriculture and regional development policy. While the French government has not removed itself entirely from these areas, funding from Brussels has come to dominate these two sectors and both the Common Agricultural Policy and the policies that guide the structural funds have led to harmonization of both agricultural and regional policies throughout the EC/EU. Thus in both of these important areas the French and other national governments have given up their capacity for independent action.

France's participation in the European economic integration process has obligated it to forfeit its capacity to use monetary policy, fiscal policy, the exchange rate, commercial policy (tariff and non-tariff barriers), agricultural policy, and regional policy as means of combating high rates of unemployment, economic stagnation, or other domestic economic objectives. This is clearly a considerable concession in relation to the gains that are expected to be achieved through economic integration. Whether this is a rational trade-off for the French is impossible for an economist to say, since avoidance of another war in Europe was one of the primary objectives of the process. What can be said is that participation in the European economic integration process has made it increasingly difficult for the French government to adopt policies that will effectively reduce unemployment or have an impact on incomes.

Incomes, Their Distribution, and Globalization

When the economy was closed to substantial international linkages, the distribution of income of any nation was to a significant degree the result of a political decision made autonomously by that nation's citizens. Marketable skills, education, inheritance, social position and a host of other factors all contributed to the income of all individuals and to the degree of inequality among the various deciles or quartiles of the population. But overriding this economics-based process of income determination was the income redistribution accomplished by government through a variety of tax and transfer mechanisms. The latter was, of course, subject to decisions made in a democratic political process. Thus the income distribution of each nation was unique and in conformity with the values and traditions of that society. Globalization changed this situation dramatically, as open borders allowed internationally generated forces to dominate traditional domestic political accommodation among income classes. In the specific case of France, not only have exogenous economic forces gained supremacy in income determination but the political response to them has become lodged in a decision-making structure in Brussels in which France is but one voice among fifteen.

The distribution of income among income classes is not the only manifestation of this surrender of national control. Globalization has also caused a restructuring of the economic well–being of France's regions and industries. Each region and industry must now confront global economic rationality more or less on its own. For some this entails exciting new freedom of action and opportunities for new activities; but for others it brings only marginalization and decline. These consequences of globalization on France's regions and industries will be developed in Chapter 7 below. In this chapter we will limit our treatment to changes in the distribution of income during the past three decades.

Later in this chapter we will examine the data for the distribution of income in France and for its changes during the post-war period. One of the primary features of the changing demographic situation in France is the growth of the immigrant population. While normal immigrants suffer hardship in all countries to which they migrate, Saskia Sassen finds that France's record has been better than almost any other European nation. She argues that through most of their recent history the French have considered immigrants to be a positive contribution to the labor force and the productive capacity of the country. Furthermore, once they arrived, 'the rational, state-centered, and assimilationist conception of nationhood that was implemented with the French Revolution,...,led to an inclusionary stance regarding foreigners who resided in France.'[4] This is in accord with the argument of Loïc Wacquant that the French *banlieu*, or low income/immigrant quarter of the city, is quite different in nature from the American ghetto.[5] He argues that the US racial ghettos are isolated sociologically and physically, and subjected to violence and degradation to a much greater degree than are their French counterparts. In spite of this, when the economy experienced difficulty in the 1970s the welcome-mat for immigrants was withdrawn in France as it was elsewhere. This led to a new concern for low-income workers and the poor – exclusion. While immigrants are the most visible component of the excluded, there are also other categories such as youth, long-time unemployed and older workers.

The disturbing forecasts for the age distribution of the population of European nations gives the immigration question a very interesting twist. During the first half of the present century the population of the current EU is projected to decline by about 12 per cent. This poses enormous difficulties for the financing of the expected retirement and health benefits of Europe's senior citizens and replenishment of the tax paying labor force. Germany alone would require an annual inflow of 500,000 workers just to keep its working–age population steady. France is the only country, with the exception of Ireland, that is expected to experience a population growth, even though that is only about 2 per cent.[6] If it is going to be able to avoid serious social and fiscal problems Europe is going to have to become much more welcoming to migrants, whether they come from Eastern Europe, Africa or Asia. France both has a better record to date than most of the other EU countries and is faced with a situation that is less dire. By contrast the United States is expected to have a population growth of about 25 per cent. The situation of the excluded will be taken up later in this chapter after we have examined unemployment.

A French or a Continental Problem?

Before we close this initial section of our discussion of France's less than stellar performance regarding unemployment and incomes during the past two decades, we must raise the question as to whether the problem is a French or a continental European one. Only after this has been done will we be able to examine France's experience and policy options. For many economists in the Anglo-Saxon or neo-classical world the answer is simple: both France and continental Europe are burdened with an economic system that results in higher costs of production and these additional costs price European goods out of many markets.[7] The cost increases are alleged to be due to higher social charges (government taxes and other levies), generous unemployment schemes that reduce the incentive to seek work, excessively numerous holidays and shorter work times, a web of labor market practices that create substantial rigidities, and high costs of hiring and firing workers. This is undoubtedly an accurate depiction of a generalized situation for continental economies but, of course, no such picture can do justice to the rich variety in detail that exists among the individual economies. To take just one point, unemployment in Sweden and the Netherlands, at 6 and 3 per cent respectively, is currently considerably below that of the EU average (10.2 per cent) or of that of its largest economies. France, Germany, Italy and Spain all have unemployment rates in excess of 10 per cent (although that for Western Germany is about 8 per cent). What is important here is not just high labor costs but the combination of labor costs plus some off-setting characteristics, such as a suitable infrastructure, labor education and training that gives workers certain skills, work place discipline, and so forth. So the question of the effectiveness of the continental labor market situation is rather more complex than it would appear to be at first glance. While there is something one can refer to as the continental values and policy system, it is differentiated to the degree that we can identify elements which are specifically French in nature and which do enable one to evaluate the effectiveness of French policy in the area of employment and incomes. Furthermore, one has to assess the practical implications of such rigidities. That is, do they actually create unemployment? Or do they do so only as a consequence of increasing the supply of labor and, as a concomitant, increasing total employment? These matters are important and they will be addressed later in this chapter.

Behind any evaluation of the economic performance of France by American critics is a contrast in basic values that must be recognized and that will color any conclusions regarding employment and income policies. As Amartya Sen has put it: 'the values of American society allow an indifference with regard to the poor that is unthinkable among Western Europeans, raised in the culture of *l'état providence*. However, these same American values would never accept the double-digit rates of unemployment which are experienced by several European economies.'[8] Thus, application of some set of universal values or targets to domestic policies is not possible in a way that would find acceptance everywhere. While Anglo-Saxon or neo-classical economists tend to focus exclusively on the jobless rate as an indicator of success in employment policy, many French economists counter that a large percentage of the jobs that have been created in Britain and the United States are undesirable jobs, offering low pay, few if any benefits, and with neither security nor hope of advancement.[9] They also argue that one of the primary consequences of the Anglo-Saxon approach to economic policy is a distribution of income that is becoming increasingly distorted, with fewer wealthy individuals gaining a larger and larger share of total income and with the middle and low-income classes losing out.[10] The previous sub-section has given data that support at least some of this counter-argument. Neither of these situations is seen to be either desirable or acceptable by the French for France. France's experience with both unemployment and the distribution of income will be the primary subject of this chapter.

All commentators agree that there are two basic models present in the 1990s: the American or Anglo-Saxon model of flexibility and the trans-Rhinean model of rigid structures and processes. Bertola and Ichino place the situation of high, intractable unemployment in the context of national economies making the transition from the latter to the former. At the end of the 1980s, they argue, Britain was a model of flexibility, Italy was caught in transition from one to the other, and France was 'consistently..."rigid" through the (decade).'[11] Jean-Marc Le Gall, however, argues that Europeans want to make this transition toward a market economy and to insert the economy in global exchanges, but they refuse the dictatorship of the market and its social costs that they consider to be too high.[12] Our conclusion must be that while there is a continental model, the French economic system is sufficiently unique to ensure that whatever problems there are with employment and incomes they must be considered to be French in nature.

FRANCE'S EXPERIENCE SINCE 1945

France emerged from the Second World War ill–equipped to confront the fundamental structural, institutional and mental transformations that it was about to face. The first 45 years of the twentieth century were extraordinarily harsh on the whole of Europe. Two wars and the depression made this one of the most disastrous periods in all of European history. The smaller countries of Northern Europe were open and flexible enough to be able to make the necessary adjustments to the exigencies of post-war economics, but the Iberian peninsula failed to free itself from fascism. The United Kingdom was in a state of decline that was partly due to self-inflicted attachment to an over-valued currency that privileged the financial sector but was disastrous for manufacturing and partly caused by its inability to adapt to its diminished global position. Germany suffered enormous destruction but had the advantage of being forced to restructure its economic and political institutions and processes under the supervision of the United States. As soon as the Cold War developed, within five years of the war's end, it became necessary for the United States to ensure that West Germany, positioned on the border with the competing Soviet-dominated world, would be a shining example of what could be accomplished under democracy and capitalism. Alas, France was not in such a position, nor would it have accepted this subordination to the United States.

While the inter-war period began with a modernization of manufacturing technologies and an expansion of a small number of firms such as Renault, Peugeot, Rhône-Poulenc and Schneider, France remained attached to its traditional structures of small firms, family–run retail shops, and an archaic agricultural sector.[13] None of this would seriously be challenged until after the Treaty of Rome in 1958. The economy was actually in trouble before the depression, although it did not plummet to the depths that were seen in the United States and Germany. During the depression most governments made efforts to moderate or to counter its impacts; the French government was less convincing or effective in its initiatives than were others. Both the political leadership and the business community were convinced that the economic downturn was caused by the large government budget deficit and the deficit in the external balance. The policies they chose – reductions in government expenditure and beggar-thy-neighbor policies with regard to the rest of the world (currency devaluation and restraints on imports) – were actually pro-cyclical in nature and only exacerbated matters both for France and for her trading partners.

The last few years before the outbreak of war were marked by devaluation (1936), an expansion of the role of the state in the economy (including nationalization of some industries and increased regulation of wages and working conditions – the Matignon Accords of 1936), and a failed general strike in 1938. By 1939, industrial production had regained its level of 1929 and unemployment was on the way down. War broke out before it could be determined whether France had actually turned the corner economically, but there can be no doubt that the changes in economic structures, processes and thinking that would be so important in the post-war period simply had not been achieved.

From 1945 to the EEC (1958)

If we begin our examination of the employment situation in France with 1949, omitting the immediate period of recovery, the record as shown in Table 5.1 is rather spectacular. The absolute number of unemployed during 1949–58 actually declined by over 50,000 and the rate of unemployment never exceeded 1.6 per cent of the available labor force. During the period the total labor force grew from 19,496,000 to 19,826,000 but the military draft expanded from 280,000 to 567,000 so the available labor force actually declined slightly.[14] The table also indicates that, as was typically the case for industrialized economies, there were inter-sectoral shifts out of agriculture. In France, agricultural employment declined between 1949 and 1958 from

Table 5.1: French employment, 1949–58

Year	Available labor force	Agriculture	Industry	Non-productive	Unemployed Number	%
1949	19,288	5,555	11,011	2,481	241	1.2
1950	19,285	5,438	11,059	2,517	271	1.4
1951	19,325	5,320	11,258	2,521	226	1.2
1952	19,299	5,204	11,305	2,543	245	1.3
1953	19,223	5,090	11,248	2,585	300	1.6
1954	19,305	5,007	11,348	2,640	311	1.6
1955	19,302	4,487	11,484	2,688	283	1.5
1956	19,238	4,668	11,638	2,714	212	1.1
1957	19,271	4,454	11,914	2,742	161	0.8
1958	19,239	4,284	12,021	2,772	183	1.0

Notes:
1. Absolute data are in thousands.
2. Non-productive includes financial institutions, domestic service and government.
3. Industrial includes goods and services.
4. Available labor force is equal to the total labor force minus those drafted for military service.

Source: J.-J. Carré, P. Dubois and E. Malinvaud, *French Economic Growth*, Palo Alto, CA: Stanford University Press, 1975, Appendix tables 4 and 5

28.8per cent of the available labor force to 22.5 per cent, while industrial employment grew from 57.1 to 62.5 per cent and that of the non-productive sectors grew from 12.9 to 14.4 per cent. Between 1949 and 1958 employment in manufacturing grew by 4.3 per cent. Within this sector there were some significant developments: employment declined in solid mineral fuels and gas by 24 per cent and in textiles, clothing, and leather by 19 per cent, but grew by 40 per cent in building materials and glass, by 19 per cent in non–ferrous minerals and metals, and by 26 per cent in mechanical and electrical industries. These changes were due in part to the evolving technologies of the post-war economy and in part to the requirements of France's colonial wars 'which absorbed more than a quarter of the government budget and necessitated imports of costly defense material.'[15]

This was an important period for workers as it saw the introduction of Social Security (1945), the end of war-time rationing (1949), the minimum wage – the *Salaire minimum interprofessionnel garanti* or SMIG – (1950), the third week of holiday (1956), and unemployment insurance (1958). This was a period in which the notion of a welfare state was being introduced throughout Europe. The effect of measures such as the minimum wage, unemployment insurance, and social security was to cause the theoretical market–determined earned income and the actual disposable income of an individual to diverge. The distribution of income and the extent of poverty would increasingly become matters of public policy rather than solely matters of individual skills, initiative, and luck.

From the EEC (1958) to OPEC (Mid-1970s)

This period was bracketed by the two events that have most dramatically changed economic life in France since the end of the war: the signing of the Treaty of Rome and the OPEC price increases. Most observers see the opening of the French economy to increasingly free exchanges of goods and services as the equivalent of a revolution.[16] During 1959–79 exports grew from 12.8 per cent of GDP to 20.7 per cent and grew at a rate twice as fast as that of domestic production. The rise of trade with EEC members relative to that with traditional colonial economies stimulated the restructuring of French production that was already under way, as noted above. Labor continued to leave agriculture for construction, transportation, services, finance, and government. Agricultural employment declined from 22 to 11 per cent of the labor force between 1958 and 1972, employment in industry rose from 62.5 per cent to 73 per cent, and that in finance, domestic service and government rose from 14.4 to 16 per cent. Within manufacturing solid mineral fuels and gas and textiles, clothing, and leather continued their slide, while the strongest gains were seen in the industries mentioned in the previous section as well as in chemicals.

The rate of unemployment continued to be impressively low and remained below 2 per cent until the end of the 1960s. Nonetheless the trend is clearly upward from 1964 with the rate rising from 1.1 to 2.8 per cent. Thus, even prior to the price increases by OPEC beginning in 1973, the employment picture in France was showing signs of some marginal deterioration. In this instance the difficulty was internally generated rather than the result of an external shock. The main domestic event at this time was the unrest and riots of May 1968. A clear indication of the economic disruption that was caused by 1968 can be gained from the days lost to strikes. The annual average of days lost to strikes for each of the five-year periods before and after 1968 was 3.2 million, whereas for 1968 it was over 15.0 million. In the wake of this disturbance:
1. the production of goods was halted for at least a month;
2. the government increased the money supply;

3. additional charges were assessed on business firms;
4. salaries were increased (with the *Accords de Grenelle*); and
5. after the departure from office of General de Gaulle, the currency was devalued in 1969.[17]

All of these actions contributed to an outbreak of inflation and to a rupture in the agreements that had kept the economy on track and unemployment almost non-existent.

Table 5.2: Unemployment, France, 1958–72

Year	1958	1959	1960	1961	1962	1963	1964	1965
Rate of unemployment	1.0	1.3	1.2	1.1	1.2	1.4	1.1	1.3

Year	1966	1967	1968	1969	1970	1971	1972	
Rate of unemployment	1.4	1.8	2.0	2.3	2.4	2.7	2.8	

Source: *Annuaire Statistique de la France*, Paris: INSEE, various issues

From OPEC (Mid-1970s) to the Early 1980s

In 1973 the oil-exporting countries of OPEC tripled the price of a barrel of oil to $10 and they tripled it again in 1979. The consequences for the industrialized world of these actions were rapid increases in the rate of inflation, to a rate in excess of 10 per cent for France during 1973–9, and a diversion of financial resources from the purchase of the entire array of goods and services to petroleum products. The latter effect triggered a slow-down in economic growth and in job creation. The impact on the employment situation in France is clear from the figures in Table 5.3. In the decade following the first price hike the rate of unemployment more than tripled and the problems of long-term and youth employment became unavoidable features of the economic picture.

One of the first responses in France to higher unemployment was a reversal of the generally positive evaluation of the presence of immigrants. The right–wing, somewhat fascist party *Le Front National*, led by Jean-Marie Le Pen, was born at this time; it was able to obtain 15 per cent of the votes in some national elections and to win the mayor's office in some towns in the south. One of the party's central arguments was that immigrant workers would gain employment by lowering the wage at which they were willing to work. This would lower wages for French workers and it would also reduce the number of jobs available to them. At a time when the effects of

Table 5.3: Labor market indicators, France, 1973–82

Year	Unemploy- ment, % of labor force	Long-term unemploy- ment share of total	Youth unemploy- ment, %	Jobs vacant (000)	Employ- ment % 1985=100
Column:	(1)	(2)	(3)	(4)	(5)
1973	2.7	21.6	4.0	252	100
1974	2.8	n/a	n/a	205	100
1975	4.0	n/a	n/a	109	100
1976	4.4	n/a	n/a	124	101
1977	4.9	n/a	n/a	104	101
1978	5.2	n/a	n/a	87	101
1979	5.9	30.3	13.3	88	102
1980	6.3	32.4	15.1	89	102
1981	7.5	32.4	17.0	69	101
1982	8.2	n/a	n/a	84	102

Sources: Columns 2 and 3: OECD, *Country Surveys: France*; Columns 1, 4 and 5: *Main Economic Indicators*, Paris: Organization for Economic Cooperation and Development, various issues

globalization on incomes and employment of workers in industrialized economies was being hotly debated, and when terms such as de-industrialization, restructuring, down-sizing, and so forth were entering the popular vocabulary, the anti-immigrant position of Le Pen and his party struck a positive note with a committed minority of the French population. However, a couple of interesting observations in this regard can be made from the data in Table 5.4.

First, the number of foreigners in France reached its peak in the early 1980s. This is clearly represented in the net flows to France from Africa, with the largest figures being 48,053 in 1980 and 45,225 the following year. For the next four years the average annual flow was only about 14,000. On the face of it, it would appear that the reaction to the presence of immigrants occurred well after their numbers had begun to decline. But there was a second and more unsettling aspect of the number of immigrants in France - its composition by origin. The share taken by Europeans fell to less than half of its 1946 figure and Asians crept up a bit while other sources remained insignificant, but Africans rose to over one-third of immigrants by 1975 and became the single largest group in 1990. It is clear that the reaction to immigrants turned negative when the flows were constituted by black and north Africans rather than southern Europeans.

When unemployment was low and labor markets were extraordinarily tight, immigrant labor was considered to be an economic resource that enabled

Table 5.4: Foreigners in France, by country of origin, selected years

Country of origin	1946	1975	1982	1990
By Percentage				
— European	88.7	60.7	47.6	40.6
of which:				
Spanish	17.3	14.5	8.8	6.0
Italian	25.9	13.4	9.2	7.0
Polish	24.3	2.7	1.7	1.3
Portuguese	1.3	22.0	20.7	18.1
— Soviet/Russian	2.9	0.4	0.2	0.1
— African	3.1	34.6	43.0	45.4
of which:				
Algerian	1.3	20.6	21.7	17.1
Moroccan	0.9	7.6	11.9	15.9
Tunesian	0.1	4.1	5.2	5.7
— American	0.5	1.2	1.4	2.0
— Asian	4.0	3.0	7.8	11.8
Of which:				
Turkish	3.6	1.5	4.5	6.3
— Others	0.8	0.1	--	0.1
Total (000)	1,744	3,442	3,714	3,597

Source: *Annuaire Statistique de la France*, Paris: INSEE, various issues

the economy to grow; as unemployment became an important question in economic policy, immigrants became a threat to French workers and immigration policy also became an issue. Data for 1969 show that foreign workers were primarily employed in one sector: construction and public works – 40.8 per cent, and that only 31 per cent were professional or technical workers and 40 per cent were laborers. Finally, the impact on French labor would appear to be focused on a small segment of the labor force; however, it is also true that few French workers would wish to have the low pay and low status jobs to which most immigrants are confined. We will discuss this in greater detail in the next section, when the issue of foreign workers becomes more of an issue politically.

From the Early 1980s to the Present

After its attempt to apply the sort of interventionist policies that would be possible only in a closed economy and having failed to achieve the desired impact on unemployment, the Mitterand–Mauroy government (1981–4) changed its approach. This has already been discussed in Chapters 2 and 3 above and will not be reviewed here. However, the rest of the decade witnessed two additional devaluations of the franc (1983 and 1986), a wage freeze (1982), a plan of austerity in government finances (1982), and finally, under Prime Minister Chirac, privatization and deregulation (1986). The employment situation faced by these governments was the worst of the

Table 5.5: Labor market indicators, France, 1983–97

Year	Unemployment % of labor force	Long-term unemployment share	Youth unemployment	Jobs vacant	Employment 1985=100
Column:	(1)	(2)	(3)	(4)	(5)
1983	8.4	42.2	19.7	80	101
1984	9.8	42.3	n/a	46	100
1985	10.2	46.8	25.6	46	100
1986	10.4	47.8	23.4	49	100
1987	10.5	45.5	23.0	54	101
1988	10.0	44.8	21.7	63	101
1989	9.4	43.9	19.1	76	103
1990	8.9	38.0	15.1	79	104
1991	9.5	36.9	25.6	62	104
1992	10.0	35.2	19.1	53	103
1993	11.6	34.2	24.6	54	102
1994	12.3	38.3	27.4	50	102
1995	11.6	45.6	25.9	57	104
1996	12.5	40.0	24.3	n/a	103
1997	12.2	41.0	20.9	n/a	104
Column:	(1)	(2)	(3)	(4)	(5)

Sources: Columns 2 and 3: *Country Surveys: France*; Columns 1, 4 and 5:*Main Economic Indicators*, Paris: Organization for Economic Cooperation and Development, various issues

post-war period and, as is indicated in Table 5.5, deteriorated well into the 1990s. The rate of unemployment rose from 8.4 per cent to over 12 per cent, and youth unemployment proved unresponsive to the policy measures that were implemented. Long-term unemployment remained stubbornly high, with the number of workers out of work for at least one year rising from 740,000 in January 1991 to over 1 million during the fall of 1993 and remaining above 1,150,000 from mid 1997 on.[18] Perhaps the key indicator of how poorly the economy was performing is the steady drop in the number of job vacancies. The data given in Table 5.6 draw the striking contrast between the EU and Japan and, especially, North America in the area of job creation. As a consequence of the ability of, for example, the United States to create new jobs, employment since 1980 has increased there by 25 million and unemployment has fallen from 7.1 per cent to 5.6 per cent. In the European

Table 5.6: Comparative statistics, Group of Seven, 1970–95

	Unemployment (% of labor force)				Total employment (millions)			
	1970	1980	1990	1995	1970	1980	1990	1995
France	2.5	6.4	9.1	11.7	20.3	21.4	22.1	21.9
West Germany	0.5	2.8	5.0	6.5	26.1	26.5	28.0	27.7
United Kingdom	3.1	7.0	7.0	8.8	24.3	24.7	26.6	25.7
Italy	3.3	4.4	10.2	12.0	19.1	20.2	21.1	20.0
Japan	1.2	2.0	2.5	3.2	50.1	54.6	61.7	63.9
Canada	5.7	7.5	8.1	9.5	7.9	11.1	13.2	13.5
United States	4.9	7.1	5.6	5.6	78.7	99.3	118.8	124.9
European Four					89.3	92.8	97.8	95.3
North America					86.6	110.4	132.0	138.4

Source: *Statistical Abstract of the United States*, various issues

countries included in the table about one-tenth as many jobs have been created. The rate of unemployment has increased in each of them, and it would be over 10 per cent in Germany if the eastern part of the country were included. This table demonstrates the undeniable validity of the EU concerns with Euro-sclerosis and Euro-pessimism that were beginning to be articulated at this time.

During this period the restructuring of production that was induced by liberalization of markets continued to have its impact on employment by industry or sector. In Table 5.7 the nature of this restructuring is shown for the decade 1977–86. Clearly, the movement away from agriculture and industry toward traded services and government (non-traded services) continued. The three components of industry showed virtually the same declines in the aggregate: intermediate goods, −23 per cent; equipment, −19

Table 5.7: Employment by industry or sector, France, 1977–86

Sector	1977	1980	1983	1986	1986/1977
Agriculture	1,980	1,821	1,651	1,513	76.4
Industry, ex. construction	6,036	5,744	5,402	5,004	82.9
Construction	1,873	1,829	1,621	1,498	80.0
Trade	2,508	2,547	2,558	2,554	101.8
Transport & telecomm.	1,314	1,334	1,383	1,369	104.2
Traded services	3,690	3,970	4,151	4,423	119.9
Non-traded services	3,452	3,686	3,938	4,198	121.6

Source: *Annuaire Statistique de la France*, Paris: INSEE, various issues

per cent; and consumer goods, −19 per cent. However there were some significant shifts in employment at a less aggregated level: of industries with at least 100,000 employees only electricity, gas and water grew − by 17 per cent. Ferrous metals and steel employment declined by 40 per cent, employment in construction materials, automobiles, textiles and clothing, and leather and shoes all declined by 27-31 per cent; metal working, mechanical goods, and paper products declined by 22 or 23 per cent; and chemicals, wood products, and rubber and plastic goods employment declined by 13–17 per cent. Electrical and electronic goods employment remained unchanged. These structural changes in employment will be identical to changes in production only if rates of productivity gains are the same in all sectors. This is not likely to be the case, as will be shown in the next chapter.

Thus there were significant structural changes in sectoral employment both within industry and between industry and the services sector in general during this period. Only if labor markets are sufficiently flexible and worker retraining and relocation mechanisms are effective enough can such substantial restructuring of employment be accomplished without the creation of a large number of unemployed workers. We will examine this situation for France later in this chapter. But at this point it is sufficient simply to note the magnitude of the problem.

As has been stated above, globalization should have some impact on the distribution of the returns to labor as globally based economic forces supplant domestic processes in wage and salary determination. Data for the distribution of income will be offered below, but the impact on salaries during the recent past is shown in Table 5.8. The gap between top and bottom salaries increased by 6 per cent during the single decade 1984–93. It should also be noted that the increase in the gap between deciles 1 and 7 is equal to that for just the top two steps. So the top salaries are pulling away from the rest of the structure. One might consider this to be a positive or a negative factor, depending on: (a) whether one speaks from the vantage point of capital or of labor; or (b) the extent to which one accepts that restructuring guided by changes in relative prices of goods and factors of production is a mechanism that should be given relatively free reign. Nonetheless, it has been generally the case in industrial societies that increasing inequality in earnings brings social and political strife. If the current trend continues another decade or so this may be the cause of either unrest in France or a diminished willingness to let the globalization process continue without increased social control of it.

In a situation in which some workers believe they are not being treated justly, the presence of foreign workers inevitably becomes a political issue. This issue was introduced in the previous section but figures for 1990 enableus to be more specific as to the impact their presence has in France.

From Table 5.9 it is clear that workers from other EC countries are more likely to be higher rather than lower skilled, while the opposite is true for

Table 5.8: Distribution of salaries, France, 1984–93

Decile	1984	1988	1990	1991	1992	1993	1993/1984
1	45,600	53,700	58,300	60,900	62,900	64,100	1.41
2	51,700	61,300	66,700	69,400	71,700	73,200	1.42
3	57,500	68,500	74,500	77,500	80,100	81,900	1.42
4	63,100	75,000	81,600	85,200	88,000	90,000	1.43
5	69,200	82,100	89,400	93,700	96,800	99,100	1.43
6	76,700	90,700	98,700	103,800	107,200	109,700	1.43
7	85,700	101,700	110,800	117,300	121,300	124,200	1.45
8	100,700	120,700	131,600	139,100	143,900	147,600	1.47
9	132,700	159,400	174,800	184,400	191,400	196,000	1.48
D9/D1	2.91	2.97	3.00	3.03	3.04	3.07	1.06

Note: Data are in current francs.

Source: *Annuaire Statistique de la France* (1994), Paris: INSEE

Table 5.9: Foreign workers in France, skills, 1990

Origin of workers	Total		Lower skilled		Higher skilled	
	Number	%	Number	%	Number	%
All countries	1,620,189	100.0	989,446	100.0	630,740	100.0
European Community	678,395	41.9	381,782	38.6	296,613	47.0
Other	941,794	58.1	607,664	61.1	334,130	53.0
All countries		100.0		61.1		38.9
European Community		100.0		56.3		43.7
Other		100.0		64.5		35.3

Source: *Annuaire Statistique de la France, 1990*, Paris: INSEE

workers from other, predominantly African, countries. If we confine our attention narrowly to economic considerations, we would argue that foreign workers could have an impact on wages and unemployment to the degree that foreign and domestic workers are substitutes. If the labor market for these two categories of workers is segmented there will be little impact. As was noted above, few French workers would accept employment in the jobs that are available to African immigrants. In 1990 the total labor force was 25,286,711, of which 2,204,900 were unemployed. Foreign workers in France numbered 1,620,189, or 6.4 per cent of the total labor force. If these workers constituted a one-year increase in the labor force there would undoubtedly have been significant impacts on French workers. While the Mariel boatlift increased the Miami (US) labor force by about this much (7 per cent) in 1980, that labor market was not sufficiently segmented for there to be a lasting impact on wages.[19] However, in France the total number of foreigners (workers as well as those not in the labor force) doubled between 1946 and 1975 and 15 years later was larger by only another 4 per cent (see Table 5.4). Therefore it is clear that since 1975 French labor has not been under the pressure of increased competition from foreign workers and it is more compelling to argue, as will be done shortly, that other factors have determined the negative impacts on jobs and wages that have been experienced by French workers.

THEORETICAL APPROACHES TO UNEMPLOYMENT

The persistence in France of high unemployment, long-term unemployment and the difficulty of youth in gaining access to jobs has generated a great deal of interest among economists and policy specialists in the causation of these problems and in the most suitable policy responses to them. In this section of the chapter we will review this debate, focusing on the primary approaches to the issue, leaving the discussion of policy, past and prescriptive, until we have also examined the related problem of the distribution of income. The basic dichotomy in these approaches is between those that are centered on micro–economic explanations and those that see macro–economic aspects as being of greater importance. Since this debate concerns problems that are not exclusively French in nature, the literature that will be referred to will include work that has been done elsewhere as well as in France.

Explanations Focusing on Micro-economic Conditions

Micro-economic explanations place primary emphasis on labor market rigidities and on factors that force up the total cost of hiring French workers. This is the approach that finds its greatest support outside France, among British and American economists and in the policy studies of the OECD; within France both the micro- and the macro–economic approaches have their adherents. The way these two approaches are reflected in French policy will be examined later in this chapter.

As noted, the micro–economic approach is composed of two distinct elements. Labor market rigidities make it difficult for an economy to react to the rapidly changing global context in which it must function. By their nature, changes in technology, in market access, and in institutional practices cause some industries, factors and regions to decline in viability while others are able to expand. These changes can be accommodated only if resources can be transferred from declining to expanding lines of production. If this is not possible, industries, factors and regions in declining sectors will suffer unemployment, income loss and marginalization; the expanding sectors may be unable to gain access to factors of production and will, therefore, not be able to realize the potential that is before them. The economy will experience rising unemployment in some sectors and sluggish growth, and factor supply bottlenecks will cause inflationary pressures. The rigidities may be the result of a preference for immobility on the part of workers, policies with regard to pensions or other social benefits that restrict mobility, protectionist measures supported by entrenched or insider workers in expanding sectors, and so forth. By contrast, the primary factor cost-increasing pressures come from, for example, taxes, social charges, minimum wage laws, and costs related to firing workers. The effect of these measures is to increase the labor cost of production and, since these costs must be passed on to the consumer, to reduce the competitiveness, in both domestic and foreign markets, of the goods that are produced. No structure composed of a diverse variety of taxes and other charges is neutral with regard to its impact on the various sectors of production; therefore the result will always be a distortion of the structure of production. To the extent that the exchange rate and domestic prices are flexible, the primary result of both labor market rigidities and higher costs of production will be lower real per capita incomes. If these prices are also inflexible, the economy will experience unemployment and slow growth.

The reports of the OECD have presented the micro–economic argument consistently, at least since its Jobs Study was issued in 1994. While the target was primarily Europe, France was taken to be a prime example of a country that could benefit from this approach. Perhaps the key statement in the report was:

> Structural unemployment grows from the gap between the pressures on economies to adapt to change and their ability to do so. Adaptation is fundamental to progress in a world of new technologies, globalization and intense national and international competition. The potential gains may be even greater than those which flowed from the opening up of economies after World War II. But today, OECD economies and societies are inadequately equipped to reap the gains. Policies and systems have made economies rigid, and stalled the ability and even willingness to adapt. [20]

Explicitly excluded as causes of unemployment were: (a) technological change; (b) imports from low-wage countries; and (c) increased intensity of competition.[21] The overall thrust of the policy recommendations for OECD member countries was, first, enhancing the ability to adjust and to adapt, and second, increasing the capacity to innovate and be creative.[22]

These recommendations were tailored for France in the two most recent OECD country surveys devoted to that country. The 1997 survey offers a set of policies that are fully in line with the spirit of the Jobs Study.[23] First, it is argued that the minimum wage is too high in France because it is used as a mechanism for achieving income distributional goals and that it should be lowered so as to encourage more employment. Additional employment-conditional benefits could be added to achieve the distributional goals. Furthermore, it should be differentiated by age of worker and by region of the country. Second, unemployment benefits should be reduced as to both duration and payment to the recipient. Especially for low-income workers the existing system can reduce the incentive to find new employment. Third, generous early retirement programs should be reconsidered since 'the scheme aims to reduce unemployment but has no effect on employment.' Fourth, expensive lay-off requirements reduce the willingness of large firms to hire workers. Finally, the French labor code sets a wide variety of constraints on, for example, working hours that limit the flexibility of production to respond to change. In general, the French system, as seen by the OECD, often results in a very small income differential between work and inactivity, is marked by high taxation that reduces the incentive to take initiative, is characterized by too many schemes that have heavy compliance and monitoring costs, and seeks goals that could be achieved with other policies more effectively and at lower cost.

The 1997 report was rather unimpressed with the efforts of the government, but by 1999 the OECD had become much more conciliatory.[24] While the Jospin government had taken several policy steps the OECD believed were appropriate, it was also noted that the decision to proceed with EU Monetary Union had forced the issue in a beneficial way. It was noted that 'commendable efforts are under way to reduce the traditionally heavy burden of administrative and fiscal constraints that hinder entrepreneurship,' 'privatization is compelling [public] enterprises to achieve greater financial transparency,' some of the subsidization programs were being directed at only the most vulnerable groups, and a variety of 'measures have been taken to try to improve labor market performance.'

While many non-French analysts agree with this evaluation, some have tried to discriminate among aspects of French policy. For example, British economist Charles Bean agreed with most of the OECD's assessment of the problem but was more open to policy solutions that were related to a country's local policy culture. He argued that although such policies may improve the functioning of the labor market over the medium term, additional specific measures may be required. Explicit mention was made of Sweden's active labor market policies. Spending money in the short run to get unemployed workers into training programs or short-term jobs, he argued, results in a cost of unemployment that is no more expensive for Sweden than is the relatively laissez-faire approach for the UK - both are 2.6 per cent of GDP.[25] Implicit in this analysis is the notion that the French, too, can find their own unique approach to dealing with labor market rigidities. Stephen Nickell examined the impact of a variety of labor market rigidities and concluded that some of them do have a negative impact on employment, others do not.[26] Examples of those that do are:

1. generous unemployment benefits of long duration since they reduce the incentive to seek employment;
2. situations in which there is a high level of unionization and no coordination between either unions or employers in wage bargaining;
3. high overall taxes or a high minimum wage with high payroll taxes; and
4. poor educational standards for low skilled workers.

However, the following do not appear to generate unemployment:

1. strict employment protection legislation and general legislation on labor market standards;
2. high unemployment benefits as long as there is pressure for workers to seek employment, perhaps by limiting the duration of benefits; and
3. a high level of unionization as long as there is a high level of coordination in wage bargaining.

Nickell's more finely nuanced study leads him to conclude: 'it is clear that the broad-brush analysis that says that European unemployment is high because European labor markets are rigid is too vague and probably misleading. Many labor market institutions that conventionally come under the heading of rigidities have no observable impact on unemployment.'[27]

Three French economists, Daniel Cohen, Arnaud Lefranc and Gilles Saint-Paul, came to a similar conclusion, arguing specifically that it was France's high firing costs that tended to depress the demand for labor and thus to increase unemployment.[28] However, they also argued that the unemployment problem was concentrated primarily among young, low–skilled workers; indeed they state that 'French society puts all the burden of flexibility upon these workers.' They present data, for 1989–90, that show that the rates of unemployment according to four levels of education are almost identical for French and US workers aged 25–49, and that high rates of unemployment are concentrated among all but the most highly educated young workers (16–24 years old) and the least educated older workers (50–64 years old). Hence their conclusion that French unemployment rates are determined not by generalized labor market rigidities but are due rather to a small number of measures that have negative impacts on specific segments of the work force. This, they argue, should be taken as a guide for French policy—makers.

Another French economist who is skeptical of the validity of the labor market rigidity argument is Jan-Marc Le Gall who wrote that:

> Putting into question the minimum wage, the mechanisms for compensating the unemployed, etc., does not seem to be the solution for constraining the increase in unemployment in Europe, even if some modifications are necessary to avoid some if the perverse effects of these measures. He refers to a report by Matteoli, which concluded that France is characterized by a set of labor market regulations that are complex rather than rigid.[29]

Explanations Focusing on Macro-economic Conditions

The macro—economic approach is also composed of two somewhat less distinct lines of analysis. The Keynesian version focuses on aggregate demand while the exchange rate version emphasizes relative structures of prices of goods, as do the micro—economic approaches, but the cause of this is lodged in the working of the macro—economy. Expansion of aggregate demand will, of course, have its impact on domestic employment and production but it will also affect the external balance and the exchange rate. So the two versions are linked together.

The Keynesian approach

The primary alternative to the micro—economic analyses just presented is the Keynesian approach. According to this position, unemployment is caused by insufficiency of aggregate demand for the goods produced by labor. Fewer workers are required to produce a reduced quantity of output; the redundant workers have no place to go but to the ranks of the unemployed. The portrait of economic performance that was presented earlier in this chapter lends an immediate credibility to this position. During the 1970s, following the increases in petroleum products, there was a diversion of available purchasing power to petroleum from goods and services produced by French, and European, labor. This caused a drop in aggregate demand that began the dramatic rise in the rate of unemployment. The clearest statement of this position is given by Edmund Malinvaud in an article published in 1986, at a time when the inflationary impacts of the OPEC price increases had generated considerable pessimism about the performance of the industrialized economies. While recognizing that the high labor cost and labor market rigidities have a role to play, his econometric analysis shows them to have a small, even insignificant power to explain France's unemployment. Malinvaud conducted an econometric study of the causation of French unemployment.[30] His first point is that there is no evidence of a mismatch in the demands for and supplies of workers; rather there it is a shift towards a general situation of excess supply of labor that is important. Second, he rejects the explanation that reduced mobility (a labor market rigidity) is a significant causal factor of frictional unemployment. He notes that mobility has always been low in France and that this has been exacerbated in the time of his study by a deterioration of employment prospects: employed workers move little nowadays because they cannot find better jobs. Finally, increased frictions in the labor market should be indicated in an analysis of the relationship between the vacancy rate and the rate of unemployment – the Beveridge curve. A study of the appropriate French data is disappointing and tells us nothing useful. His conclusion from this study is that:

> The rise of unemployment is first and foremost due to international conditions: a long period of stagflation, disorder and depression at the world level, and an inability of Western Europe to maintain its competitiveness and to organize the coordination of economic policies of its various members. But it is also due to an inadequate policy response in France. Faced with the prospect of mounting unemployment, public opinion and governments did not want to sacrifice other objectives in order to contain it; or perhaps they did not want to recognize this unpleasant prospect and did not understand what the real trade-offs were.[31]

French policy-makers were to blame because they gave in to pressures for a high and quick *de facto* indexation of wages to the cost of living as a response to the OPEC induced increase in inflation. This was complicated by the desire of President d'Estaing (1974–5) to create social harmony and peace, and by the increase in the minimum wage and full compensation for the reduction in the work week by President Mitterand (1981–2). To the extent that high wage costs are a factor in higher rates of unemployment, they were allowed by the government, Malinvaud states, in order to maintain the cohesion of French society, and to teach economics to an unwilling public. The policy reversal adopted by the Mitterand government in 1983 reduced the up–ward pressure on French labor costs and therefore improved profit margins for producers.

The international conditions enumerated by Malinvaud had the effect of depressing aggregate demand throughout Europe, and the change in French domestic policy did nothing to ameliorate them. His econometric study leads him to the conclusion that the results 'reinforce my personal prior belief, which is shared by many others and gives a dominant role,...,to the causal chain running from world demand and autonomous domestic demand to the demand for goods, then to the demand for labor. Each one of the other factors appears by comparison to be marginal.'[32]

Support for this position, covering Europe as a whole, for the period that follows Malinvaud's study is given by Valerie Symes. Since her work is not specifically on France only the general conclusions will be noted. The context for the later 1980s and the 1990s is the movement toward some form of monetary cooperation or, ultimately, monetary union. For monetary integration to occur national economies must be made to conform to similar indicators of macro–economic performance – inflation, growth, government deficits, national debts, and so forth. This process also gives higher priority to the objectives of central bankers, and primary among these is low inflation. Symes argues that:

> Tight monetary and fiscal conditions in most European countries in the 1980s, followed by the fiscal requirements for EMU in the 1990s, have resulted in a depressing aggregate demand in Europe, whilst the expansion in the European economy in the second half of the 1980s was based largely on the sudden growth in the world trade resulting from expansionary policies in the United States. It is based on these observations of the effects of macroeconomic policy that there has been an increase in discussion on the positive role that expansionary macroeconomic policy should play in reducing the rate of unemployment in Europe. [33]

Malinvaud himself endorsed this explanation of French unemployment as recently as 1998, when he noted that several countries have reduced their rate of unemployment during the previous 15 years, and that they have done this through persistent use of policies that have both stimulated the expansion of demand and promoted the development of supply.[34] This is in a commentary on work done by Olivier Blanchard and Jean-Paul Fitoussi for the Conseil d'analyse économique in which the authors conclude that 'since the beginning of the 1990s, a weakness of global demand caused a weak growth of production and an increase in unemployment that exceeded its equilibrium level. Unemployment in France today is undoubtedly Keynesian in nature.'[35] Jean-Marc Le Gall wrote that a growth rate of at least 2.7 per cent per year was required just to stabilize the rate of unemployment in Europe.[36] The conclusion of this group of analysts is distressing in that it indicates clearly that the solution to unemployment in France, and in much of the rest of Europe, to a significant degree lies beyond the capability of individual national governments to resolve. We will return to this aspect of public policy later in this chapter.

A counter view is given by Jacques Lesourne who notes that the relationship between a point of economic growth and job creation is not a universal constant. For him the question remains that of France's limited ability to create employment when demand is strong, such as was the case in 1993. He concludes: 'The increase in the number of unemployed is not at all mysterious. It results from the inadequacy of response of French society to demographic, economic and technology changes that are known to all.'[37]

Over-valuation of the exchange rate

The last approach to the problem of unemployment in France and the second of the macro–economic approaches we will examine agrees that French goods are priced out of international markets and that the reduced net demand for traded goods has cost French workers jobs. But the cause of the loss of price competitiveness is seen to be the over-valuation of the exchange rate.[38] This moves the entire structure of French prices up *vis–à–vis* structures of foreign prices causing a decline in exports relative to imports. Reducing the demand for labor reduces the local currency wage for those who are employed, but for the producer confronting structures of foreign currency prices the overvaluation of the French currency increases the foreign currency cost of that labor. For the demand for domestic labor to increase, and for unemployment to be reduced, the foreign currency cost of labor must come down and this will only happen if the currency value is reduced to its purchasing power parity value. The primary exponent of this approach, Gérard Lefay, argues that:

> the quadrupling of the rate of unemployment, in Europe, is considered as normal and is attributed to the excess of wage rigidities,…,The use of the non-accelerating inflation rate of unemployment, as a justification for policies of wage austerity, is only a new illustration of the efforts that have been undertaken to mask the monetary causes of the structural slowing of European economic growth.[39]

Data for the trade balance just prior to the time of Lefay's article (1996) would appear to weaken his argument. As may be remembered from Table 4.5, France's trade balance improved between 1990 and 1994, two years before Lefay's article was published, from a deficit of Fr124.4 billion to a surplus of Fr27.1 billion. The only area of deficit was in trade with NAFTA; that was only Fr12.2 billion and was actually reduced from a deficit of Fr31.2 billion in 1990. So there does not appear to be a close correlation in evidence between high and slowly rising unemployment and a deteriorating balance of trade.

A factor that makes evaluation of Lefay's argument difficult is the fact that France has joined the European Monetary Union. As was noted at the outset of this chapter, in doing so France is now in the position of having virtually no national policy tools that can be used in the battle against unemployment: monetary policy, the exchange rate, fiscal policy, commercial policy, regional policy, and agricultural policy have all been made largely subordinate to decisions made in Brussels. Of importance to the mechanism, he emphasizes, is the interest rate and exchange rate policy of the European Central Bank. Central banks modeled on the US Federal Reserve Bank and the German Bundesbank, as the ECB has been, have as their primary function the control of inflation. This means that the interest rate will generally be higher than that desired by those who seek to reduce unemployment and, due to inflows of capital attracted by the higher interest rates, the exchange rate will be correspondingly higher as well. That is to say, the currency will be over-valued in Lefay's terms. This was close to the unanimous expectation when the Euro was introduced. Most commentators expected that the Euro would be a strong currency, with all of the economic weight of 360 million consumers behind it, and that it would challenge the dollar for supremacy in international finance. In fact, however, the value of the Euro has declined during its first year from its initial value of \$1.17 by close to 30 per cent. So the structure of French prices cannot be said to have become inflated due to exchange rate over-valuation. During that time, January 1999 to January 2000, French unemployment drifted down a bit, from 11.6 per cent to 10.8 per cent. But there have been several significant changes in policy, the application of technologies, industrial structures, and so forth, so a direct causal linkage cannot yet be assigned. We will need another three or four years of data before this causation can be examined.

INCOME AND ITS DISTRIBUTION

Earlier in this chapter we briefly mentioned the issue of the impact of globalization on the distribution of income in France. In studying the economic well–being of individuals in any country it is necessary to examine both the earnings (wages and salaries) that are received from economic activity and the incomes that are available for supporting consumption and saving. The difference between the two is the array of taxes and transfers that are part of the fiscal policies of all governments. We will begin with earnings and will then turn to total incomes.

When the impact of globalization was raised earlier it was suggested that as markets were opened to freer movements of goods and factors of production and as global economic forces gained greater force the distribution of earnings would become less egalitarian. Economic theory tells us that if a country has skilled labor in abundance it will have a comparative advantage in producing goods that use intensively that skilled labor. Even though the earnings of skilled labor are higher than those of unskilled labor, increased production of skilled labor intensive goods will increased the demand for skilled labor and will bid up its wages relative to those for unskilled labor. In this way the distribution of income becomes even less egalitarian. This does in fact appear to have taken place. Data that are available to us indicate the following pattern of change over time. In 1950 the ratio of the top decile of the private sector wage structure to the bottom decile was about 3.4. This ratio grew throughout the 1950s and into the 1960s, indicating that the distribution of earnings was becoming less egalitarian. It peaked in 1966 at 4.1 and fell to 3.1 in 1985, after which date it increased so that by the end of 1992 it had risen back to 3.4.[40] The reversal of the long-term trend occurred in the period of the policy changes following the disturbances of 1968, the inflation caused by the OPEC price increases, and the initial policies of the socialist administration of Mitterand in the 1980s. By 1983 the latter policies had given way to acceptance of the need to conform to the exigencies of globalization and the distribution of earnings began again to move toward greater inequality.

Dominique Redor has put this into an international perspective in a study of industrial earnings in the United States and nine countries throughout Europe for the years 1978–80.[41] As expected, the United States was the most inegalitarian and Denmark the most egalitarian. France was second to the US with the UK and Belgium tied for third place and Germany tied with Hungary for seventh. The ratio of the top to the bottom decile of industrial earnings for France, 3.4 to 1, was considerably higher than for other European countries: Belgium was 2.6 to 1, Germany was 2.3, and Denmark was 2.0. Looking just at the ratio of average earnings for manual and non-manual workers, Redor found again that France was the most inegalitarian of the European countries studied: the ratio for France was 1.70 to 1, Belgium was 1.49, Germany was 1.38, and Denmark was 1.30. This is, of course, a static rather than a dynamic view but it does help us to understand the distribution of income in France.

The increased inequality in salaries shown above in Table 5.8 is mirrored by changes in earnings by state employees. The basic salaries have not shown any movement between 1982 and 1990, but various wage supplements available to state employees have caused the ratio of net wages between the top and bottom deciles to rise by over 2 per cent during that period. However, in contrast with the private sector, all of this dispersion has been concentrated at the lower end of the wage structure, with the mid to bottom ratio rising from 1.43 to 1.50, or by almost 5 per cent, while the top half actually declined marginally from 1.58 to 1.57.[42]

When we consider the dispersion of total incomes it becomes clear that the policies of successive French governments have had a powerful effect.

Reductions in income would be due to taxes and social security contributions. Between 1960 and 1990, taxes grew slightly from 22.7 per cent of GDP to 24.4, but social security contributions rose during the same period from 9.8 per cent of GDP to 19.4. As a consequence, the total percentage of deductions rose from 32.5 to 43.8 per cent of GDP during this 30-year period. During 1960–84 total deductions rose by 12.6 per cent but they declined during 1984–90 by 0.8 per cent, so that the entire increase occurred in the earlier 24-year period. Social welfare expenditure rose during 1970–85 from 18 per cent to 27 per cent of national income, but only by an additional three percentage points between 1985 and 1993.[43] On both sides of individual incomes (earnings plus social expenditures minus taxes) the biggest increases occurred prior to 1985. Concialdi concludes:

> From 1962 up to 1975, the relative position of all categories above the average showed a downward tendency, while the position of groups below the average remained unchanged,....,or improved substantially,....,Changes between 1975 and 1979 look much smaller. As a result, the ratio of the upper group to the lower one declined, from 2.9 in 1962 to 2.5 in 1975, and was still 2.5 in 1979. Between 1984 and 1989, there was no tendency towards a decline in income inequality,....,These data show a sharp decline in income inequality from 1962 to 1979. Together with aggregate figures published from various social groups, these statistics support the widespread view of a continuous long-term fall in income inequality in France. However, the fall in income inequality does not seem to be very strong after 1979,....,,Between 1975 and 1979, the distribution of gross income per household became less unequal, but the trend reversed itself somewhat in 1979–84. Taking into account redistributive effects, we find income inequality continued to fall between 1979 and 1984.[44]

We can extend Concialdi's analysis by a few years with the results of a study done by four researchers for an OECD publication. Oxley, Burniaux, Dang and d'Ercole examined the distribution of income in 13 industrialized countries. They concluded that, for a period that was essentially the 1980s (for France it was 1979–90), 'taxes and transfers, taken together, reduced inequality in the latest year in all countries,' and 'the increasing role of the tax-and-transfer system slowed the growth in poverty rates after taxes and transfers in all countries.'[45] In France, the tax-transfer mechanism improved disposable income for the bottom three deciles by 1.2 per cent, and reduced it by 1.7 per cent for the middle four and by 0.5 per cent for the top three. Thus, it led to a decline in income inequality during this period. If we look at the poverty rate, it increased in France between 1984 and 1989 by 1.6 per cent before taxes and transfers, but fell by 2.1 per cent after the fiscal adjustments are taken into account.

The general conclusion one can make regarding the distribution of income in France is that inequality was reduced during the 1960s and 1970s; earnings became less egalitarian from 1980 on but this was reversed by the tax-transfer mechanism, that is by government policy. This is consistent with the hypothesis that globalization had the effect of causing earnings to become polarized and that government saw its role as being that of offsetting to some degree the domestic impacts of the opening of borders to movements of goods, services, capital and labor. This is an important issue and it will be with us throughout the remaining section of this chapter.

FRENCH POLICY DURING THE FOUR POST-SECOND WORLD WAR PERIODS

It will become clear in this section that a succession of French governments, whether of the left or the right politically, have introduced an impressive array of policies that have been aimed at reconfiguring the employment situation. This body of policy has sought to reduce unemployment in the aggregate as well as among specific segments of the workforce, to alter the structure of employment by industry or skill, to offset the generally disruptive impacts of the opening of markets, and to limit the reduction in income faced by those who have become unemployed. As Jean-François Eck has noted, these policies can be grouped under three distinct headings: 'prevention of unemployment, reduction of unemployment, and income maintenance.'[46] From this review of French policy, two issues will emerge: first, while policies have been introduced with a specific goal in mind, in their application they are often blurred in their impact; and second, with such a wide and diverse set of policies on the books, one can wonder whether in an increasingly market-oriented economy: (a) the extent of intervention has not been excessive, and (b) the frequent changes in policy have not created excessive uncertainty, thus slowing investment and job creation. These are very important questions; but first we must examine the recent history of employment policy in France.[47]

There was little need for a policy to counter unemployment in the period between the end of the Second World War and France's entry into the European Economic Community, since the rate of unemployment never exceeded 1.6 per cent of the available labor force (see Table 5.1). Indeed, according to Jacques Lesourne, employment policy was first developed only after unemployment began to rise in 1967.[48] Nevertheless, this was an important period for workers as it saw, as was noted above, the introduction of Social Security (1945), the minimum wage – the *Salaire minimum interprofessionnel garanti* or SMIG − (1950), unemployment insurance (1958), and the third week of holiday (1956).

It was in the second period leading to the OPEC price actions in the 1970s that France began to develop an extensive set of policy measures designed to deal with unemployment and its consequences. While the rate of unemployment appears to be marvelously under control from the perspective of today, between 1966 and 1969 it did rise by 85 per cent from 1.4 to 2.6 per cent. From then it rose every year until it peaked in 1987 at 10.5 per cent. At first, this unemployment was thought to be a problem that was transitory rather than structural in nature. The major policy action taken was in the third category of Eck's typology − compensation for those who became unemployed. The unemployment compensation scheme had been set up in 1958 with benefit amounting to just 35 per cent of the last wage and this was to last for only nine months. The National Employment Fund was established in 1963, to counter the employment consequences of industrial restructuring, and other efforts were made shortly thereafter to promote employment and professional training among adults.

Only after the difficulties began to mount in the 1970s did policy start to be implemented in all three of Eck's categories. In the decade beginning with 1973 the rate of unemployment rose without pause from 2.7 to 8.2 per cent. One set of actions aimed at reducing the supply of labor. This included a program, in 1974, of making immigration more difficult. In another initiative, workers were encouraged to retire at an earlier age; firms were encouraged to reduce the number of workers above a certain age (in 1972 it was set at 60 and then it was lowered to 55 years of age in 1977) and the benefits to older workers who were laid off were increased. On the other hand, the unemployment compensation program was progressively liberalized until in 1974 the benefit was doubled to 70 per cent and this could be received for up to two years. If the cause of the unemployment was economic the benefit authorized rose to 90 per cent of the last wage. Finally, in 1975 a law was passed that made it more difficult to gain authorization to lay off a worker, and a review had to be conducted to determine whether the employer had legitimate economic grounds for the dismissal.

During 1976–7 it was recognized that it would not be possible to return to the normality of *les trente glorieuses* and that a fundamental rethinking of employment policy was in order: henceforth, the emphasis would be placed on the return to equilibrium and the restoration of competitiveness with a central role given to monetary stability.[49] Thus, equilibrium replaced full-employment as a goal and policy was, first, to seek to halt the progressive increase in unemployment and, second, to make the unemployment compensation scheme less generous and easily obtained. Macro–economic policy aimed at aggregate demand was given reduced priority. Policies aimed at reducing the labor supply continued to be a priority. In 1977, money was rather ineffectually offered to foreign workers to induce them to return to their land of origin, and inducements were offered to older workers who were laid off simply to accept compensation in lieu of seeking another job. Concomitantly, the age at which these benefits could be received was progressively reduced toward 55 years of age. Additionally, there were special programs for workers in industries, such as steel, in which restructuring pressures were especially strong – here the age for enrollment was reduced to 50.

The situation of young workers received attention and a program of Granet (the name of the secretary of state for employment) apprenticeships was introduced in 1975. But more importantly it was explicitly recognized that much of the difficulty faced by young workers was due to the inadequacy of the French educational system when it came to preparing them for a job: their productivity was below that which would make them attractive to employers. Unfortunately, this is still being presented as a problem 25 years later.

On the eve of the Socialist victory in the elections of 1981 France had in place a wide array of unemployment policies aimed at specific categories such as older workers, young entrants into the labor force, and workers in declining sectors of manufacturing. While they had done little to slow the increase in unemployment itself, there had been an improvement in the standards of living of those out of work.[50] There were policies designed to reduce the active labor force through encouraging earlier retirement and reducing the number of immigrant workers. And compensation to those who became unemployed was made considerably more attractive than it had been. Once implemented, programs were often replaced by new programs with a slightly different objective. The intention seems to have been to put in place a program for every category of worker in need. In 1980 the rate of unemployment surpassed 6 per cent for the first time and youth unemployment was 15.1 per cent. While these figures were unsettling in themselves, the budgetary impact of the policies was not yet unmanageable. Within five years, however, unemployment had jumped to 10.2 per cent and 25.6 per cent of young workers were unemployed. Furthermore, those who remained unemployed for more than a year had increased by 70 per cent to 46.8 per cent. The new government of Mauroy took office with a philosophy which mandated that unemployment be reduced substantially and that the burden of unemployment be eased on workers who were seen to be the victims of forces over which they had no control. Unfortunately, the unemployment figures were deteriorating significantly and the financial burden of the planned initiatives would prove to be heavy indeed.

During 1981 and 1983, the government adopted a four–faceted employment strategy. First, there was to be a macro–economic expansion based on increased government spending. Second, about 170,000 public sector jobs were created, there were specific employment stimulating initiatives in the textile and small–scale manufacturing sectors, and increased assistance was given to small business creation by the unemployed (begun earlier by Raymond Barre). Third, the available work was to be spread over a larger number of workers through a reduction in the work week and an increase in the statutory paid holiday to five weeks. The work week was initially to be reduced to 35 hours by 1985, but 39 hours was as far as it went. According to the Bank of France these two measures may have resulted in as many as 145,000 additional jobs over a period of three years.[51] There was also a reduction in the maximum legal length of the workday. Fourth, the legal age of retirement was reduced to 60 and partially compensated early retirement was allowed between ages 55 and 59; the number of those who took advantage of this option rose from about 200,000 to 700,000 workers between 1980 and 1983. At the other end of the age spectrum, youth completing the school system without gaining marketable skills were offered a series of apprenticeship programs designed to make them attractive to employers. The policy of substitution of older workers by younger ones had a positive impact, but given the forecasts for the aging of the French population this was not likely to be effective in the long run.

Unfortunately, things did not go as Mitterand and Mauroy had planned and hoped. Macro–economic expansion generated inflation and put the franc under considerable pressure and, as we have noted in Chapter 4, it was devalued in 1981 (8.5 per cent), 1982 (10 per cent), and 1983 (8 per cent). The government was forced into a policy of retrenchment and austerity. The increased number of unemployed caused a financial crisis in the unemployment compensation fund (UNEDIC – Union Nationale pour l'Emploi dans l'Industrie et le Commerce) and it was forced to deny benefits to 200,000 unemployed workers. In 1983 the program that aimed to reduce labor supply through removing older workers from the labor force was cancelled. There were cutbacks in programs to aid specific sectors under restructuring. The benefits of 90 per cent of salary for those who were laid off due to economic reasons was replaced by a program of special allotments that declined over time, as an incentive for the recipients to return to the ranks of the employed. In this period of crisis, Lesourne states, the political class finally recognized that unemployment was not transitory but rather that it was structural. It would be a feature of France for some considerable time, and it would be necessary to increase labor market flexibility, improve education and training, and to accept the restructuring of economic activities.[52]

After the crisis of the early 1980s, French policy–makers were forced to narrow their focus to programs aimed at giving initial employment to young workers and at offering retraining opportunities to older workers. Due to difficulties in industries such as steel, shipbuilding and automobiles, the number of authorized lay-offs rose from 366,000 in 1983 to 440,000 two years later, so the macro–economic situation was only making things worse. Something had to be done and the government began to reduce the rigidities in the French labor market through, for example, the introduction of employment contracts with a fixed duration. Thus employers could hire workers without the concern that they would not be able to reduce the workforce if demand for their output should fall. Additional measures were aimed at internships/apprenticeships for young workers so they could increase their employability. The major innovation during the late 1980s was the introduction of the RMI or *revenue minimum d'insertion*. This was a minimum income that was made available to those without employment and was designed to ease the burden of unemployment.[53]

The employment situation in France continued to deteriorate into the 1990s. Unfortunately, the fiscal situation of the government also continued to deteriorate and reductions in expenditures were necessary. Employment policy became dominated by the reduction in the cost of labor to employers in an effort to make their goods more cost competitive and to stimulate the hiring of workers. Efforts were also made to make the labor market less regulated. In addition to the domestic fiscal constraints, the creation of the European Monetary Union required that France adhere to the convergence criteria which mandated that budgetary deficits and the national debt both be reduced, to 3 per cent and 60 per cent of GDP respectively. Having lost virtually all of its macro–economic policy tools – fiscal, monetary, tariff, competition and exchange rate policies – the government had little option but to resort to the labor market flexibility policy formula of the OECD and of many liberal economists. Fortunately the economy of the United States grew rapidly during the decade. Because of these two factors French unemployment has steadily declined in recent years so that by the spring of 2001 it is poised to drop below 9 per cent for only the second time (1990 being the other) since 1983.

After examining the past two decades, two researchers have concluded that there has been little fundamental institutional change and that: 'All in all, the French labor market remains heavily regulated in comparison to the Italian and Spanish ones, where many elements of flexibility were introduced throughout the second half of the 1980s and the early 1990s.'[54] Nonetheless, the effect of France being drawn more completely into a globalized economic environment has been a clear loss of a particularly French approach to employment policy. Membership in the EU and now in Euroland has forced

France increasingly to work cooperatively with other EU nations to address the high unemployment that has been the scourge of Europe for the past quarter century. The next decade promises to bring a dramatically new policy environment both for France and for the other economies that are participating in the European integration process.

NOTES

1. John Maynard Keynes, 'National self-sufficiency,' *Yale Review*, vol. 26 (1933), pp. 755–769.
2. For a review of this process, see Peter Kenen, *Economic and Monetary Union in Europe*, Cambridge: Cambridge University Press, 1995.
3. This is well discussed in: Rainer Masera, 'Single market exchange rates and monetary unification,' in Alfred Steinherr (ed.), *30 Years of European Monetary Intergration*, New York: Longman, 1994, pp. 286–297.
4. Saskia Sassen, *Guests and Aliens*, New York: The New Press, 1999, p. 64.
5. Loïc J.D. Wacquant, 'Banlieues françaises et ghetto noir américain: de l'amalgame a la comparaison,' *French Politics and Society*, vol. 10, no. 4, Fall 1992, pp. 81–103.
6. 'Fewer and wrinklier Europeans,' *The Economist*, January 25, 2000, p. 52.
7. The standard view is given in Roger C. Altman and Charles A. Kupchan, 'Arresting the decline of Europe,' *World Policy Journal*, Winter, 1997–8, pp. 3–5. For a more sophisticated analysis, see Stephen Nickell, 'Unemployment and labor market rigidities: Europe versus North America,' *Journal of Economic Perspectives*, vol. 11, no. 3, Summer 1997, pp. 55–74.
8. A.K. Sen, 'Inequality, unemployment and contemporary Europe,' *International Labour Review*, vol. 136, no. 2, pp. 155–172.
9. Erik Izraelewicz, *Ce monde qui nous attend*, Paris: Bernard Grasset, 1997, ch. 7; Robert Holcman, *Le Chômage*, Paris: La documentation Française, 1997, p. 117.
10. Daniel Cohen, *Richesse du monde, pauvretés des nations*, Paris: Flammarion, 1997, p. 67.
11. Guiseppe Bertola and Andrea Ichino, 'Crossing the river: A comparative perspective on Italian employment dynamics,' *Economic Policy*, vol. 21, October 1995, p. 414.
12. Jean-Marc Le Gall, 'Emploi et chômage en Europe: une nécessaire clarification,' *Revue politique et parlementaire*, vol. 98, no. 985, October–December 1996, p. 25.
13. Michel Zylberberg, 'De la guerre à la depression (1914–1939),' *Cahiers français*, no. 255, March–April 1992, pp. 10–21.
14. The numbers do not add up exactly as the military draft figure is the average for the year.
15. Jean-François Eck, *Histoire de l'économie française depuis 1945*, Paris: Armand Colin, 1996, p. 5.

16. André Gueslin, *L'économie ouverte 1948–1990*, (number 4 in the series Nouvelle histoire économique de la France contemporaine), Paris: Éditions La Découverte, 1994, p. 8

17. Eck, *Histoire de l'économie française*, p. 38, and E. Malinvaud, 'The rise of unemployment in France,' *Economica*, vol. 53, no. 210(S), 1986, p. S215.

18. *La politique économique de la France*, Paris: Ministère de l'économie des finances et de l'industrie, 1999, p. 42.

19. Robert H. Topel, 'Factor proportions and relative wages: the supply-side determinants of wage inequality,' *Journal of Economic Perspectives*, vol. 11, no. 2, Spring 1997, p. 63.

20. *The OECD Jobs Study*, Paris: OECD, 1994, <www.oecd.org/sge/min/jobs94/intro.htm>

21. OECD, <www.oecd.org/sge/min/jobs94/part2a.htm>

22. OECD, <www.oecd.org/sge/min/jobs94/part3a.htm>

23. *OECD Economic Surveys: France, 1997*, Paris: OECD, 1997, ch. III.

24. *OECD Economic Surveys: France, 1999*, Paris: OECD, 1999, ch. II.

25. Charles R. Bean, 'European unemployment: a survey,' *Journal of Economic Literature*, vol. *XXXII* (June 1994), pp. 573–619.

26. Nickell, 'Unemployment and labour market rigidities,' p. 72.

27. Ibid., p. 73.

28. Daniel Cohen, Arnaud Lefranc and Gilles Saint-Paul, 'French unemployment: a transatlantic perspective,' *Economic Policy*, vol. 25, October 1997, pp. 267–285.

29. Le Gall, 'Emploi et chômage,' p. 23.

30. The results are given in Malinvaud, 'The rise of unemployment in France,' pp. 208–216.

31. Ibid., p. S213.

32. Ibid., p. S208.

33. Valerie Symes, 'Unemployment in Europe: a continuing crisis,' in Valerie Symes, Carl Levy and Jane Littlewood (eds), *The Future of Europe*, New York: St. Martins Press, 1997, p. 236.

34. Edmond Malinvaud, 'Commentaire,' to the report by Olivier Blanchard and Jean-Paul Fitoussi, *Croissance et chômage*, Conseil d'analyse économique, Paris: La documentation Française, 1998, p. 39.

35. Olivier Blanchard and Jean-Paul Fitoussi, *Croissance et chômage*, Conseil d'analyse économique, Paris: La documentation Française, 1998, p. 10.

37. Le Gall, 'Emploi et chômage,' p. 19.

37. Jacques Lesourne, *Vérités et mensonges sur le chômage*, Paris: Éditions Odile Jacob, 1995, pp. 118 and 124.

38. Gérard Lafay, 'Les origines internationales du chômage européen', *Revue d'économie politique*, vol. 106, no. 6, November–December 1996, pp. 943–966.

39. Ibid., p. 958.

40. Pierre Concialdi, 'Income distribution in France: the mid 1980s turning point,' in Peter Gottschalk, Björn Gustafsson and Edward Palmer (eds), *Changing Patterns in the Distribution of Economic Welfare: An International Perspective*, Cambridge: Cambridge University Press, 1997, pp. 239–264.

41. Dominique Redor, *Wage Inequalities in East and West*, Cambridge: Cambridge University Press, 1992, pp. 54–61. This was originally published as *Les Inégalités de Salaire a l'Est et l'Ouest*, Paris: Economica, 1988.
42. Concialdi, 'Income distribution in France,' p. 246.
43. Ibid., pp. 250–253.
44. Ibid., pp. 255–256.
45. Howard Oxley, Jean-Marc Burniaux, Thai-Thanh Dang and Marco Mira d'Ercole, 'Income distribution and poverty in 13 OECD countries,' *OECD Economic Studies*, no. 29, 1997/II, pp. 273 and 277.
46. Eck, *Histoire de l'économie français*, pp. 160-165.
47. Any review of French employment quickly becomes replete with references to programs and agencies, each of which is identified by a set of letters. This can be extremely confusing to a non-specialist. For this reason only minimal reference to specific entities is made.
48. Lesourne, *Verités et mensonges*, p. 156.
49. DARES, *Les Politiques de l'Emploi en France depuis 1974*, Paris: La documentation Française, no. 509, 26 February, 1997, p. 2.
50. Lesourne, *Vérités et mensonges*, p. 158.
51. DARES, *Les Politiques de l'Emploi*, p. 3.
52. Lesourne, *Vérités et mensonges*, p. 161.
53. For a discussion of this and its relation to the minimum wage see 'RMI et SMIC: étude sur l'apport financier de l'accès à l'emploi,' *Problèmes économiques*, Paris: La documentation Française, no. 525, 1997, pp. 13–19.
54. Bertola and Ichino, 'Crossing the river,' p. 391.

6 Economic Structure, Restructuring and Development of Output

Until the mid-1970s, the French economy was managed and structured by the state. Since then, firms of all sizes have been gradually freed from the intervention of the state, and nationalized firms have finally been privatized and forced to confront the competition of the market. As has already been noted, the first period was marked by a very high rate of economic growth. However, it is not true, as some have suggested, that the last quarter-century has failed in this regard. The average rate of growth of GDP per capita has been only about 2 per cent per year, but the initial point was so high that the later period created wealth to a greater extent than was true of 1945–75. We will demonstrate shortly that this is explained by the profound changes that have occurred in the operations of French firms.

Table 6.1: Gross domestic product per capita, in constant 1990 dollars

	1950	1973	1997
France	5,200	12,900	18,900
United States	9,600	16,600	23,900
Japan	1,900	11,000	20,700
Germany	4,300	13,200	19,900

Source: Angus Maddison, *L'économie mondiale 1820–1992: Analyse et statistiques*, Paris: OECD, 1995

However, the growth that has taken place during the past-quarter century has been accompanied by an exacerbation of inequality, even though gross revenues have increased decade after decade. Public opinion as expressed by the media and by the policy establishment is united in the view that the state has acted as a buffer against the forces of trade liberalization and technological change. The paradox is that this is the same French state that was the first to modernize the productive system and to support financially the advancement of technology. It is also the government that decided to open its economy to the liberalized trade of the European integration process, the deregulation of financial markets, and global trade liberalization through the GATT and then the WTO. To take just two examples, French telecommunications and transport are today among the most advanced in the world. It is clear that the strong growth of *les trente glorieuses* has allowed the financing of an extensive effort that has extracted considerable cost from the French people, in terms of taxes and unemployment. But it is also clear that this effort has borne fruit in the high productivity of today's labor force.

In spite of this, or perhaps because of it, there is today simultaneously a shortage of qualified labor and relatively high unemployment, especially among youth, women, immigrants, older workers and those with obsolescent skills. The long-term trend in productivity is one cause of the loss of employment in traditional activities as well as the cause of the development of activities now included in what is referred to as the new economy. If the number of workers had remained constant for the past 20 years, productivity gains would have allowed a 50 per cent increase in production. However, French workers devote fewer hours to their job today than ever before. In 2000, time on the job represented only 15 per cent of waking hours in comparison with 50 per cent in 1945, and the work week has been reduced by about 10 hours in 35 years (36.7 hours per week in 1997 in comparison with 46.1 in 1963). French workers on average choose voluntarily to work fewer hours due in part to technological progress and to a generous social system, and young workers involuntarily due to the increased barriers to entry to the labor market that they must confront.

This contemporary mutation of the French production system and labor force has occurred in a context that was rather confusing. What was taking place was not immediately clear to workers, their employers, investors, or the heads of firms themselves. As Erik Izraelewicz has written, toward the end of the century 'the United States and Europe were passing through a period of profound restructuring of relative prices – a period that brings to mind the earlier industrial revolutions.'[1] Production units were seeking their critical size, with mergers taking place on a global dimension – in France as elsewhere. In France the average annual number of mergers grew from 32 during 1950–8 to 74 for 1959–65 and 136 for 1966–72.[2] More than just the number of them, it was the nature and the scale of mergers that had changed. The refocusing of activities and the size of firms, reorganization among and within firms, the dramatic opening of previously protected markets, an expansion of the number of units of production, research and distribution (including, of course, development of the world-wide web and electronic commerce), transnational mergers and acquisitions – all of this was new. The integration of both industry and finance are of primary importance here. What was involved was the usual process of a market economy – continual restructuring; that is, the things that Joseph Schumpeter saw as causes of creative gales of destruction: innovation, external scale economies linked to markets and internal scale economies linked to the accumulation of capital and access to labor. However, what was new was the speed at which these changes were realized, five to ten years earlier than they were anticipated. One response was the suggestion of Jeremy Rifkin that we were facing the end of work.

France began to adapt to the market economy toward the end of the 1950s, when European economic integration gradually opened the production and consumption to competition and when the government started its process of easing control over the operations of firms. But a diminishing degree of control was present for the next 30 years. The wave of nationalizations initiated by the Mitterand government at the beginning of the 1980s retarded the liberalization of large firms by one or two decades in spite of strengthening forces of globalization and market liberalization. It is, however, a curiosity that at the same time that the government nationalized several manufacturing firms it was liberalizing financial markets, in the face of a crying need for saving and liquidity in the 1980s and at the same time the necessity to battle against inflation. It was thus necessary to open financial markets to attract international capital and this could only be done with a strict, feasible and stable monetary system. The nationalization of 43 firms in 1982 was done entirely on political grounds; the new socialist government had to make concessions to the Communist Party to retain their support in the Parliament. Furthermore, the dominant ideology of the left since the end of the Second World War insisted that the state should play a central role in the economy. During the 1980s however, the Commissariat au Plan became simply a consultative and policy analysis body. The state soon distanced itself from any firms in difficulty, and the planning apparatus *per se*, in place for almost 40 years, gradually disappeared. The years 1983 and 1984 mark the date of both a virtual revolution in French capitalism and the abandonment by the government of the interventionist ideology. The roots of this revolution in thinking and in action date from the economic crisis of the mid-1970s.

Between the opening of goods markets in 1958 and the liberalization of the 1980s, France experienced the petroleum shock of 1973 and the ensuing economic crisis of 1974–5. During this period of global recession, it was essential to reconsider many activities, there was an increase in business failures and unemployment began its long and steady increase. Small and medium-sized firms came to acquire increased importance, especially because of their relative flexibility and adaptability. This is explained by the fact that the division of labor in a small enterprise typically involves individual workers whose skills are relatively less specific than in a large firm and there is less rigorous separation of tasks. In addition, information is transmitted at much lower cost within the firm than if it is accessed externally and can better facilitate decision-making and direction. Finally, with investment being less important on average in smaller firms, the shock and the crisis had less effect on their average costs. The share of large firms in non-agricultural production diminished throughout the ensuing two decades. This situation was stabilized with the mergers and acquisitions activity of the 1990s.

To summarize: the petroleum shock of 1973 was followed by restructuring, then nationalization, and finally by privatization. We must recall that following the war, the French state nationalized, among others, 34 insurance companies, the Bank of France, and the four primary commercial banks. A new form of French capitalism emerged in the 1990s with the denationalization movement. The state reduced its presence in the economy, share-holders grew in importance in company decision-making, and globalization asserted itself within a Hayekian catalystic process, both in the destructive and creative sense. In 2001, with a few exceptions such as France Télécom, Air France and EDF, French enterprises resemble those of other G-7 economies. We will now examine this period of change, first in the aggregate and then by sector of activity.

EVOLUTION OF THE FRENCH ECONOMY IN THE AGGREGATE

After 30 years of expansion that accompanied economic reconstruction following the Second World War, the French economy abruptly ground to a halt as a consequence of the two increases in the price of petroleum in 1973 and 1979. This crisis led directly to a fundamental reconsideration of the nature of French economic institutions and the role of the state. In this section we will examine both of these events and then, briefly, the nature of recent economic growth.

The Economic Crisis of 1974 and the Transformation of 1983–4

The economic crisis that began in 1974 constituted both a turning point and a point of transition. The years prior to this event can be characterized as the establishment of a French economy that was both modern in its technology and open to the rest of Europe in both production and consumption. In the years that followed, the two movements were continued and made ever more pervasive. It is agreed today that the crisis of 1974 was the event that triggered the reforms of the past 25 years. Globally, since each national economy was affected differently by the crisis, the relation of each nation or region to the global economy has been modified distinctively, and perhaps a bit unpredictably.

Thus, Japan was less affected by the crisis than other countries because of the dynamism of its exports, its production and its innovation, and because of the support given by its Ministry of International Trade and Investment. The United States managed rather well due to its high and increasing expenditures on research and development and the strength of investment. On the other hand, the economies of the European Community were the most powerfully affected of the three.

The crisis of 1974 hit France suddenly and with great force. As was noted in the previous chapter, unemployment doubled from 2 to 4 per cent in just a year and a half, and there was a fall in the rate of growth in goods production, shipbuilding, steel, electronics, textiles, among others, but not in the service sector. It was the shock of deindustrialization and the powerful competition of the newly industrializing countries of Asia and South–East Asia that traumatized the French economy.

The Analysis of the Transformation

There are five key aspects of the transformation of French capitalism following the economic crisis. First we must examine household consumption. In the aggregate, French household consumption expenditures, after taxes, were constrained and even, on a couple of occasions, reduced. This relative impoverishment was expressed in a restructuring of the composition of consumption expenditures and in the behavior of households. There was an introduction and rapid expansion of discount department stores and of factory outlets. As a concomitant, there was a reduction in expenditures on housing. Investment responded negatively to these changes and this had an impact on innovation. Countering this was an increase in public expenditures, primarily social transfers and subsidies to nationalized firms, during 1975–9 and again during 1982–3 that gave an illusion of continued growth and strong demand.

Investment was crucial during the first phase of opening the French economy to the outside world as the state intervened extensively in the effort to enhance the competitiveness of domestic producers. During the 1960s and the first part of the 1970s the state promoted large-scale mergers and concentration of production, and created a number of large firms such as Saint Gobain-Pont à Mousson, Péchiney-Ugine-Kuhlmann, BNP, UAP, SIDELOR, and SNIAS. In the words of Pierre Rosonvallon, 'it was in the Prime Minister's office, the office of the President, and at the office of the Minister of Industry, on rue de Grennelle, that the industrial restructuring initiative was decided.'[3] One of the central ideas was that of creating several national champions as there were only three French firms among the 50 largest firms in the world in 1974 and five in 1977. By the end of the 1970s several of France's largest firms began with state participation to develop acquisitions of foreign firms. In reality it must be admitted that the French productive system was not very competitive at this period. The crisis of 1974 actually resulted in no transformation in this regard. It was not the initiative and wish of the state that could force the necessary changes, but rather a profound change in the French political and economic culture was required.

The slow-down in the growth of investment is very noticeable from 1974 on, especially in research and development. French expenditures on R & D during 1974–82 were lower than those of any other OECD country. The Conseil Economique et Social noted, in 1984, that 'investment in human capital in the form of R & D has a return, in terms of subsequent production, that is superior to that of investment in machinery and equipment.' In the private sector, where gross profit is rather low, the tax system favors indebtedness rather than innovation. It was during 1975–80, under the influence of Giscard d'Estaing, that taxes and other charges on firms had their period of greatest increase in France. It is therefore not surprising that the dynamism of innovation was more drastically diminished, in all areas, than was the case in other industrialized countries. At the same time, the financial returns of firms were more significantly lowered in France than in these other countries. Alternatively, because of intergenerational social transfers (due to a sharp increase in public sector borrowing) current household consumption rose most rapidly during 1974–82, more so than in other countries, and this in spite of increases in taxation. This was accompanied by an expansion of exports, primarily toward the rest of the EU, in itself an indication of a new behavior on the part of French firms, both large and small. In France before 1974, the 250 largest firms supplied about 50 per cent of total exports. The share of small and medium-sized firms grew steadily during the 1980s and 1990s, in part because they were able to react more rapidly than the large firms to sudden changes in their environment. Finally, in the 1990s the years of mergers and acquisitions brought forth the large conglomerate and cross-border firms that have become so prominent in today's economic structure. At the same time, large industrial groups are transforming themselves into micro-groups of small and medium-sized entities. In 1980 there were only 600 of them but they had grown to approximately 5000 in 1995.

The structure of French production of goods and services as well as the structure of the firms themselves weas radically modified during the 1980s in ways that generated economies of scale. Two factors were at work here: first, the conquest of foreign markets while some domestic markets were abandoned; and second, the waves of privatization and deregulation which were followed by a process of restructuring that was not directed by the state.

With regard to the first factor, the competitive devaluation of the 1970s had a positive impact, at least in the short term, in spite of a rate of inflation that was higher in France than in other countries (with the exception of Italy) during 1974–84. This inflation was to some extent imported even though the exchange rate was floating at the time. French exports began to experience a better reception in foreign markets in the 1980s. This contributed to a restructuring of productive activities, as well as of the firms themselves. Concerning the second factor, the privatization that followed the nationalization of the 1980s completely changed France's competitive position in global markets, the methods of business organization and management, and their means of financing. Increasingly independent, they regrouped themselves and consolidated their activities during the 1980s and then instituted further mergers and formed networks during the next decade.

In summary, looking back over this period one can distinguish the positive effects of two types of economy of scale. With the formation of the European Economic Community this expansion of the market brought with it the economies of scale that were observable during the 1960s. The crisis of 1974 forced a process of restructuring on French industry that not only weeded out the weak firms but also led to consolidations, mergers and other inter- and intra-firm actions that continued strongly until the 1990s. The policy of support to firms in difficulty was gradually abandoned from the 1970s. Waves of privatization together with financial and money market liberalization, both at the regional and the global level, in turn permitted economies of scale with regard to the use of factors of production.

Today, globalization, which for France can be seen as primarily a consequence of European economic integration, offers to domestic firms both types of economies of scale. As is the case with the large domestic market of the United States, production costs are lowered with enlargement of the market (external economies) and also with the size of the firm itself (better access to capital and to labor, as well as internal economies). However, in contrast with the US, European firms face one of the highest tax burdens, the most obvious example being that on energy.

The beneficial consequences of scale economies, it must be remembered, take place in the context of a continuing process of technological progress that is increasingly capital intensive in nature. In both the medium and the long term the rate of accumulation of capital has always been more rapid than that of the growth of the labor force. In France there have been two clusters of technological progress and innovation, after the Second World War and after the reforms of 1982, separated by slow-downs resulting from the process of restructuring. The slow-down related to 1974 is distinguished not only by its magnitude but also by a change in its very nature. Perhaps this presages a future era of New Technologies in Information and Communication (NTIC).

The central factor that has facilitated new developments is that of finance. According to Christian Stoffaës: 'the evolution of the method of financing industrial activity is an essential key to competitiveness and restructuring.'[4] The competitiveness of French industry has suffered from state-directed financing throughout the post-war period; all this changed in 1983–4.

In 1984 France enacted a new banking law and this moved the economy from one of bond financing to one of equity. At the same time the government began to reduce its support of the large nationalized firms. Until 1984 (and the failure of one of these firms, Creusot-Loire), the French economy was characterized as capitalism without capital. This state control was exercised through the use of specialized banks and above all by the public treasury.[5] Before 1984 firms had no choice but to borrow if the state chose not to support them. The monetary and financial markets that are so familiar today simply did not exist as effective institutions at that time. Some branches of activity, such as public works and defense, were entirely dependent upon contracts for purchases by the state or upon massive subsidization, such as was the case with shipbuilding and coal mining. These latter industries were ultimately nationalized in the manner of the steel industry following a rescue plan, in 1978–9, which cost taxpayers tens of billions of francs. The crisis of 1974 had reinforced the will of the government of Giscard d'Estaing to adopt a position of a paralyzing hyper-management in the micro-economy in parallel with a destabilizing stop-and-go macro-economic policy. At this time the government decided virtually everything of importance: appointment of the senior management of the 250 large state-managed firms; authorization or prohibition of mergers; basic direction of investment; and financing of investments and company losses. For example, Matra was obligated by the government to diversify into publishing! In Marxian terms, this was an economy of state monopoly capitalism. The apex of this movement was reached in 1982 with the Mitterand government's law on nationalizations.

Suddenly, in 1983, the newspaper *Le Monde*, at that time favorable to the socialist government, devoted its first page on two consecutive days to a vigorous panegyric to private enterprise, profit-seeking and the entrepreneur. This was a total break with the ideology used in the electoral campaign of François Mitterrand and the Socialists in 1981, which stressed the wall of money and the entrepreneur-exploiter. It was a truly fundamental ideological revolution that was to have its impact during the ensuing 15 years.

In 1986 the government lost its majority and for two years France was in the situation of co-habitation, with a socialist President and a conservative Prime Minister and government. The new government introduced a wave of privatization of public enterprises beginning, as Table 6.2 shows, with Saint Gobain. Share values of the affected firms rose considerably following their privatization. For example, UAP rose by 400 per cent in five years, Saint Gobain by 250 percent over the next 13 years, and CCF by 60 per cent over 12 years; however, Machines Bull managed only 16 per cent during the next two years and ended up in the loss column by 2001.

Finally, in 1999 French capital was able to finance a number of start-ups that had never been attained before. At last venture capital gained a prominent position. Some laws and regulations were relaxed and additional state supports were introduced. Risk capital companies and investment funds became more numerous. The experience of the Anglo-Saxon world and funds

Table 6.2: Full or partial denationalizations of large french firms, 1986-2000

Year	Firms
1986	Saint Gobain
1987	Alcatel Alsthom, CCF, Havas, Paribas, Osociété Générale, Suez, TF1
1988	Matra, Hachette
1993	BNP, CLF, Rhône-Poulenc
1994	Elf Aquitaine, Renault, UAP
1995	Péchiny, Seita, Usinor Sacilor
1996	AGF
1997	France Télécom, Machines Bull
1998	CNP Assurances
1999	Air France, Crédit Lyonnais, AéroSpatiale Matra, Thomson Multimédia
2000	Caisses d'Epargne (now a cooperative)
2001	Banque Hervet

Source: *Les Echos*, January 7, 2001

supplied by US pension funds pushed this activity until France was placed third in the world, although still far behind the US and Britain, which raised 50 times as much capital. The US remained the primary direct and portfolio investor in France and these investments provided employment for over two million French workers. These investments also accounted for about 40 per cent of the value traded on the CAC 40, the French version of the Dow Jones Index. The French legal structure remained considerably more rigid than that of the US or Britain, and less supportive of innovation. It is therefore not surprising to note that European capital flows primarily to the UK. In 1997, 771 million euros of risk capital was invested in the UK, 336 in Germany, and 198 in France. The Netherlands had 163 million euros, Belgium 133, Spain 41 and Italy only 31.[6]

State funding has had a significant impact on research and development and productivity in France, indeed the state has been responsible for over half of R & D in France during the post-war years. This situation was totally changed by the economic liberalization that followed the 1974 crisis when technological advance was slowed for both R & D and investment in production. This meant that renewal of equipment was slow and the rate of economic growth was reduced. As can be seen in Table 6.3, the negative impact of an aging capital stock contributed to a slowing of the growth rate to just 2.20 in the mid 1970s. Confirmation of this is given by the strong correlation between productivity and economic growth during the period 1950–84. The Conseil Economic et Social also noted that during this period this relationship generated a rate of growth that was higher in France than in the other industrialized countries. Furthermore, the relationship between growth and employment in France for this period was also much stronger. It

Table 6.3: Contributions to growth in GDP, 1951–84

	1951–73	1974–84
Employment (number of workers)	0.15	−0.30
Duration of work	−.0.30	−0.80
Labor skills	0.40	0.70
Immigration of professional workers	0.50	0.30
Capital equipment value	1.30	1.30
Age of capital equipment	0.25	−1.25
Residual (technical progress)	3.10	2.25
Average annual rate of growth	5.40	2.20

Sources: J. J. Carré, P. Dubois, and E. Malinvaud, *La Croissance française*, Paris: Le Seuil, 1972; and J.F. Eck, *Histoire de l'économie française depuis 1945*, Paris: Armand Colin, 1988

was only after the mid 1980s that the relationship between growth and employment and productivity was changed. The relationship was a familiar one: higher productivity generated the growth that in turn created more employment; so strong productivity meant more employment. On the other hand, an unprecedented increase in the capital/labor ratio fed the increase in labor productivity. However, the partial price indexation of salaries in France has for long constrained the creation of employment.

Finally there were developments in employment, investment and the distribution of income. As the 1970s began, the nature of new job creation changed, because of a transformation in the structure of skills and specialties required, developments in electronics and information technology and their application in the service sector, and the opening of the economy to market-based competition. Professional training adapted only with a lag, and increased unemployment was a result. In the face of the extraordinary increase in the number of unemployed during the 1980s French governments made the mistake of attempting to redistribute the existing jobs, using policies such as reduction in the number of hours in the work week, lowering the age of retirement to 60, early retirement, and so forth. As a consequence of the reduction of the work week from 40 to 39 hours, 15,000–30,000 new jobs were created according to the government[7] or 17,000 as estimated by the business press.

It should also be noted that the economic crisis increased the importance of small and medium-sized firms. In relation to large firms, they find it easier to respond to a macro-economic environment of uncertainty or rapid restructuring. This explains why large French producers did not react to the international crisis as well as the suggestion that they lacked the means to do so. The initiatives aimed at redistribution of work also constrained a spontaneous restructuring along the lines of Schumpeter's creative destruction, but they did induce the large firms to begin a period of mergers and acquisitions that encouraged the government to pursue its policy of privatization and of giving large publicly owned enterprises their autonomy. This can be seen in a positive light by arguing that this step, perhaps inadvertently, resulted in the French economy avoiding the disintegration that otherwise would have occurred.

During 1998–2001 additional laws were enacted that reduced the work week from 39 to 35 hours. This time the financial environment favored the expansion of investment, as was indicated by a lowering of the rate of self-financing from 98 per cent in 1997 to 94 per cent in 1998. Finally, it must be noted that the social charges paid by French firms were the highest of the major OECD countries: as a percentage of GDP French employers paid, in 1996, 19.7 per cent, their counterparts in Germany paid 15.5 per cent, and in the UK it was 6.2 per cent, with an EU average of 12.2 per cent.[8]

The Contributions to Economic Growth

The rapid economic growth experienced by France during 1945–75 is easily explained by post-war reconstruction and then by the opening of the economy that followed the formation of the European Economic Community. Accompanying both of these events was a perhaps more fundamental cause of the increase in the quantitative growth rate and in the diversification of domestic production: the long-term trend of increased productivity. As Table 6.3 indicates, both the modernization of productive capital and advances in technology contributed to the technical progress that accounted for 57 per cent of economic growth until 1973 and all of growth during the following decade. We can also examine the contributions to GDP growth of the principal components of aggregate demand, as is done in Table 6.4. Two of

Table 6.4: Components of aggregate demand and growth in GDP, 1971–98

	1971	1980	1990	1995	1997	1998
Household consumption	3.0	0.8	1.4	0.9	0.4	1.9
Public sector consumption	0.6	0.4	0.4	...	0.2	0.3
Total investment	1.7	0.6	0.6	0.4	...	1.0
Inventory	−1.0	−0.2	0.2	0.4	0.1	0.4
Foreign trade	0.5	−0.3	−0.2	0.3	1.5	2.0
Annual rate of growth	4.9	1.4	2.4	2.0	2.2	3.2

Sources: Annuaire Statistique de la France; and *Comptes Nationaux*, various issues, Paris: INSEE

the main things to note from this table are that the surplus in the external trade account has reinforced domestic final demand in recent years, and that private demand and investment have taken up the slackening of public sector demand. Finally, Carré, Dubois and Malinvaud decomposed growth in GDP according to employment, capital and productivity (Table 6.5). With the shock of the crisis of 1974 the importance of employment in quantitative terms as a causal

Table 6.5: The Carré, Dubois and Malinvaud calculation of contributions to GDP growth

	1951-1973		1974-1995	
	Annual average	Quarterly variation	Annual average	Quarterly variation
Growth in GDP	5.4	0.82	2	0.94
Employment	1.1	0.37	0	0.56
Capital	1.5	0.23	1	0.15
Productivity	2.8	0.74	1	0.61

Source: M. Bernard Barbier, *Perspectives de l'économie mondiale à l'horizon 2005*, Paris: Delegation du Sénat pour la Planification, Rapport n° 315, 1996

factor in GDP growth has disappeared. In qualitative terms, however, the human factor reappears, albeit indirectly, toward the end of the century. It is this factor that is so productive in the new economic growth and which had nothing to do with the growth of *les trentes glorieuses*. Later, it appeared that investment in human capital was reduced in reference to the acceleration of technical progress. However, we do not have the means at our disposal to demonstrate this rigorously. The capital-consuming nature of technological progress became obvious in the last quarter of the century as compared with the post-war years when technical progress amounted to twice the share of investment in total economic growth (2.8 per cent vs. 1.5 for the earlier period). Additionally, the quarterly fluctuation of investment has clearly been reduced following 1974. It is necessary to take into account that the character of growth and of technological progress have changed profoundly during the past 25 years. What is called the new economy is fed by rapidly advancing information technology and the perhaps unrealistic expectations as to what it can accomplish. It is too soon to suggest the result of a movement that has yet to show its impact after several years. It is also necessary to take into account the fundamental differences between sectors of the economy, specifically between the growth of industrial production and that of services in general and of services linked to information technology.

The decomposition of growth of GDP in terms of sector or of branches confirms the progress of deindustrialization and the shift to the services sector following 1974. Between the 1970s and 2000 agricultural output fell from 5.0 per cent to less than 2.5 per cent as a share of GDP. At the same time the share of manufacturing (excluding construction) fell by 23 per cent (from 37 to 28.4 per cent) and services rose dramatically from 58.3 to 69.4 per cent. These movements are observed in most industrialized economies. If we take a longer view and examine employment, between 1949 and 1999 agriculture's share fell from 29 per cent to 4 per cent, and services rose from 36 per cent to 71 per cent. Manufacturing rose from 35 per cent in 1949 to 38 per cent in 1973, and then fell to 24 per cent by 1999.

THE CONTINUING RESTRUCTURING OF FRENCH OUTPUT

If one wishes to highlight one single date in the evolution of French industrial enterprises it would have to be 1984, the year of the *plan de rigueur* which was the response to the disastrous consequences of the economic and social experiments of 1982–3. Since that time, even if the governments did not draw attention to their actions, they all searched to a greater or lesser degree to deregulate and to liberalize activities and markets. Thus the rate of tax on profits fell from 50 per cent to 42 per cent in 1987 and then to 33 per cent in 1993. French capitalism of 2001 has little in common with the Colbertism that was established in the post-war years and reinforced between 1960 and 1983. Furthermore, since 1999 France has made a significant effort to catch up to the other industrialized economies with regard to NTIC, innovations, mergers and start-ups. This must be considered another radical transformation of the entrepreneurial landscape of the hexagon.

The Concentration and Expansion of French Firms

French capitalism began to be modernized around 1960, it was freed of the obligation to function within the financial sphere of the state and the public treasury in 1984, and it became global in its outlook following the privatizations of the 1990s. Today it is hardly possible to speak of a French model any more than of a Rhinean model of capitalism. Toward 1960, cooperative ventures among firms became popular. In these structures each firm would hold shares of the other. In this fashion firms were able both to protect themselves from hostile takeovers and to consolidate their relationships into functional networks. These networks were also a way of reducing the risk inherent in an uncertain climate and of diversifying the activities of each member of the group. Industry and finance were also able to form linkages. Before the monetary and financial liberalization of the 1980s, the two large publicly owned investment banks, Suez and Paribas, constituted two significant economic poles, each of which was able to control entire sectors of French corporate capitalism; they were instruments of control of the state that was still tied to a Colbertist model of intervention. With regard to the service sector, several large distribution companies (major department store chains, supermarkets, and so forth) created, with or without the participation of the banks, their own instruments of consumer credit. Some failures, such as that of Crédit Lyonnais, the collapse of land and building prices beginning in 1990, and the growth of shareholder power and involvement brought to an end the existing business structure. The era of strengthened growth centers and of financial–industrial groups was over. The practice of cooperative ventures increasingly took the form of exchanges of shares, with or without new stock issuances, in the search for critical regional or global scale with a recentering of activity on one or a few principal areas. Thus, during a period of 40 years French capitalism experienced two major mutations, with the intervening years being devoted to a balancing of nationalization and privatization.

In 2001 we see a French capitalism that is aggressive, competitive and international, in which a growing number of world-class groups are at the center of the stage. The two primary causal factors were, in summary, liberalization of the markets through deregulation and privatization, and the opening of the markets to continental and global competition. Both of these factors began to have their impacts with the onset of the 1990s, and we must remember that France was the last of the industrialized countries to completely abandon control of capital movements, and that only in 1990. Even if France has the largest number of industrial entities in Europe, in 2001 there is only one of these groups in the top 100 companies in the world – Elf.

The privatization movement was supported by Minister Dominique Strauss-Kahn and this inspired a wave of mergers and acquisitions, both domestically and internationally. That this was not a new phenomenon but was rather an acceleration of existing tendencies is demonstrated by the developments in the financial sector. Liberalization of financial institutions and markets during the 1980s resulted in diverse forms of restructuring. The first stage of liberalization was followed by the arrival of foreign banks and other financial institutions, with the number of new foreign firms increasing by 20 per cent between 1984 and 1988, and by a reduction in the total number of individual financial firms by 44 per cent over a period of 10 years. By the end of the 1990s great strides had been taken by French firms in the areas of bank–insurance mergers (for example, CNP and Prudential) and consolidations (such as that of Lazard Frères or CDC-Groupe Caisse d'Epargne), while on the European scene there were mergers to create even larger firms such as HSBC, Deutsche Bank-Dresdner Bank and the Royal Bank of Scotland. The 1999 takeover by BNP of Paribas succeded but its attempt to do the same with Société Général did not. Table 6.6 shows that in just 14 years the total number of credit granting firms in France fell by 40 per cent. This table gives a clear illustration of the rapid concentration that reduced the number of firms while loan activity developed significantly. The liberalization ushered in by the Socialist governments of the 1980s can be seen as having substantially restructured the several branches of financial activity.

Table 6.6: Number of credit granting institutions in France

Year	Banks	Specialized financial institutions	Total
1984	1012	989	2001
1988	877	1229	2106
1993	590	1059	1649
1994	587	1021	1608
1995	573	872	1445
1996	550	832	1382
1997	547	726	1273
1998	517	692	1209

Sources: Comité des établissements de crédit et des entreprises d'investissment—Banque de France; *La Tribune* September 17, 1999

The transnational mergers of today, occurring primarily in the automobile, chemical, pharmaceutical, petroleum, defense and information technology industries are, unfortunately, often accompanied by reductions in the employment of all elements of the workforce from senior executives to production line workers. Public opinion has turned against these large multinational firms and the French media are replete with images of heartless world companies and critiques of savage American capitalism such as those of Forrester that were discussed in Chapter 1. As is shown in Table 6.7, these mega-mergers hide a reality that is also characterized by large numbers of small and medium-sized companies with fewer than 500 employees that employ 2/3 of French workers, as is also the case in the United Kingdom and Germany. However, the French structure is distinguished from that of other countries by the predominance of firms employing 20–99 workers. In the United Kingdom very small firms, employing 10 or fewer workers, are responsible for more job creation than is true on the continent. This is the result of the taxation policies of the Thatcher and Blair governments.

In the US, firms of 500 or fewer workers account for 57 per cent of jobs in comparison with 2/3 in France. There are currently almost 2,300,000 firms in France, of all sizes and legal forms. All but 200,000 of them have fewer than

Table 6.7: French firms and the number of employees, 1991 (%)

	1—19	20—99	100—499	500+
France	29.1	21.0	16.2	33.7
United States	24.6	18.8	16.2	43.1
Germany	25.9	18.7	18.2	37.2
Italy	58.2	13.2	9.9	18.7
United Kingdom	33.0	16.1	17.2	33.7

Source: *Annuaires Statistiques de la France*, Paris: INSEE, various issues

10 employees and half of them have no employees at all, and between 1995 and 1998 the percentage of all firms that were in this smallest category rose from 92.6 to 93.05. As one would expect, it is in commerce and services to households that the largest proportion of small firms are found. The area in which the French firm structure is lacking is in the number of new firms. The rate of start-ups is weaker than in other industrialized economies. During the past decade there have been about 50,000 legal bankruptcies per year and the number of start-ups has fallen from 309,000 in 1990 to 271,000 in 1997. According to an OECD study, Canada, Israel and the United States each have a start-up rate of 6.9 per cent, Italy and the United Kingdom have 3.4 per cent, and France joins Denmark, Germany and Japan at the bottom with a rate of 1.8 per cent.[9]

In Chapter 2 it was noted that manufacturing firms subcontract a growing number of services in order to focus more narrowly on the principle activities. The new firms of the 1990s were especially narrowly specialized, and those in the information technology sector were specialized in either hardware, software or application. The hardware firms are considered to be in the industrial sector while the other two are in services. Even though the service sector value accounted for 70 per cent of all value added in 2000, it was manufacturing that captured most of the interest of economists and of government. Manufacturing has held the central place in the French economy, in part because it is the primary client of the service sector (see Chapter 2) and in part because the evolution of these firms reflects the evolution of the economy in general.

Manufacturing

Table 6.8 gives a general overview of the development of several major sectors of French manufacturing prior to the reforms of 1984. With few exceptions, the pattern has been one of the deindustrialization that has characterized most industrialized economies. The years prior to the reforms

Table 6.8: Annual growth rates of French manufacturing branches, 1970–84

	1970–73	1973–79	1979–84
All manufacturing	6.5	2.6	0.4
Armaments	5.4	16.4	11.5
Electronic appliances	13.0	8.4	6.7
Synthetic textiles	10.9	−4.1	−3.5
Steel	3.0	0.3	−4.7
Iron ore	−1.5	−8.3	8.7

Note: Figures are percentage change in constant 1980 francs.

Source: *Annuaires*, Paris: INSEE, various issues

can properly be considered to be disastrous. Following the Second World War the state financed and planned the reconstruction of the transportation and communication infrastructures. Some delays were experienced, for example with the state telephone network, but these were dealt with successfully during the 1970s. The coal sector was placed under state control in order to keep it from collapsing, although ultimately this did happen under competition from another state-controlled sector of energy – nuclear power. Concurrently with reconstruction France became an industrial nation through development of its heavy industry, petroleum and mechanical sectors, as well as plastics and chemicals. While the crisis of 1974 slowed the pace of development and the modernization of industry, in reality it was the omnipresence of the state in virtually all major industrial firms that put this sector in difficulty by 1984. Many firms were forced to close plants or lay off workers or relocate to other countries. During the 12-year period 1974–86 the textile and steel industries reduced their employment by 60 per cent, and in shipbuilding the figure was 80 per cent. European countries imposed steel production quotas and a strong consensus developed in support of the necessity to restructure this very large sector, without arriving at a strategy for returning it to market competition. In the steel industry only Usinor and Sacilor were salvaged by means of considerable support from the French state. This steel crisis was felt throughout Europe, as can be seen from the data in Table 6.9.

Very large public sector budget deficits, a current account balance of payments deficit, a substantial increase in social transfers and the national debt, and some unfortunate policy choices account for the decision of the government to perform a complete about-face in its policy posture in 1983. During the following decade French industry was gradually freed of the constraints of state control. Firms were able to refocus their activities toward

Table 6.9:   Employment in the steel industry, major european countries,
*   selected years*

	1974	1980	1986
France	160,000	110,000	60,000
Germany	130,000	200,000	140,000
United Kingdom	190,000	130,000	55,000
Italy	95,000	95,000	60,000
Belgium	70,000	45,000	30,000

Source: La Tribune de l'économie, December 8, 1987

those in which their competence was clearer and this restructuring involved further lay-offs, largely through out-sourcing of many service activities which, in turn, put downward pressure on wages. Several of these firms were actually able to become world leaders in their sectors of the economy, for example L'Oréal, Michelin, Bouygues and Air Liquide. This phase of restructuring has been characterized as a refocusing of industry, but in fact many firms in wood and paper, shoes, textiles, shipbuilding, and computers have been forced to close. The several decades of Colbertism have facilitated the reconstruction and modernization of French industry, but this was followed by costly lay-offs and restructuring and by investment and public subventions that led to misallocation of resources, labor and capital. But times have changed, and today France resembles quite closely the other economies of the OECD.

The return of industrial vitality
In Europe it was the industry of three Nordic economies, Sweden, Norway and Finland, that was the most dynamic during the 1990s. Excluding construction and public works, output rose by 15 per cent. During this decade French industry was situated in the middle of EU members with a growth of only 4 per cent, or 7 per cent if construction and public works are included. We have already noted that France has been experiencing deindustrialization, as is true of most of the industrial economies, even though in absolute figures output continued to grow by almost 30 per cent between 1973 and 1990 and by an additional 16 percentage points by 1999, and capacity utilization increased from 79 per cent in 1993 to 85 per cent in 1999. Overall growth of French output rose by 4.5 per cent in 1999 while industrial output grew by 5.1 per cent, although it declined in 1998 and most of the industrial growth came toward the end of 1999. Manufacturing employment actually fell by 50,000 in 1997 and stagnated until the end of 1999.

In the longer term the advances of 1999 masked a significant disparity. As was noted in Chapter 2, French deindustrialization is both relative and continuous. Manufacturing has suffered substantial losses in some of its major traditional areas of specialization: consumption goods such as clothing, household appliances and medicines as well as industrial equipment such as shipbuilding, machinery and electronics. The areas of strength have become food processing, with a growth of 13 per cent between 1990 and 1997, automobiles (14 per cent growth), high value-added intermediate goods (chemicals, plastics, wood, finished metal products, electrical components, and electronics which grew by 8 per cent) and non-petroleum energy (21 per cent growth). Recently privatized Usinor has become the largest producer of steel in Europe and the world's second largest producer of stainless steel.

The majority of industrial activities have been concerned with the wave of mergers and acquisitions that began in 1998. Hoechst and Rhône-Poulenc (which became Aventis), Suez and Lyonnaise des Eaux, Havas and CGE (which became Vivendi), Axa and UAP, Groupama and GAN are just the most publicized of the mergers. It was noted above that large industrial firms and banks had chosen to become linked during the 1960s. The recent mergers were a new development for an extensive list of companies in banking, insurance, aeronautics, defense production, pharmaceuticals and chemistry, and automobiles. It appears that these initiatives were motivated more by concerns of security or defense than of the creation of value. The French metallurgy industry must be seen as a special case as it vacillated between nationalization and privatization. Actually the French steel firm Usinor (after the merger of Usinor and Sacilor) is the largest firm in this industry in Europe. Its production (in 1998) of 25.6 million metric tonnes exceeded that of Corus (22.5), Arbed (20.1) or Thyssen Krupp (14.8). Steel production has long been at the head of French heavy industry. This industry was the property of the state until the 1990s, although it was restructured in the 1970s. In 2000 there were only 40,000 workers, down considerably from the 160,000 employed in 1970. It was not a competitive industry for France and was becoming more and more burdensome for the taxpayers. For example, the return per worker was double in Germany and in Japan triple the return in France. For these and other reasons, the 'third industrial revolution' in France has been simultaneously similar to that of other industrialized countries and a cleaning-up of the industrial system.

The third industrial revolution and small and medium-sized firms
François Caron coined the term 'third industrial revolution,' and France at the turn of the millennium is marked less by differences from the processes experienced in other industrialized economies than by some disquieting lags in French development. This is essentially a revolution that blended in the initial phase both the secondary and tertiary sectors, that is, manufacturing and financial firms, then the phenomenon of outsourcing, and more recently the producers of hardware and software, of communication and of maintenance.

The history of an industrial revolution often begins with localized initiatives. This may consist of artisanal alternatives to mass production, generally organized in cooperative networks – new groupings of small and medium-sized firms. The firms are small and are generally staffed by highly skilled workers. Rather than produce the standardized products and services that occupy the rest of the industry, the new enterprises are by nature aimed at narrowly defined markets and are themselves highly flexible and adaptable to change. As is argued by Sabel and Seitlin, innovation, strengthening of market position and expansion of production offer these firms the chance to succeed in spite of the cost and other advantages enjoyed by larger mass production firms.[10]

What was true in the first two industrial revolutions of the eighteenth and nineteenth centuries concerning the birth and growth of firms in the 'new economy' remains true today. When a new firm fails, a lack of audacity is more likely to be the cause than the inherent strength of the position of an established mass producer. It can also be caused by the harmful industrial policies of the government, as was the case with French government commitments during the twentieth century to technologies that proved in reality to be non-viable. The importance of this sort of erroneous decision is due to the dominant role played by the state in the French economy and in the consequent mass production of goods and services such as the telephone system or national system of education. Furthermore, the state has appointed as the leaders of state-controlled enterprises individuals who were politically favored but not professionally distinguished.[11] Some observers, such as French Minister Claude Allègre, point to the conservative role played by national lobbying groups, uniting both industrial firms and their workers, that oppose the liberalizing initiatives of Brussels.

The industrial restructuring of the last decade must therefore been seen as, on the one hand, the internationalization of French capitalism and, on the other hand, the actions of groupings of smaller French firms. This phenomenon of groupings of small firms is quite specific to France. Between 1985 and 2000 the number of small firms belonging to one or more such groups has multiplied by a factor of five and their balance sheet assets have become quite impressive. In contrast to this, large industrial groups are simply the result of mergers and acquisitions of some firms by others. Neither structure is to be found in construction or in commercial or household services.

Investment and human capital during the past 25 years
Motivated by the upturn in the growth of foreign demand and rebounding from the oil shocks of the 1970s, investment grew considerably in France between 1985 and 1989, although the magnitude of this recovery varied considerably according to sector. It was especially important for the services,

for transportation and for intermediary goods, but appeared for other sectors only toward 1988 and less strongly. Investment showed instability beginning in 1989 with the build-up to the recession of 1993–5 that affected all sectors of the economy. Weakness of domestic demand is in large part responsible for this decline in investment. Its wild fluctuation is indicated in Table 6.10. The decline of 1997 was certainly the result of the Asian financial crisis, but the economic recovery was under way, both domestically and globally (a weakness of growth in two of France's largest partners, Italy and Germany, was offset by growth in the United States), and credit progressively became less costly and easier to obtain until the end of 1999, at which point the interest rate rose by 200 basis points the following year. During 2000 capital investment has been the result of decisions by large firms of more than 500 employees; these firms doubled their investment between 1999 and 2000, helped by strong demand and a less restrictive monetary policy.

Table 6.10: Annual percentage change in manufacturing investment

	1991	1992	1993	1994	1995	1996	1997	1998	1999	2000
Percentage change in investment	+1	−9	−18	−3	+9	+1	−1	+6	+6	+9

Sources: *Bulletin Mensuel du Trésor*, no. 113, October 1999; *Investir*, no. 1362, February 21, 2000

During the past 20 years French industrial investment has been subject to dramatic fluctuations. It grew by 5 per cent annually during two periods, 1984–90 and 1995–2000, that corresponded with periods of strong growth of household consumption. Purchases of household equipment and appliances have continued to progress so that today 96 per cent of households have a telephone connection (as opposed to 21 per cent in 1973), 34 per cent have a dishwashing machine (up from 5 per cent), 92 per cent have at least one automobile (in contrast with 62 per cent), and color television ownership is up between 1973 and 2000 from 8 per cent of households to 92 per cent. Household purchasing power, after taxes, has increased in every year since 1973, with the exceptions of 1980, 1983 and 1984. The big items of 2000 were cell phones, Internet connection for a computer, DVD players, game players, VCRs, audio systems, cars and microwave ovens. Thus has France joined the capitalist consumer culture.

According to the OECD, the rate of growth of investment in France has been rather weak from the crisis of 1974 until the late 1990s when it rose to

4–6 per cent per year. In terms of investment, during the past 20 years France
has been passed by its principal trading partners, as is shown in Table 6.11.

Table 6.11: The evolution of manufacturing investment, selected countries

Country	1980	1990	1997
France	100.0	134.5	124.6
United States	100.0	126.9	184.0
Germany	100.0	135.3	134.6
United Kingdom	100.0	186.4	199.7
Japan	100.9	215.8	221.7

Sources: *Statistical Yearbook*, Paris: OECD, various issues; *Annuaire Statistique de la France*,
Paris: INSEE, various issues

When we turn our attention to human capital, its development over time
shows less instability. Nonetheless, the French experience is not well adapted
to the needs of the developing new economy. In particular, the new
information technologies and their managerial applications have not met the
industryies needs, and too many university graduates and skilled workers have
developed the wrong specialties, for example in textiles and printing, in which
the demand for labor is declining. Conversely, an insufficient number of
workers are gaining skills in specialties for which demand is increasing, such
as computers. As a consequence, there is a polarization of the labor force
between those who are well suited to the new economy and those who are
wedded to yesterday's economy. This imbalance is found equally among
small and medium-sized firms and large industrial groups.

There is, of course, a category of firm for which the modernization
movement, specifically that of information technology, has had little or no
impact. In these firms, whether small or large, workers have not been able to
appropriate for themselves the results of innovation that to them remain
foreign. They have had neither a stimulating association nor applied training
in their specialization. By contrarast, those firms that have successfully
managed their evolution have adopted a new mentality, and the initiative and
the training of their workers have proved that the motor of their economic
advance has been based primarily in their labor force.[12] These are the firms
that are the best performing in French industry and, it goes without saying, in
the services and new information technologies. The improved returns of these
firms were linked to the appearance of structures of independent small teams,
high quality research, and flexibility of working hours which was actually
facilitated by the recent laws concerning the 35-hour work week.[13]

The productive structure has progressively become one of a collection of
networks, the members of which are often rather small and specialized firms,
operating in the same context as large entities that develop into new global-

scale groups. The most striking characteristics of these new enterprises, whether large or small in size, is their intensive utilization of new information technologies, computers and robots, telecommunications, outsourcing, restructuring and downsizing, and accelerated development of networks and various forms of partnership. Outsourcing has been partially integrated into networks, even though this is less noticeable among the largest firms.

The recent evolution of French industry is a good example of the theory of competition rent[14] (price minus cost): rent-seeking in competitive markets operates both through innovation (with prices highest for the first to enter the market) and through price (the reduction of average cost). The reshuffle of market shares and relative prices that was observed at the end of the 1990s concerns not only the economic situation of firms but also that of regions and nations. Contrary to common belief, more intense competition has led to more restructuring among developed countries themselves than it has between developed and Third World countries. Data indicate that 0.6 per cent of the workforce of European economies has been affected by competition from Third World economies and that this represents only a very minor share of unemployment that approached 10 per cent EU-wide during the late 1990s. Migration of skilled workers indicates that competition is considerably more intense among the industrialized economies. For example, young French skilled workers emigrate primarily toward London or Silicon Valley.

Furthermore, since the crisis of the 1970s we have seen a new type of footloose company. These firms no longer identify themselves as companies of any particular nation, they respond to price changes that are the result of exchange rate changes, they concern themselves with organizational planning and with differences in profit taxes, and they move and displace workers as readily as do their shareholders. This has been one of the primary sources of economic development of Scotland and of Ireland during the past two decades. Before this phenomenon French governments sought to ease the burden of adjustment on human beings by slowing the pace of deregulation in Europe, and by slowing the pace of lay-offs and restructuring throughout state enterprises and the public service. Thus a large protected sector was maintained in France, at least until about 1995. The contemporary transformation of economic activity in France has not been accomplished without some pain. Given that capital is far more flexible and mobile than labor, especially in France, and that it takes a longer period of time to recycle a worker than capital, the restructuring is accordingly done with pain to individuals and with costs to geographic areas. Those who are incapable of making a swift and easy transition to new employment are destined to remain among the under-employed or to give their place to more qualified workers.

New information technologies have had a powerful impact on the French economy, an economy that now looks more and more like that of the United States; however, with some enduring particularisms: a taste for cultural and educational innovation, accompanied by a speed of adaptation and of experimentation that exceeds that found elsewhere, at least according to the economic press. It is nonetheless true that France lags in Internet connection, with a rate of only 16 per cent in comparison with the EU average of 23 per cent, and rates for the United Kingdom and Germany of 27 and 29 per cent respectively, and far behind the 51 per cent registered in the United States.[15] In the so-called third industrial revolution, that is now having its impact on virtually all countries of the world with the exception of most of Africa and some parts of Asia, the European Investment Bank has taken over many firms that have failed, whether public or private in ownership. A rescue fund of 15 billion euros for 2000–2 has been established, following a decision that was taken at the Lisbon Summit (March 2000) with the intention of developing an economy founded on innovation and knowledge. If one includes all the financing that is being undertaken by other European institutions the fund approached 40 billion euros. The specific areas to be supported include: modernization of telecommunications; development of European networks of communication; assistance to the creation of companies in the area of information technology; encouragement of sources of venture capital; and development of an effective network of European universities, firms and research institutes. The private sector has been slowed in its efforts at modernization by the relatively high costs of local telephone communication maintained by France Télécom. In 2000 the medium and long-distance rates were lowered by more than 20 per cent and in 2001 the government put an end to the monopolistic linkage between the local and FT systems. Banks, insurance companies and firms in the stock market are in the process of moving significantly onto the Internet and competition among them is becoming intense. In 2001, the odds are against the success of many French Internet brokers and Internet access providers.

This sort of environment is evidently favorable to the creation of start-ups of rather small firms, a factor that makes clear the heterogeneity of French structures of production. Venture capital has developed very rapidly in France through the organization of large fairs at which ideas about projects and entities with capital to risk can encounter each other. In France 97 per cent of all firms are medium, small, or very small firms. With regard to large firms, new information technologies clearly favor rapid development of Internet services and multi-dimensional networks as bets on the future – the retail firm Carrefour is a prime example of this. The SNCF (national railways) and the postal system have formed an alliance to become the second largest package service in Europe. In general it can be said that the year 2000 marks a change of mind of the CEOs of French firms of all sizes in favor of the Internet and Intranet. There are now a large majority of them who recognize the necessity of changing their operational strategies toward both their suppliers and their customers, regarding sales and public relations, and are in favor of establishing networks and alliances with other firms. To take just one example, about 17 per cent of the growth in business engagement in information services is accounted for by administrative computer services integrated in the firm, related to logistical chains, or to management activities related to clients. Computers and their maintenance represent about Fr400 billion spent in France during 1999 (out of a GDP of Fr9,000 billion). By comparison, electronic commerce in France equals only 1per cent of its importance in the United States. Finally, it can be noted that the growth of many regional, and even cross-border, specializations is related in many cases to the growth of new information technologies.

While France has developed very well in mobile telephony, while Internet usage grows at a rapid pace, and while computer use gains yearly in domestic and professional applications, biotechnology is somewhat retarded in its growth. It seems as though the government has made a decision to back away from support of research and production in this area. The United States, however, is preparing itself to make major advances in this industry.

Agriculture

Urbanization has progressed in France as it has in other developed countries. Following the end of the Second World War, 40 per cent of the workforce was in agriculture. Rural France has for long constituted a profoundly conservative pole of social stability in the face of the several industrial and social crises that have buffeted France and was, for example, actively engaged in the protectionist policies of Jules Méline at the end of the nineteenth century. At the outset of the twenty-first century the French firm is a true profit- and efficiency-seeking productive enterprise that is hampered in its operation by the legal monopolies that continue in the distribution of its output. The modernization of the 1950s both stimulated an out-migration from agricultural areas and increased the productivity of those who remained.[16] Legislation of the next decade made it rational for farmers to borrow to purchase equipment with subsidies from the state. The government promoted a restructuring of agricultural lands with the Sociétés d'aménagement foncier et d'établissement rural which were accorded priority in the purchase of farmlands. Without nationalizing agricultural land the state was able to reshape French farming by the use of methods that were very technical in their rationale but also often contested. Another law established with this same objective was the Groupement agricole d'exploitation en commun. In order to keep labor on the land and to slow the aging of the rural population a retirement fund was established, which was financed for the most part by tax revenues of the state.[17]

Another feature of the 1950s was the fact that the volatility and hence the uncertainty of prices for agricultural goods led to the first public demonstrations (barriers on public roads) by farmers, and to the management of agricultural prices by the authorities, first by the French government and after 1962 by the Common Agricultural Policy of the European Economic Community. A new movement toward protectionism was under way. From its beginning the agriculture policy of Brussels was devoted to regulation of production and imports in a Europe that was heavily dependent on imports of food. After 1984 policy was revised toward the support of agricultural revenues, and subsidies replaced market interventions (and the practice of price floors). The net result of all of these measures was overproduction in several areas of agricultural production. Then in 1986 and again in 1992 further reform was introduced and production quotas were introduced as well as a freeze on the cultivable land: 10–15 per cent of land was mandated to be fallow. The Common Agricultural Policy is destined to disappear in the next few years, with Europe having been transformed into a continent that can not only feed itself but also produce a considerable surplus for the export market. As subsidies are replaced by tariff equivalents it will become necessary to reconfigure export prices so they conform to world prices, and the surpluses of cereals and beef are likely to come to an end.

Concurrently with these changes in agriculture rural France continues to suffer from out-migration. Entire villages have fallen into ruin and, as Henri Mendras as written, it is the end of the French peasantry. Those who remain are increasingly aged, although many of them have become quite entrepreneurial, competent administrators and accomplished in their use of the new technologies. The number of farms has fallen from over 1.2 million in 1980 to 660,000 in 2000, but the size of those that remain has increased considerably. In 1955, of 2.3 million farms only 20,000 had more than 100 hectares, while in 1997, 76,000 of 680,000 farms were of that size.[18] Even though it has doubled during the past half–century the average size of French farms remains rather small. In 1997 this figure was 38.5 hectares; however, the average size for EU farms was only 17.5 hectares. Obviously there has been a dramatic concentration of many smaller farms into large and more efficient operations. Even with all of these policy changes and restructuring France remains the EU's largest single producer of agricultural goods, as Table 6.12 indicates.

During this period, agriculture has shown a tendency to shift from diversified farms to those that are increasingly specialized. Certain monoculture has required substantial investment of capital and the fluctuations of the economic cycle and of prices have aggravated the human, social and economic difficulties that have confronted French agriculture. For example, periodically the price of pork falls below the cost of its production. But the investments, once made, are irreversible and the exit costs for those who leave can be quite high. In a very real sense, farmers have been

Table 6.12: Land under cultivation (in millions of hectares)

Country	1980	1997
France	29,300	30,210
Spain	23,500	29,600
Germany	12,200	17,300
United Kingdom	17,100	15,900
Italy	15,900	15,700
European Union	120,000	137,300

Note: Some 1980 figures are estimates. EU figures are for 15 members.

Source: *Annuaire Statistique de France,* Paris: INSEE, 1999

abandoned by the growth of the rest of the French economy. Their standard of living varies in accordance with crop prices, which have deteriorated from an index (1995 = 100) of 213 in 1960, to 190 in 1970, to 140 in 1980, to 110 in 1990 and finally to 90 in 1999.[19] In actuality, the conditions of life of French farmers have posed a problem for the government for at least 50 years. During the 1950s the policy was that of trying to induce the young to remain on the land, primarily through bonuses to stimulate the departure of older farmers. But the deterioration of prices and of farm living standards has continued unabated. Even during periods of full economic expansion the number of farms has continued to decline and the majority of smaller farms have seen their revenues fall. Some sectors of French agriculture are destined to disappear, causing considerable difficulty for some regions and departments. This is especially true for activities such as cereals and beef since they are products that are standardized and subject to competition in global markets. It will be necessary for agricultural areas throughout the world to confine their production to products in which they actually have a comparative advantage, whether through price or quality, as is the case for wine or cheese in France.

As Table 6.13 shows, while Germany is the largest producer of pork in the EU and Spain is number one in sheep, France is dominant in oil seeds and

Table 6.13: French share of EU agricultural production

	All livestock	Of which cattle	Cereals	Oil seeds	Vegetables	Fruit	Wine
Share of EU (%)	15	25	30	57	13	16	35
Rank in EU	1	1	1	1	3	2	2

Source: *Comptes nationaux*, Paris: INSEE. 1998

is ranked first, second or third in several major sectors. Agricultural production has increased at a diminishing rate since 1974 with a strong aggregate recovery in 1993–4 that was not experienced by all sectors. For example, cereals virtually collapsed between 1990 and 1994 when the value of output declined from Fr54 billion to only Fr34.5 billion, however there was an increase to Fr41 billion in 1997. Livestock experienced a crisis without precedent, due to increased competition from foreign producers, with revenues unchanged between 1990 and 1997. Beef and veal were the hardest hit, largely because of the concern with mad cow disease.

It appears that commercialization of agriculture and its distribution has made difficult both the lasting improvement of the standard of living of French farmers and restructuring and concentration of agricultural holdings. Agricultural producers regularly complain that their vegetables, fruits or meats sell at retail for several times more than they themselves receive for them due to the substantial mark-ups imposed by intermediaries. As an example, Table 6.14 gives a representation of the relationship of revenues gained by various elements for 1 kg of apples. With three intermediaries, the market price is 2.5 times that received by the grower.

Table 6.14: Revenues by participant in the food sector for 1 kg of apples (francs)

Participant	Revenues
Farmer/producer	4.64
Packaging	1.89
Transportation	1.39
Super market	3.36
Value added tax	0.62
Price to the customer	11.90

Source: *Bulletin d'information*, Continent Supermarkets, 1999

As the world's principal food exporting nation France has benefited enormously from globalization of this industry. This position has been maintained during the past 15 years, as Table 6.15 indicates. France holds an important position in ocean fishing because of the length of its Atlantic coastline. As with agriculture, fish prices have had a tendency to fall due to increasing international competition for products that are essentially standardized or homogeneous. The number of fishermen has also declined in recent years, from 19,800 in 1990 to 13,400 seven years later. Ship size has increased from 23 to 27 tons during the same period while their number has fallen by 28 per cent.[20] As is the case with manufacturing, concentration in the fishing industry has been pursued in order to achieve economies of scale. And as is true for agriculture, fishing has experienced the same situation regarding prices and revenues.

Table 6.15: Selected agricultural exporting countries, by share of the world market.

Country	1983	1997
France	8.4	9.3
United States	8.2	9.0
Netherlands	8.9	8.5
Germany	6.7	6.1
Spain	1.9	3.0

Source: ANIA (Association Nationale des Industries Agro-alimentaires), in *Les Echos*, November 4, 1999

Energy

The final part of the primary goods sector to be examined, briefly, is that of energy. French coal production today is only a quarter of what it was in 1973, and consumption has fallen from 46 to 22 billion tonnes. Petroleum production has also fallen from 142 to 114 billion tonnes during the same period. On the other hand, electrical power (primary, hydro, and nuclear) has surged from 7.3 per cent of usage in 1973 to almost 38 per cent in 1997 and now joins petroleum with 29 per cent of total consumption. France is even a net exporter of electricity in the face of an increase in consumption since 1973 by a factor of 2.5. Overall, the country has reduced its dependence on imports of energy from 78 per cent in 1973 to about 50 per cent today. However, in terms of per capita consumption of energy France is tied with Germany at fourth place in the world, behind the United States, Canada and Oceania.

Services

Until the post-war period, this sector was characterized by the traditional trades: personal services, small shops and offices, taxis, restaurants, and so forth. Since that time, in France as elsewhere, the sector has become modernized, with firms becoming considerably larger and the labor force significantly feminized, especially in education, banking, insurance, law, commerce, and public administration. In all industrialized countries the tertiary sector in 2001 is undergoing dramatic expansion. The most dramatic changes in France have occurred during two distinct periods: that of the privatizations in 1986–8 and 1996–9, and currently through mergers and acquisitions. The last transformation of services was characterized by the establishment of networks among firms in banking, insurance, consulting, accounting, brokerage, and transportation. This has been followed by e-commerce with goods and services being sold on line. Retail distribution holds a very large place in France. The firm Carrefour is the largest distributor in Europe and in 2000 arranged an alliance with Sears and Oracle with the objective of strengthening its innovative capacity. The result of this alliance is a business-to-business supply network (GlobalNetXchange) on line between suppliers and distributors, as has already been done among European automobile firms. However, it should be noted that only 18 per cent of French firms utilize an Intranet, as compared with 100 per cent of Swedish firms.

Mass marketing has become a French specialty that is often exported, although companies such as Wall Mart have been serious competitors. Supermarket floor space has increased by over 20 per cent between 1993 and 1999, and employment has increased from 2,556,000 in 1993 to 2,663,700 four years later. If Internet commerce expands as Merrill Lynch forecasts,[21] both floor space and employment should be expected to stabilize in the near future. The largest insurance company in the world is the French firm Axa-UAP, and this has happened since the state removed itself from the insurance and banking sectors, having control only of Bank Hervet until late 2001 and several minority positions in firms that were formerly nationalized. Several banks have absorbed or created insurance firms or have succeeded in establishing partnership relations, and some insurance firms have created their own bank. These linkages were greatly strengthened following the oil spills at sea and storms of 1999.

CONCLUSION

During the past half-century French agriculture has developed from a traditional self-sufficient sector to one that is highly productive, market-oriented and European in outlook. Successive rounds of liberalization through the GATT and then the WTO have accelerated this process, which must be seen as inevitable and irreversible. At the same time the attractiveness of the countryside has been modified profoundly, with food processing, manufacturing, crafts and tourism often surpassing agriculture and grazing activities in importance. Industry has been the object of dramatic restructuring, under the control and at the initiative of the state, and then more recently through mergers and acquisitions. However, French industry has been less susceptible to the pressures of deindustrialization than has been the case in other industrialized economies. Advances in various technologies have rescued many of France's largest industrial groups and continue to do so, with Vivendi in 2000 being the most recent.

In Chapter 3 French industrial policy was shown to be often conservative or even reactionary, attempting to resist an irresistible evolution or to delay the moment of truth for ventures that were clearly doomed to failure. This is no longer the case. The obvious development of the French tertiary sector has progressed with considerable speed during the 1990s. The modernization of activities, the innovations and the increase in productivity have all received the support of the state, which has reduced its presence during the same decade. The state as producer has been replaced by the state that is generous in its support and assistance to the private sector in innovation and restructuring, and has turned its focus toward Europe and its markets. As would be expected, not all of its policies have met with success, for example Esprit in information technology and Race in telecommunication. The services sector has become diversified and noticeably modernize – one thinks of computerization and supermarket retailing – while at the same time many traditional small-scale activities have been preserved, such as small shops, tourism, and restaurants. Banking and insurance are now almost entirely privatized and have been restructured and oriented toward larger markets. Financial institutions unfortunately have retained too many of the traits of the old state capitalism, with the state retaining minority control in many instances. Among service sector activities, tourism continues to be a solid success and France remains the premier tourist destination in the world, with 80 million visitors in 2000. Finally, the evident de-socialization of consumption, facilitated by the return of economic growth, has recently exercised a net positive effect on all related activities and on competitive innovation.

NOTES

1. Erik Izraelewicz, *Les Echos*, February 21, 2000.
2. J.C. Asselin, *Histoire économique de la France*, vol. II, Paris, Editions du Seuil, 1984.
3. Pierre Rosanvallon, *L'Etat en France de 1789 à nos jours*, Paris: Editions du Seuil, 1990, p. 261.
4. Christian Sofaës, *Services publics question d'avenir*, Commissariat general du Plan, Paris: O. Jacob—La documentation Française, 1995, p. 471.
5. Cf. Maurice Parodi *et al.*, *L'économie et la société française au second XXème siècle*, Tome 1, Paris: Armand Colin, 1994, p. 197.
6. European Venture Association figures reported in *Les Echos*, May 5, 1999.
7. *Rapport du Conseil*, Paris: Conseil Economique et Social, 1984, p. 14.
8. The figures are the OECD's as quoted by Philippe Marini, *La concurrence fiscale en Europe: une contribution au débat*, Paris: Senate, 1998–1999, ch. III.
9. Cited in *Les Echos*, June 22, 1999.

10. Charles Sabel and Jonathan Zeitlin, 'Historical alternative to mass production: politics, markets and technology in nineteenth-century industrialization,' *Past and Present*, vol. 108, August 1985, pp. 133–176.

11. Andrew Jack offers several examples of this in his *The French Exception*, London: Profile Books, 2000.

12. 'Le dossier management,' *Les Echos*, February 22, 2000, p. 51. The cultural difference between French and American firms is very noticeable and widely commented upon. See Philippe d'Irribarne, *La logique de l'honneur – Gestion des entreprises et traditions nationales*, Paris: Editions du Seuil, 1989.

13. See, for example, Philippe Askenazy, 'Les 35 heures, une clé inattendue,' *Les Echos*, March 28, 2000.

14. Gary Becker, *The Economic Approach to Human Behavior*, Chicago: University of Chicago Press, 1976.

15. *Les Echos*, March 27, 2000, and *European Internet Report*, Morgan Stanley Dean Witter.

16. The Massey-Ferguson revolution led to the disappearance of small firms and to the indebtedness of those that remained.

17. Remember that the French retirement system is financed by current tax revenues rather than by capitalization – current workers finance the pensions of those who are retired.

18. *Annuaire statistique de la France*, Paris: INSEE, 1999.

19. *L'Expansion*, February 17, 2000, Paris: INSEE.

20. *Annuaire statistique de la France*, Paris: INSEE, 1999.

21. Henry Blodget, 'L'Europe a le même potentiel que les Etats Unis pour le commerce électronique,' *Connectis-Les Echos-Financial Times-L'Expansion*, February 25, 2000.

7 Decentralization: Regions and Cities

One of the most striking consequences for France of the evolution of globalization has been the restructuring of the loci of decision-making and of responsibility for economic development among the national and sub-national levels of government. As national governments have imposed constraints, consequent to trade liberalization and deregulation of markets, on their ability to intervene in their own national economies an opportunity has been created for France's regions and cities to become more entrepreneurial and self-promoting. This development has been accompanied by changes in policies at the national level and in the legal status and capacities of regions and cities. These changes have resulted in a restructuring of the national economic space, in initiatives for local development, in a demand for new infrastructure projects, and in relationships between French regions and cities and their counterparts in other countries. Finally, this new economic environment has exerted added pressure for a restructuring of economic activity throughout France and has hastened the rise or fall of specific industries, factors of production, and sub-national economies. In this chapter we examine each of these important issues.

Daniel Noin has written: 'the French economic space has not only been transformed by rapid evolution of the system of production, it has also been transformed by public officials who sought to reshape it.'[1] Thus if we are to understand the spatial restructuring of the French economy in the post-Second World War years we must examine both the effects of globalization and the decisions of French policy-makers. As has already been noted, there was a break in the performance of the French economy in the mid-1970s. The years since then can be characterized as a period in which the economy was increasingly affected by the liberalization and deregulation of markets, and by relatively dramatic changes in the technologies of production, transportation and communication. With regard to policy, changing economic conditions have called periodically for the introduction of a new law or a new approach to the management of territory that has cumulatively resulted in a momentum toward a fundamental change in French economic decision-making – decentralization. It is these events that will form the primary structure of the policy discussion of this chapter.

Since 1958 another actor has begun to insinuate itself into French regional policy – the European Economic Community-European Union. As this entity has matured and developed its competence, its funding and policy initiatives and its relation to sub-national governments have had a powerful impact that will have to be considered before we have completed this analysis. But first, we must describe the nature of France's regions and its urban economies.

THE FRENCH ECONOMIC SPACE

There are 22 regions, 96 departments and over 36,000 communes in administrative France. Map 7.1 identifies the regions and traces the departments. We have occasion to discuss many of the individual regions at many points in this chapter without making explicit reference to this map and trust the reader to use it as required. French economic geographers have been engaged for decades in the creation of a rich set of maps describing the economic activity of their country. Perhaps the most widely cited and the most impressive are those that have been done by the team of Roger Brunet for the government regional development agency DATAR (the Délégation à l'aménagement du territoire et à l'action régionale).[2] This work has given us the frequently reproduced so-called blue banana map, showing the concentration of economic activity in a crescent stretching from south-east England through the Low Countries, the Rhine corridor and Switzerland to northern Italy. North–east France is included in this relatively dynamic area. Since these mappings are so readily available they are not reproduced here. The observations that this set of maps yield can be represented summarily with a map of France that is divided as in Map 7.2.[3] The line which runs from Le Havre in the north–west to Marseille in the south–east gives a rough understanding of the economic division of the country into two distinct parts. While such geographic demarcations are usually a bit forced and obfuscate as much as they clarify in this case several valid distinctions can be made. This is due largely to the fact that the south and west of France (hereafter the west) are linked to the sea while the north and east (hereafter the east) face the land mass of Europe. This latter half of the country has been historically linked to Germany, northern Italy, England and the Low Countries in a way that has not been true of the western part. The ports on the Atlantic Coast have served as points of access to the western hemisphere and the Mediterranean ports have given similar access to North Africa and the Middle East. When the Mediterranean economy is strong, the Rhône River has facilitated contact between the two economies with Lyon as the focal point of trading activity. Thus the east has been linked to areas of industry, finance and commerce, while the west has been dominated by trading, shipping, fishing and

Map 7.1: The regions of France

agriculture. This division has been strengthened by the further development of the blue banana, high-activity crescent, as a consequence of the integration of markets and production encouraged by the formation of the European Economic Community and the European Union.

When we examine the two parts of this map several important observations can be made. First, there is the nature of settlement and

habitation. The eastern part includes the largest urban centers in France –
Paris, Lyon, Marseille and Lille, the four urban centers with populations
exceeding 1 million inhabitants, while in the west there are only the less
important cities of Bordeaux, Toulouse, and Nantes, with populations of
between 500,000 and 750,000. Of the ten most densely populated of France's
22 regions, only Brittany is in the west. This is shown in Map 7.3. During

Map 7.2: The economic division of France

the past two decades, however, the most rapid growth in population has
occurred along the Atlantic Coast, along the Mediterranean and in the south-
east from Lyon southward.[4] Population growth due to births is directly
correlated with city size, with the smallest towns experiencing an annual
growth rate of 0.15 per cent while Paris recorded a rate of 0.84. However, just
the reverse is true with migratory flows. Here urban areas suffered an outflow
of 0.08 per cent (with 0.24 for Paris) while rural areas gained 0.67.[5] The net
movement into Paris has fallen from an inflow of 700,000 during 1954–62 to

an outflow of roughly the same magnitude during the 1990s.[6] As can be noted from Figure 7.1, the growth of population between 1962 and the predicted figures for 2015 is limited entirely to suburbs and to smaller towns. Large cities grew by 2.5 million between 1962 and 1975 but are projected to be stagnant for the rest of the period; rural areas show a steady decline from 2.9 million in 1962 to only 1.9 million by 2015. Suburbs and smaller towns grow

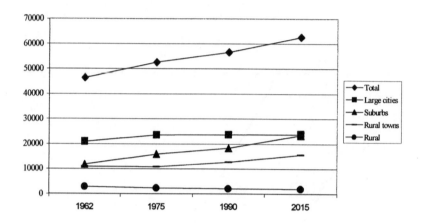

Source: DATAR, *Débat national pour l'aménagement du territoire*, Paris: La documentation Française, 1994, p. 20.

Figure 7.1: Distribution of the French population, 1962-2015

from 22.7 to 38.9 million.[7] This will be discussed further later in this chapter, but it does suggest that the rural to large city migration that characterized the post-war years has been halted and been replaced by movement to smaller cities.

Second, with the exception of the wine-growing area of Champagne, all the departments in which the agricultural labor force exceeds 15 per cent of total employment are in the west. Conversely, with few exceptions the departments in which manufacturing accounts for at least 25 per cent of the labor force are all concentrated in the east. Of France's 22 regions just five in the east, Île-de-France, Rhône-Alpes, Lorraine, Alsace and Nord-Pas-de-Calais, account for over 51 per cent of industrial output and over 46 per cent of industrial employment. Industrial activity has been drawn to the coal-rich areas along the Belgian and German borders, and to the large markets of these densely populated areas. As a consequence, the largest manufacturing centers and those with the largest individual facilities are located in the east, although Aérospatiale is in Toulouse and Citroën has a large plant in Rennes.

The third point that can be made using Map 7.2 is the location of high-technology activities. The three largest concentrations are in Paris, Lyon and Grenoble, and important centers are developing in Sophia-Antipolis, near Nice, in Strasbourg and in Villeneuve-d'Ascq on the Belgian border, and the most impressive infrastructure of science parks, technopoles and centers of

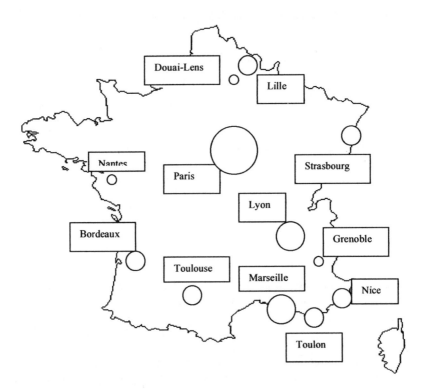

Map 7.3 Major population centers of France

innovation is located at numerous places throughout the east. In the west, the area of Toulouse-Montpellier has important technopoles and the Multipole technologique régional du Languedoc is located there. Furthermore, it has been the policy of the government for the past 30 years to build up the universities and research and development establishments outside the major urban centers and this has helped many of the smaller cities of the west. In fact a map of the number of university students in France would show a rather even distribution throughout the country, although Paris dwarfs any other urban area.[8]

Fourth, data on output per employee indicate that productivity is highest in the regions of the east with Île-de-France, Rhône-Alpes, Alsace and Provence-Alpes-Côte d'Azur at the head of the ranking. Productivity in regions of the west is, with the exception of Centre, below 90 per cent of the national average.[9] Labor productivity tends to be directly correlated with city

Table 7.1: Population of France's largest cities

City	1999	1990
Paris	9,622,507	9,318,821
Marseille-Ais-en-Provence	1,349,772	1,230,936
Lyon	1,348,772	1,262,223
Lille	1,000,000	959,234
Nice	888,784	516,740
Toulouse	761,090	496,078
Bordeaux	753,931	696,364
Nantes	544,932	496,078
Toulon	519,640	437,553
Douai-Lens	518,727	323,174
Strasbourg	427,245	388,483
Grenoble	419,334	404,733

Source: Forte extension des villes entre 1990 et 1999,' *INSEE Première*, no. 707, Paris: INSEE, April 2000

size, due to the attractiveness of large cities for the private sector service activities and headquarter functions, and the concentration in urban areas of highly educated professionals and government bureaucracies. The location of France's largest cities in the east explains the productivity differences between east and west.

Fifth, the concentration of manufacturing and private sector services in the east results in a corresponding concentration of foreign direct investment and of corporate head offices there. Paris is host to 22.9 per cent of foreign direct investment in France and six other regions of the east have between 6 per cent and 10.3 per cent. Only two regions of the west, Acquitaine (Bordeaux) and Pays-de-Loire (Nantes and Saint Nazaire) have between 3 and 6 per cent and all of the others have less than 3 per cent.[10] Paris is by far the head office leader in France, with Lyon the only other major center. It is, however, also true that Paris has seen its ranking as a corporate center deteriorate in the global hierarchy from second to London at the beginning of the twentieth century to fifth at its close, behind New York, Tokyo, London and Frankfurt. Of the 50 largest US multinational firms, 31 have subsidiaries in Europe but only three are located in Paris. Daniel Noin attributes this to France's long history of anti-liberal, interventionist policy.[11] As has been argued throughout this book, France has changed its approach to regulation in response to the exigencies of globalization, but it will take some time before foreign business leaders will consider that France is as attractive as England, the Netherlands or Belgium.

Finally, commercial activity and the service sector are heavily concentrated in Paris, with Lyon a distant second. Few of these activities are located in the center of France, in the circle bordered by Paris, Lyon, Toulouse, Bordeaux and Nantes. In fact, over 48 per cent of service sector employment and over 53 per cent of service sector production is concentrated in just four of France's regions, Île-de-France, Rhône-Alpes, Provence-Alpes-Côte d'Azur and Nord-Pas-de-Calais – all in the east. These four regions also account for 56 per cent of production in the private sector, with the public sector (education, administration, transportation, and so forth) equal to or greater than the private sector in all of France's regions but Île-de-France and Rhône-Alpes, in which Paris and Lyon are located.

The basic conclusion to be drawn from examination of the two France's, is that French regions to the east of the line are more densely populated, urban, industrial, connected with the dynamic economies of the Rhine corridor, internationally engaged, and productive. Those to the west are relatively agricultural, sea-oriented, and rural. This is the understanding that has motivated French regional policy throughout the post-war period.

Another way of looking at the French economic space is that given in Map 7.4, taken from a representation of the European economic space by the Commission of the EU. Each macro-region shown in Map 7.4 is defined by its economic function, its per capita income, and its place in Europe, and is part of a region that extends into the contiguous economic space. The District of the Capitals included London, Benelux, the western part of Germany, and the Paris basin. The Atlantic Arc runs northward to Wales, Ireland and western Scotland, and southward along the Atlantic coast of the Iberian Peninsula. The Western Mediterranean begins at Gibralter and ends in north-western Italy. The Alpine region links Rhône-Alpes and Franche-Comté with northern Italy, Switzerland and southern Germany. Finally, the Central Core runs through Spain to the borders of Portugal and Andalusia. The Commission has defined each region in terms of its characteristics and its strengths and weaknesses.[12] Reviewing this schema would add details to what has just been presented but would not be in conflict with it. What it does do for us is make explicit that these French regions must be seen in the context of a greater EU or even a European economic space which exerts its force increasingly as the integration process continues.

POLICY INITIATIVES

Through the 1970s France remained one of Europe's most centralized and insular national economies. All roads led to Paris and all political initiatives emanated from the capital. France was properly seen as being composed of Paris, of provincial cities of varying size and regional importance and of sparsely populated rural areas. The roots of this structure are fixed in the seventeenth century and the policies of Louis XIV and Colbert but were perfectly consistent with the inclinations of Charles de Gaulle in the 1960s.

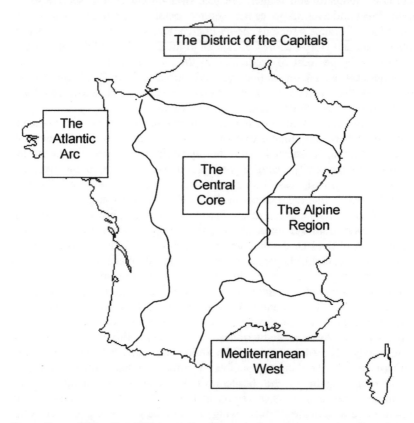

Source: *Europe 2000+, Coopération pour l'aménagement du territoire européeen*, Brussels: Commissison of the European Union, 1994

Map 7.4: The European macro-regions that include France

Fundamental to this policy of centralization was the perceived need to strengthen the nation militarily and economically in the context of struggle with competing nations, whether Spain or England or, finally, Germany. In this effort France was reasonably successful until the Second World War. Paris was unquestionably the premier city of Europe, with unrivaled supremacy in culture, fashion and intellectual life. It was a powerful center of business decision-making and of finance. The provincial cities developed their specialized economies, grew as regional centers and became characterized by their own individualized assets.

However, not all was as idyllic as it appeared to visitors. Shortly after the conclusion of the Second World War a government agency, the Délégation générale de l'équipement national, issued a report in 1948 in which it was argued that the concentration of industrial activity in large agglomerations was creating unhealthy conditions, congestion, and threats to social stability.[13] Gaining greater publicity was the book by Jean-François Gravier, *Paris et le désert français*, which was published in 1947.[14] In this work Gravier set the opulence of Paris against the relative backwardness of the rest of the country and began a discussion of geographic inequalities that is still with us today. It was indicative of a new mentality that activities should be evaluated using the economist's notion of efficient allocation of resources rather than the status or grandeur of the nation as a primary criterion. As a result of this critique of the consequences of centralization an agency was created in 1948 that was charged with management of the spatial distribution of economic activity (regional development) in France, the Direction de l'aménagement du territoire. Then in 1950 a budget line, Fonds national d'aménagement du territoire, was established that would provide financial support for various initiatives. In 1955 the national program was restructured into programs for 22 newly created regional entities.

The crucial development in regional policy was the establishment in 1963 of the Délégation à l'aménagement du territoire et à l'action régionale (DATAR). The 1960s and 1970s are generally considered to be the glory years for DATAR, since increased attention was given to regional development and this agency of the central state was completely in charge of planning and implementation of initiatives approved by the Interdepartmental Committee for Regional Policy (CIAT). The primary objective of CIAT was that of transferring employment opportunities and offering various subsidies for industrial relocation to the less developed areas of France; however, all areas were given attention. Priorities were increasingly governed by the state of the economy. The period of low unemployment and rapid growth extended into the early 1970s, so government revenues were readily available to fund projects, and addressing the east–west imbalance could be almost the sole priority. After the economic downturn in 1973 increased attention had to be given to areas throughout the country that were experiencing the negative consequences of higher energy costs, de-industrialization and global restructuring.

The first effort was to reduce the economic weight of Paris. This will be examined in greater detail below, but for now it will suffice to note that both Gravier's book and the establishment of DATAR set the context for discussion of policies that could reverse the flow of skilled people and high-level economic functions from all reaches of the hexagon to the capital. In 1964 an initiative was begun to make six provincial cities increasingly attractive to firms and to develop their social, educational and cultural assets. The cities chosen were: Lille, Nancy, Lyon, Marseille, Bordeaux and Nantes. In 1970 four others were added: Clermont-Ferrand, Dijon, Nice and Rennes. The largest and most suitably situated of them, Lyon, Lille and Marseille, were projected to enhance their competitiveness with cities of similar size in neighboring countries, cities such as Frankfurt, Milan and Barcelona.[15] This initiative has had some success, especially with Lyon and Lille, but at the cost of generating some ill-will with smaller cities in their region which felt they were becoming dominated by the chosen *métropoles d'équilibre*, as the ten were called. This called forth a program of investment in 73 cities with populations between 20,000 and 100,000. These *villes moyennes* received funding to rehabilitate older housing, to create pedestrian walk ways and shopping streets, to conserve their architectural heritage, and to redevelop their town centers.

A final program of this period was the development of so-called new towns. One of the primary objectives was to reduce pressure on the larger cities that were experiencing robust expansion and to restructure their suburban areas. Thus, all the new towns were established in close proximity to Lille, Lyon and Mareille and in the Parisian basin. Funding for this program included support for rapid transport systems, development of commercial centers and other infrastructure projects. The results were mixed, for example the town near Lyon, L'Isle d'Abeau, never took off since it was too distant from the city, and the towns in proximity to Paris grew to the point of becoming part of the continuing problem of the Parisian basin rather than the solution to it.

The end of *les trentes glorieuses* in the early 1970s brought with it a set of new economic realities that forced a major change in the conduct of French regional policy. We have already noted what must be considered to be the impacts of globalization: de-industrialization and restructuring. Existing regional specializations that provided a comparative advantage in a relatively closed and managed economy lost their validity in this newly developing environment. The changes in the technologies of communication and transportation caused the economic impact of distance to be reconsidered and improvements in production technologies resulted in a spatial restructuring of economic activity. By this time the European Economic Community had passed its fifteenth birthday and was responding to these changes by enhancing its own regional development and agricultural support programs. Gradually national governments began to cede policy formulation to sub-national levels of government and to recognize the growing role of Brussels in cooperative ventures with cities and regions.

In 1981 the Socialist government of François Mitterand was elected to power. With an understanding of these dramatic changes and with thoughts of increased participatory democracy and of returning power over the state to the people, the Socialists began a serious plan of decentralization. The minister in charge was Gaston Defferre and during 1982–3 he introduced several important reforms. The regions were given increased participation, that is legal competence, in overall economic planning and in regional planning, thus breaking the absolute control exercised by the national government in these matters. Proportional representation was introduced in all local elections as a means of reducing the power of mayors and other local authorities. It also meant that the mayor would be confronted by a democratically elected opposition that would also be experienced in governance should there be a change in the party that formed the government. Prior to this reform local governments were made up entirely of one party in a first-past-the-post system. Local communities and departments were given increased responsibility for planning in rural areas and in mountainous areas, two geographical categories that were felt to have distinctive situations and concerns. Finally, the Socialists brought to an end the so-called *cumul des mandats*, or the ability of one individual to hold simultaneously several elected positions in different levels of government. This reform limited the influence one individual could accumulate and it forced him or her to chose between local, regional or national responsibilities.[16]

The most important law, Droits et Liberté des Communes, des Départements et des Régions, was introduced on March 2, 1982. Jean-François Eck states that this law 'gave realization for the first time to an authentic decentralization.'[17] It consisted of five principle points:[18]

1. the power of the prefect, the representative of the central state, in regional development was abolished;
2. this power was transferred to the president of the elected *conseil général*;
3. the region was recognized to have full competence and was administered by its own elected *conseil regional*;
4. the central state transferred sets of policy competences to the commune, the department and the region; and
5. the several financial programs that had been administered by the central government were transferred as block grants to the local authorities.

Gérard-François Dumont puts it slightly differently and sees the funding of the state being structured around four principles that are directly linked to laws passed in 1972 and 1977:

1. aid to areas in difficulty was reaffirmed but the procedures for getting access to it were significantly improved and the powers of local authorities were strengthened;
2. while the powers of the central state were confirmed the powers of local authorities were clarified;
3. the regions were given responsibility for economic development at the regional level; and
4. local authorities were given greater freedom in the granting of indirect assistance, although some of these initiatives were given more precise limits.[19]

One observer has written:

In the administrative history of France, these measures are of a magnitude that is without precedence since the beginning of the nineteenth century. No other individual has reshaped so many aspects of public policy. Gaston Defferre, minister of the interior and of decentralization, thus joins Napoleon Bonaparte, but in presenting an initiative in exactly the opposite direction.[20]

He also noted that in contrast with other reforms of the period, the 1982 law was imposed from the center with no experimentation beforehand and with no consultation with the regions or other local authorities.

These reforms authorized local authorities to offer a variety of subsidies, locational inducements, guarantees for loans, and support for building and infrastructure initiatives. During 1982–9 expenditures by local authorities on infrastructure and facilities rose from 131 per cent of that of the central government to 189 per cent. They were also given authority to give companies partial or full exemptions from certain financial obligations or taxes. Unfortunately, the coordination among the various levels of government was not always as clearly defined as it should have been. Catherine Grémion concludes that especially at the lower levels of government the marriage between the elected and the bureaucrats was a forced marriage, that many of the administrators were poorly qualified, that large cities managed better than their smaller and poorer counterparts, and that "decentralization led to a balkanization of public policy" at this level.[21]

Albert Mabileau is equally critical of the implementation of the 1982 reforms. He argues that 'decentralization is not yet impregnated in the spirit of the French, and that lasting changes will come only in the long term.'[22] However, he is optimistic about the future. He suggests that decentralization has brought a change from the principle of rationality that has been in place since the nineteenth century to the principle of complexity in which multiple levels of government are involved in decision-making. According to Mabileau France has experienced a localization of national policy and a nationalization of local policy and considerations of efficiency have given priority to a logic of proximity in policy-formulation and administration – similar to the logic of subsidiarity that has become so important in the European Union. What has emerged that remains to be resolved is the conflict between the national interest and the local interest. Local interest unconstrained has always been viewed in France as anarchic and destructive of the well-being of the French people. He concludes that 'one sees the emergence of new values at the local level; the logic of proximity that is linked to considerations of productivity and efficiency.'[23]

Both Grémion and Malibeau wrote on the eve of the second round of major reforms – those of May 1991 and February 1992. These new laws had the effect of reviving the process of decentralization. The 1991 law was formally limited in its scope as it gave to Corsica 'laws for preservation of its cultural identity and for defense of its economic and social interests.'[24] But in its Girondian spirit it led directly to the law of February 6, 1992, which completed the process initiated in 1982 and dealt with the shortcomings that were noted by Grémion and Malibeau. Its 135 articles clarified the division of responsibilities and competence among the various levels of government, it made the prefect more responsible for managing this division of labor, and it greatly enhanced public access to the process of policy making. Bruno Rémond argues that the 1992 law 'amplified the shock wave created by the 1982 decentralization law, and it opted for a vision that was more convivial and more collegial. In his view, France decentralized in order to become more democratic.'[25]

Little done by the French state is devoid of its political connotations and decentralization was no exception. Having come to power the Socialists had to chart their own course if they wanted to retain office past the first mandate. While it was necessary to make some accommodation with the Communists they also wanted to draw a clear line between the two parties and their ideologies. Ronald Tiersky captures this succinctly:

> For the Socialists, decentralization was thus a double good: on the one hand, a classic French struggle, endorsed by all republicans, to liberalize the state; on the other hand, a Socialist battle against Leninism and Stalinism inside the French left. Decentralization would simultaneously undo the excessive French centralization of state power and impose their own Socialist conception to the Communists.[26]

However, he goes on to conclude that 'the French left in the Mitterrand era succeeded excellently at what was French in their program, above all in rallying and reforming the republic, but only poorly in what was Socialist.' Perhaps the economic and political situation in which France found itself from this period on made such a programme no longer achievable.

Finally, in 1995, Interior Minister Charles Pasqua tried to revitalize DATAR and the state role in regional policy with the Loi d'orientation pour l'aménagement et le développement du territoire. This law was designed very ambitiously to give citizens in all parts of France equality of opportunity and to reduce the inequalities in the conditions of life that were linked to geography.[27] It aimed to accomplish these goals through the introduction of programs aimed at areas that remain the focus of policy today: troubled suburbs, isolated rural areas, and what were referred to as fragile zones in declining industrial basins. There were programs for remote mountainous areas and for the Atlantic coast – the littoral. This latter initiative gained considerable attention, perhaps because of the activity of some of the universities located there. An example of this is the work done by Claude Lacour at the University of Bordeaux on *l'arc atlantique*, or the cities of the Atlantic littoral.[28] A policy of positive discrimination was to be carried out primarily by easing the fiscal burdens of firms operating in these areas with the intention of countering certain specific handicaps of these areas. Unfortunately, budgetary considerations have constrained implementation of these measures, and they were to be introduced in an environment that was less accepting of central state intervention than it was in 1982. Nonetheless, Daniel Noin has concluded that 'regional policy can no longer be the sometimes incoherent addition of multiple demands prescribed by the elites; instead they are invited to consider policy ordered by and which meets the long term needs of the affected populations.'[29]

In spite of all of this, Claude du Granrut reminds us that 'decentralization preserved the unitary character of the state, which remains sovereign.' The process involves the state transferring responsibilities to lower levels of government, rather than responsibilities being taken from it, and the sub-national entities administer rather than govern.[30]

The new economic and political climate of the 1990s has been such as to give priority to two aspects of regional development which we will now examine: expenditures on infrastructure and the policies of the European Union.

Economists have long understood the importance of infrastructure, communications and transportation in particular, in the determination of the location of economic activity. Until recently, investment in infrastructure was used to integrate areas that were rich in raw materials or had promising markets into the economic area of the dominant economic powers. The economic viability of such colonies as Canada and Australia or those in Africa and Asia hinged on their ability to develop cost-efficient ways which would aid mutual access between them and the imperial center. In recent decades, investment in infrastructure has been instrumental in making distant underdeveloped parts of the world efficient areas for production of manufactured goods. With good transportation and communication structures, and increasingly with a suitably educated labor force, low-wage countries have become very attractive as sites of production of goods that had hitherto been manufactured in established industrial countries, such as France. This has given rise to the phenomena of deindustrialization and global restructuring, that we have already discussed above.

When we look at France we find that the traditional rail and road network was adequate to meet the needs of the day, but soon proved to be a hindrance to economic development. The state met the challenge with a substantial expansion of rapid transportation options. During the past 30 years the autoroute network has been expanded eight-fold and the Train à Grande Vitesse (TGV), the high-speed rail system for which France is so justly renowned, was introduced in the early 1980s. While the autoroute system provides service for all regions, the TGV lines service primarily a relatively small number of larger cities. Air service has expanded during the post-war years, in part because of the subsidies given by the state to provincial/regional airports and small air carriers in the belief that this would provide a crucial stimulus to local economic development. Nonetheless, a map of air traffic would show that it is dominated by six major links between Paris and the following cities: Marseille, Nice, Toulouse, Bordeaux, Montpellier and Strasbourg. We will examine the impacts these transportation initiatives have had on regional development later in this chapter. Far less significant transversal linkages are based on Lyon with connections to Lille, Nantes, Bordeaux, Toulouse and Nice. As we will note below, the air link between Paris and Lyon has lost out to competition from the TGV service. This multi-modal high speed transportation network has undoubtedly allowed for a more efficient production and distribution system to be developed during the past three decades. However, the most important question relates to the impacts it has had on the spatial distribution of economic activity throughout France and the impacts this has had on individual cities and towns. We will return to this question shortly.

Within the economic space of the European Community/Union the development of a significantly more efficient transportation system has also had powerful economic impacts. First, the mere speed of the new trains reduces the time each traveler must allocate to the trip. While an hour here or an hour there may seem trivial, if one can manage to do the round-trip between Bordeaux or Lyon and Paris in one day rather than staying over in a hotel the savings becomes more apparent. In contrast to air travel, with its trip between the center city and the airport and the waiting and queuing one does, virtually all of rail travel time can be devoted to some form of work-related activity.

Second, moving goods and people faster has important consequences for both the center, Paris, and the provincial cities. Unfortunately these consequences are not as clear-cut as one would like. Faster and more frequent travel, and better telecommunication, may enable the center to extend its reach into the rest of the country, in which case Paris gains relative to other cities. Decentralization may then mean no more than the extension of the control by Paris into other regions through a subsidiary office that is in effect little more than another floor in the headquarters office. On the other hand, Ian Thompson has noted that having a TGV line between Paris and Lyon has resulted in little of this sort of decentralization. For Lyon and other cities 'the TGV gives the peripheral regions a greater opportunity to develop their own initiatives.'[31] The net effect is uncertain in the abstract, and we shall have an opportunity to examine it more closely later in this chapter when we study the experience of Lyon. What appears to be clear, however, is that the TGV connection is in itself not sufficient to have a positive impact on a town or city. Daniel Noin puts it very bluntly: 'The grand transportation infrastructure projects have benefited primarily the large cities.'[32] For a city to benefit from being a stop on a TGV line it has to have something that makes it attractive in its own self. For example, Tours has benefited from its TGV connection with Paris, now just one hour away, whereas its neighboring city Vendôme has not. Some professionals choose to live in Tours and commute to jobs in Paris and others do just the opposite. Tours is a university town and has all the attractions that come with that status, it has an attractive historic district, and it is a center of a distinctive food and wine culture; it is an attractive place for professionals to live. Thus during the first years of the TGV service, from 1982 to 1990 the rate of population growth of its region, Center, was seventh highest out of 22 regions. Of those seven regions, four were in the high population growth of southern France; only Île-de-France (the region of Paris) and Upper Normandy had higher rates of population growth.

Third, with the older pre-TGV and pre-autoroute system the space between urban centers was a continuous transition between larger and smaller towns with each deriving some benefit from the flow of traffic. Some of this benefit was simply that of meeting the needs of travelers passing through, but some of it was also an attractive location for lower-level economic activities. With high-speed rail and road travel the stops are far less frequent and the flow of traffic gives absolutely no benefit to locations that are not already rather large and that justify a halt in the traffic flow. Thus the newer system may lead to the marginalization of smaller towns which have no access or, in the words of R.W. Vickerman, 'the long-term effect is towards an economic core of a set of discontiguous metropolitan regions.'[33] This also suggests that towns near a major urban center or between two of them, but with no immediate access to the TGV, may actually be in the periphery, in an economic rather than geographic sense, whereas a town that is quite distant from, say, Paris or Lyon may be in the center if it has a good infrastructure linkage with that major city.

The French introduced their technologically advanced TGV system with the opening of the south-east line from Paris to Lyon in two stages during 1981–3. With newly constructed dedicated railways, speeds of up to 270 km/hour were attained. Extensions of this line were made to Valence (1992–4) and to Marseille and Montpellier (1999–2000). These are plansto continue the service from Lyon to Geneva and to Turin, and from Montpelier through Perpignan to Barcelona. The second line, TGV Atlantique, with lines to Tours and to Le Mans was completed during 1989–90, with extensions on existing infrastructure through Nantes and Rennes to the Brittany coast and from Tours to La Rochelle, Toulouse, and Bordeaux and Spain. In 1993 TGV Nord/Euro-Star from Paris through Lille to Calais and the tunnel to England completed the existing domestic network. Lille is also an important point on the Paris–Brussels Thalys line. The final projected element in the network will be TGV Est, from Paris to Strasbourg, which is anticipated to be in service in the very near future. More striking is the suggestion that the traditional structure of all lines leading to Paris be broken. As it is, if one wants to travel by TGV from Bordeaux to Marseille or Lyon, it is necessary to travel to Paris and change trains to the South-east line. So a Bordeaux–Toulouse–Narbonne line is planned. Another proposed line is from the Paris–Lyon line to Mulhouse and Basel.

In all of this there is clearly a strategy with two objectives at work. First, there is the desire to provide a fast, efficient and popular domestic rail network for France itself. Rail travel time from Paris to Bordeaux has been reduced from 4.5 hours to 3, and from Paris to Lyon from about 4.5 hours to 2, with an hourly service. Clearly it poses a challenge to both air and road travel. Second, there is the linkage of the domestic network to the rail systems of the United Kingdom, Belgium, Germany, Switzerland, Italy and Spain, thus putting France at the center of the emerging European high-speed rail system. France's position in Europe is such that it is well placed to serve as a crossroads for high-speed movements of goods and people. While Germany has far and away the heaviest highway and rail traffic, France is the link between the Iberian and Italian peninsulas and Northern Europe and the United Kingdom. The TGV now allows travelers to cross France in no more than five hours. This role will be even more significant with completion of the proposed 54 km tunnel under the Alps linking Lyon with Turin for both freight and high-speed passenger trains, which will enable north–south traffic to avoid the time-consuming Swiss and Austrian mountains, the Paris–Strasbourg link to the German system, and extension of the Paris–Bordeaux line into Spain.

Figures for traffic on the TGV south-east line from Paris to Lyon give an indication of the extent to which this initiative has been successful. Between 1980 and 1992 total passenger traffic rose from 12.5 million to 22.9 million. Traffic on conventional lines fell from 12.5 to 4 million in 1987, where it stabilized, but TGV traffic rose from 0 to 18.9 million by 1992. Thus over 82 per cent of passenger traffic was handled by the TGV, and conventional train traffic remained at 4 million passengers. All of the growth in traffic during this period was accounted for by the high-speed system. With regard to the rail system as a whole, in 1996 the TGV accounted for 24.79 billion passenger miles, and the traditional lines 18.86 billion. By 1998 the TGV traffic had increased by 29.9 per cent, while the traditional traffic fell by 12.5 per cent. Clearly the public was pleased to have the option of high-speed travel. The impacts of the TGV on both air and road travel have been considerable. As Table 7.2 indicates, air traffic has shown the largest percentage increase since 1980 while bus and rail have stagnated. Within its first decade of operation the TGV surged past air traffic and has now more than doubled it. For example, during its first decade of operation air travel between Paris and Lyon experienced a diversion of about 70 per cent to rail.[34]

Table 7.2: Domestic passenger traffic, selected years, 1980–99

	1980	1990	1995	1999
Automobile	452.5	585.6	64.3	708.4
Bus	36.0	41.3	41.6	42.7
Rail	54.5	63.7	55.6	64.5
of which TGV	...	14.9	21.4	30.6
Air	5.7	11.4	12.7	14.5

Source: *La France en bref: Edition 2000*, Paris: INSEE, 2000, p. 19

While land transportation has been stressed here, we must not forget the impact that canals have had on the movement of bulk commodities and on the location of certain activities related to them. The same must be said about sea ports and the development of efficient inter-modal transportation linking sea with both rail and road transportation. These transportation infrastructures have long been important for the French economy but have not experienced the same degree of transformation that has been true of rail and road services.

The final aspect of French regional policy we will examine is the increasing role of the policies of the European Union. While the economic integration process in Europe began with the Treaty of Rome in 1957–8, the member countries did not turn their attention to regional policy until 30 years later. The first task was, of course, that of the difficult one of creating a seamless economic space among the member nations. Regional impacts were either ignored or it was assumed that they would be ameliorated through trickle-down effects emanating from the most dynamic regions.[35] Those regions that were recognized as being unlikely to benefit from the increased growth and efficiency of the integration process were regions that were largely agricultural in their economic structure, and it was felt they would benefit from the Common Agricultural Policy, or coal and steel regions in decline, which would benefit from policies of the European Coal and Steel Community. Only in 1985 with the preparatory work for the Single Europe Act (1988) was it explicitly recognized that the integration process had the potentiality of increasing the economic strength of the already strong regions and weakening that of the already weak. Thus, the concern was raised that regional income and economic activity disparities could be widened. Decentralization in France and the increased interest of the EU in regional policy were part of a global movement that supported both initiatives and thus made them compatible and, in turn, mutually supportive.

If membership had been limited to the original six countries, only France west of the diagonal, central and southern Italy and the relatively prosperous north of Germany would not have been in the high economic activity crescent that was referred to above. But expansion of membership to 15 has added the Iberian Peninsula, Greece, Ireland, the three Nordic members and the United Kingdom. Of these additions, only south-east England lies in the crescent. At the date of membership, per capita incomes in Spain, Portugal, Greece and Ireland were considerably below those of the other members. Research demonstrates that income disparities among member nations and among regions diminished during the first two decades of the European Economic Community, but that after 1980 the rate of convergence slowed among nations and actually ceased among regions.[36] Dunford and Hudson argue that inequality among regions within member countries actually increased through the 1980s and into the 1990s.[37]

In response to this concern, the European Community introduced a package of reforms in 1988 that included increased funding and four principles for reform: concentration, programming, partnership and additionality.[38] Concentration referred to the fact that regional development funds would be spent in regions accounting for only 51.6 per cent of the EU population. Objective 1 regions would have 26.6 per cent of the population, objective 2 regions, 16.8 per cent, and objective 5b would have 8.2 per cent. Objective 1 regions received about 60 per cent of funds during 1989–93 and 70 per cent during 1994–9. Programming referred to a shift from project financing to multi-year support – three years for industrial reconversion plans and six years for all others. The principle of partnership meant that there would be explicit cooperation in planning, financing and evaluation of contracts by the EU Commission, the national state, and regional and local authorities. Finally, additionality ensured that assistance from Brussels had to be in addition to, rather than a substitute for, funding from other levels of government. This had developed into a significant problem and was projected to be even more widespread as national governments were obligated to conform to the convergence criteria for introduction of the common currency.

How did these reforms and indeed the policies of Brussels in general affect regions in France? The questions such as those relating to convergence or divergence of French regions, of changes in the urban hierarchy, and of the development of new specializations in the European economic space will be dealt with shortly. For the moment we will concern ourselves only with the expenditure of funds by the EU and the impacts on the structure of decision-making in France. Funding was to be given to six types of regions that were deemed to be in need of assistance:

Objective 1   Underdeveloped regions.
Objective 2   Regions subject to industrial decline.
Objective 3   Regions in which there was long-term unemployment and in which youth were excluded from employment.
Objective 4   Regions that were experiencing industrial restructuring.
Objective 5a Regions with needs to adapt agricultural and fishing Economies.
Objective 5b Rural regions.

With the exception of Île-de-France, all of France's regions benefit from EU funding, primarily from objectives 2 and 5b. Objective 2 funds are scattered lightly throughout the country but there are heavy concentrations in Nord-Pas-de-Calais and Franche Comté. Objective 5b funding is given to almost all departments with the exception of the large metropolitan areas of Paris, Lyon, Marseille, Nice and Bordeaux. The only area to receive objective 1 funding is that of Valenciennes-Douai in Nord-Pas-de-Calais. In addition to these programs explicitly aimed at regions, in certain conditions other programs are geographically based, and many of France's regions have benefited from them. The *Arc Atlantic* program funds development of the western coast line from Brittanny to the Spanish border. Eleven regions that are on France's land borders benefit from the INTERREG program that funds trans-border Euro regions. More will be said about this shortly with regard to Alsace and the trans-Rhine region. When Spain and Portugal entered the EEC, the Integrated Mediterranean Program gave support beginning in 1989 to regions along the south coast of France to compensate for competition they would feel from products of the new entrants.[39] The list of other projects from which French regions have benefited is too extensive to be detailed here.

There is considerable concern among EU watchers that the funding that is available will not be adequate to materially affect regional incomes. First, the total EU budget is less than 2 per cent of the combined GDP of the15 members. Thus, the allocation to structural funds cannot be enough in itself to have the desired effect. Second, with the adoption of the single currency initiative national budgets will be forced to comply with the convergence criteria that the budget deficit be no more than 3 per cent of GDP and that the national debt be reduced to 60 per cent of GDP. National budgets of most countries have been under this constraint for most of the 1990s. Third, while it was agreed in 1992 at the Edinburgh summit that these funds should be doubled over a period of seven years (1993–9), in fact funding increased between 1994 and 1999 by only 36 per cent, in real terms. Fourth, the extension of membership to Central Europe that has been agreed to in Nice will either force the EU to dramatically increase regional development funding so that new members can be treated as equals with regions of the current 15 members, or funding will have to be spread more thinly to cover both existing and new members, or a two-tier system will have to be introduced. All options have the potential for raising enormous difficulties.

SUB-NATIONAL ECONOMIES IN A DECENTRALIZED FRANCE

The policies and the events that have been discussed in previous chapters of this book and the policies of France and the EU that have just been reviewed have certainly had their impacts on regional income disparities among French regions. In this section we will begin at the most general level with the two questions of whether there has been a convergence of incomes within France and how regional economic specialization has been affected. We have already noted that the concentration of economic activity in Paris has been recognized as a factor that hampers economic development in provincial cities and their regions. Policies targeted at Paris will be the second topic of this section. Finally, during the past 10–15 years two other significant developments have emerged – the entrepreneurial city and the trans-boundary Euro-region. Space does not allow a full examination of these fascinating issues, but we will study in some detail one example of each – Lyon and the Upper Rhine region.

Convergence or Divergence?

Income and employment throughout France have been powerfully affected by the complex of changes that have been manifest since the Second World War: trade liberalization, technological change, deindustrialization, restructuring, and price shocks to mention a few. After post-war reconstruction, the rapid growth until 1974 brought a steady diminution of regional differences. Barro and Sala-I-Martin show that this convergence continued until about 1980 at which point the rate of improvement was significantly reduced. They concluded that the rate of regional convergence throughout Europe, North America and Japan was roughly 2 per cent per year.[40] Cappelen, Fagerberg and Verspagen show us that between 1980 and 1995 regional income disparities in France actually experienced a slight increase.[41] The same conclusion is reached by Camagni in his study for the Ministerial Meeting on Regional Policy and Spatial Planning of the EU in 1996. He argues that any convergence among EU regions from the mid 1980s on is due entirely to the convergence of nations, with Ireland, Spain and Portugal significantly reducing their disadvantage.[42]   Finally, after surveying this literature Armstrong concluded: 'Whatever the outcome of tests of growth theories using EU regional data sets, it is clear that free market growth processes when left to their own devices are extraordinarily slow in bringing about the equalization of region disparities.'[43]   Thus, while the explicit objective of French regional policy has been the reduction of regional per capita income disparities, progress toward it has not advanced in recent years. Furthermore, even if equalization mechanisms do work the rate of progress is such that existing disparities will continue many decades into the future. Regarding French regions Surarez-Villa and Roura offer several observations. First, both the poorest, or objective 1 (only Douai-Valenciennes) and the old industrial regions in north and north-east France have lagged behind their counterparts in other EU countries. Second, both Rhône-Alpes and Languedoc have benefited from inward migration of skilled labor and from better transportation access to the more dynamic markets of the 'blue banana.' Finally, most of southern France is part of the high growth macro-region of Northern Italy and Mediterranean Spain.[44]   Figure 7-2 gives indices of per capita income for geographically contiguous clusters of French regions for

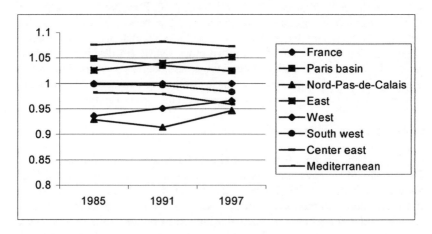

Note: The figures for France equal 1 for all three years.

Sources: Eurostat, *Basic Statistics of the Community*, and *Regions Statistical yearbook*, Luxembourg: Office for Official Publications of the Community

Figure 7.2: Regional performance, selected years

three years. Île-de-France is excluded as the data are not compatible with other regions. Île-de-France as a region is similar to Hamburg as a Land – each is a metropolitan area without an agricultural or rural component. Incomes in agriculture and in rural areas are lower than those in urban areas, so both Île-de-France and Hamburg have per capita incomes that are considerably higher than the national average. In 1993 per capita income in Hamburg exceeded the German average by 75 per cent and that in Paris exceeded the French average by 51 per cent. If a large rural area were included with the urban area both of these figures would be considerably closer to their respective national averages. This can be seen clearly in Table 7.3.

With exclusion of Île-de-France we can note the changes in per capita income in the other regional clusters. The first date is 1985, which is just as the decentralization initiative was begun. Between that year and 1997 the spread between the lowest and the highest regions diminished slightly from 0.929–1.076 to 0.946–1.072. Among the regional clusters we can note some significant movement: both East and West have improved, but Paris basin, South west and Mediterranean have deteriorated, and Nord-Pas-de-Calais slipped a bit at first but gained overall. Between 1985 and 1997 the position of Île-de-France improved by 3.5 per cent, so, while some provincial

Table 7.3: Per capita income, French regions, selected years

Region	1985	1991	1997
France	100.0	100.0	100.0
Île-de-France	149.2	149.4	154.4
Paris basin	92.6	91.2	89.4
Nord-Pas-de-Calais	82.0	80.5	82.6
East	90.6	91.6	91.8
West	82.7	83.8	84.3
South west	88.2	87.8	85.8
Center east	95.0	95.3	93.6
Mediterranean	86.7	86.2	83.7

Source: Eurostat, *Basic Statistics of the Community*, and *Regions Statistical yearbook*, Luxembourg: Office for Official Publications of the Community

regions have improved in relation to others, the gap between Paris and the provinces has, if anything, increased in spite of stated government policy. Data from the European Union indicate that regional disparities at the NUTS III or departmental level have steadily increased between 1991 and 1999 by almost 50 per cent. This was true of eight of 14 EU member countries

(Luxembourg was not included), with only Denmark, the Netherlands, Austria and Portugal showing a reduction in disparities and with Spain and Ireland unchanged.[45]

Finally, Map 7.5 shows us the performance of the regions with regard to increases in both employment and production during the 1990s. The black

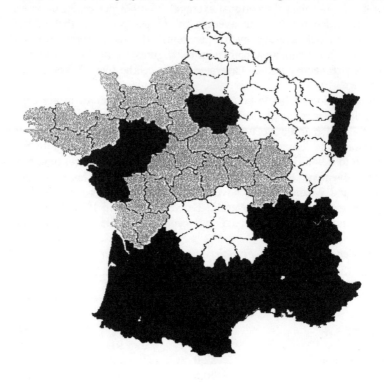

Map 7.5: Economic performance of French regions, 1990s

regions have shown the greatest strength and the white regions have been the lagging regions. The Auvergne and Limousin have historically lagged in economic performance, and the regions of the north and east are the areas in which traditional industry has been located – industry which is now suffering from restructuring on a continental and a global basis. Alsace benefits from its position next to Baden-Württemberg, as will be discussed below. Bretagne has benefited from improvements in its educational, research and transportation infrastructures and Ile-de-France is becoming a center of globalstature. The rest of the high-performing regions are in the south and are part of a general expansion of the Mediterranean economy, and benefit from the same infrastructure improvement as does Bretagne. One very interesting observation that can be made from this map is the fact that, with the exception of Alsace, the regions nearest the high-activity, blue banana corridor are doing the worst in France, while the 'peripheral' south and Bretagne are doing the best. Thus it would appear that the periphery need not be excluded from economic expansion, nor would it appear that proximity to the center is in itself a sufficient advantage.

The most widely supported explanations of successful regional growth stress investment in human and physical capital, adequate transportation and communication infrastructure, and either a capacity to innovate and create new knowledge or frictionless access to them. The infrastructure has already been discussed and the prominence of Paris in it was noted. While some provincial cities have benefited from the expansion of the system in recent decades, the most significant impacts have been on cities rather distant from Paris, such as Lyon, Marseille, Toulouse and Nice. The other major impact has been that of extending the 'reach' of Paris farther out into the countryside and to incorporate other cities within a radius of 150 miles into the Parisian orbit. In spite of much effort during the past decade, Lyon has not been able to assert itself as a major airport for international travel; connections to North America have started and then been cancelled. Proximity to Geneva as well as direct TGV connection to Charles de Gaulle airport in Paris seem to have proven to be hurdles that were too substantial to be cleared.

Higher education has been democratized since the 1960s to the degree that almost every community with a population of 60,000 or more has some educational institution, be it a university or technical institute or a specialized institute. Thirty-eight cities had some sort of university in 1995, and the share of all students who were in Paris fell from 35 per cent to 23 per cent during the period 1960–95.[46] However, moving the elite schools out of Paris has not been completely successful as the students feel a need to be in touch with the relevant ministries that are still located in the capital. We must also remember that not all institutions of higher education have the same impact on a city's economic development. For example, in Lyon Ch. Bernard University (Lyon 1) offers all of its diplomas in science, technology, and bio-pharmacy and related fields, while Lumière University (Lyon 2) and J. Moulin University (Lyon 3) concentrate their studies in languages, literature and other humanities, and in economics and business. Each university will have a positive impact on the economy of the city but each will be suited only for cities with specific roles and strategies for development. So simply spreading education more broadly throughout the country will not necessarily have the desired impact of reducing the centrality of Paris.

New Regional Specialization?

Economic theory would predict that opening the French market to competition from abroad and giving French firms access to foreign markets would lead to a redefinition of regional specialization. Some regions will experience positive impacts as their producers gain exports while others will suffer from import penetration of their previously protected domestic market. In this section of the chapter we will review some of the literature and data in an effort to gain some understanding as to the impacts that globalization has had on regional specialization within France. This impact is more difficult to determine at the sub-national level than it is at the national level because of the myriad factors that also influence changes in regional specialization. First, sub-national entities are never in control of policy since other levels of the administrative structure also have specific mandates that have impacts on economic development. Only in the unreal world in which there was perfect policy coordination and decision-makers had neither ego nor agenda would this disappear as a factor. Second, even if the region has the mandate in an area of policy it may not command the resources to enact its policies. Third, regions are often torn between the competing interests of rural and urban areas and fashioning a set of policies that meets both of these constituencies may be difficult if not impossible. Fourth, in France the success of a region or city is in part a function of the personality and access to Paris of its senior officials. An entrepreneurial city such as Lille or Lyon may be able to attract a Martine Aubrey or Raymond Barre, but those that cannot will find it difficult to make their voice heard. Fifth, the performance of any individual region will be affected by the performance of the national economy due to a variety of macro- and micro-economic conditions such as unemployment, taxation, interest rates, the exchange rate, and prices. Finally, markets are being opened at the same time that technology is advancing, the age and skill structures of the workforce are changing, other regions both in France and throughout the EU are adopting policies that affect their competitiveness, and a host of other things are happening. It is extremely difficult to sort through all these factors to determine how much of regional change is due to just one of them. Nonetheless, some researchers have been able to come to conclusions and these will be of interest to us.

At the national level, it was shown in Table 5.7 that employment in agriculture, industry and construction had all declined between 1977 and 1986 by about 20–23 per cent, that trade and transport and telecommunication were basically unchanged and that employment in services had increased by roughly 20 per cent. In Table 7.4 these figures are brought up to date. France has shown a distinct movement away from agriculture and, to a lesser degree, industry toward services. This is, of course, a pattern that is observed in most industrialized economies; it is certainly similar to the experience of Germany and the Netherlands. However, industry has had more staying power in both Italy and the United Kingdom, and employment in services has not shown the same growth in the United Kingdom as it has in the other economies. However, it is clear that employment in the three sectors of the economy have shown greater changes in France than in any of the other EU countries that have been selected. This could in part be due to higher levels of protection being in place at the beginning of the 1992 process, especially with regard to the Netherlands, and in part to the fact that France's central position has exposed it more to market forces than has been the case with Italy.

Table 7.4: Employment by sector, (% of total employment)

	1987	1992	1999	1999/1987
Agriculture				
France	7.1	5.9	4.1	0.57
Germany	5.2	3.7	2.8	0.54
Netherlands	4.7	3.9	3.7	0.78
Italy	10.5	7.9	6.8	0.65
United Kingdom	2.4	2.2	1.8	0.75
Industry				
France	30.9	29.6	24.4	0.79
Germany	40.5	39.1	33.3	0.82
Netherlands	27.1	25.2	22.2	0.82
Italy	32.6	33.2	32.0	0.98
United Kingdom	30.2	30.2	26.9	0.89
Services				
France	62.1	64.5	71.5	1.15
Germany	54.1	57.2	63.8	1.18
Netherlands	68.2	70.9	74.1	1.09
Italy	56.8	59.0	61.2	1.08
United Kingdom	67.4	67.5	71.3	1.06

Note: Figures for Italy, Netherlands and United Kingdom are for 1997.

Sources: Eurostat, *Basic Satistics of the Community*, Luxembourg: Office for Official Publications of the European Communities, various issues; Federal Statistical Office Germany, web page; OECD, *Country Surveys*, 2000

The performance of individual French regions should then be seen in the context of the evolution of employment in the nation as a whole. We have not been able to obtain the required time-series data for 2- or even 1-digit industrial classification production for all 22 French regions. However, an insight into the impact of globalization in its various forms – GATT instigated trade liberalization, the EEC/EU integration process, advances in technology and liberalization of financial markets – can be gained from examination of the increase in foreign direct investment in France. As was shown in Table 4.11, investment in French production facilities by foreign firms was a phenomenon of the 1990s. This was, of course, a decade that followed the globalization initiatives. If the defensible assumption is made that foreign direct investors are responsive to emerging regional comparative advantage, then the figures for FDI in France can be taken as indicative of changing regional specializations. Using data for the year 1997, we can see in which regions new jobs were created, as well as the major sectors that attracted that investment.

First, Nord-Pas-de-Calais, with 5,076 new jobs, led all regions. Île-de-France was second with 2,346 followed by Alsace, Rhône-Alpes, Lorraine, Centre, Picardie, Provence-Alpes-Côtes d'Azur and Poitou-Charentes, each of which gained at least 1,000 new jobs. At the bottom, with fewer than 500, were Aquitaine, Franche-Comté, Auvergne, Midi-Pyréennes, Limousin and Corsica. In Table 7.5 we present the manufacturing and other sectors that were most attractive to foreign direct investors for the nine regions (just listed) to which they were most attracted. There were also isolated specializations There were some isolated specializations that were evident among the other 13 regions: food processing in Languedoc-Roussillion, Aquitaine and Bretagne; electro-mechanic in Basse-Normandie and Pays de la Loire; wood–glass–ceramic in Champagne-Ardenne and Bourgogne; ECI in Bretagne; and distribution-logistics in Pays de la Loire and Champagne-Ardenne

Some additional insights as to what has happened to sub-national specialization can be gained from a study done by Michel Houdebine at INSEE for the period 1978–92.[47] One of the most interesting findings is that, at the level of the 96 departments, geographic concentration declined while for the 348 *zones d'emploi* it increased. Furthermore, specialization increased for large communities and *zones d'emploi* but declined for small entities. With regard to high technology, two industries were notable for their tendency toward concentration: pharmaceuticals and semiconductors. However, scientific research, electronic equipment, electronic components, data processing equipment, and aircraft engines all exhibited geographic de-concentration.

The characteristic of some regions is the result of globalization but that of others is not. For example, the relatively diverse structure of Rhône-Alpes is comprised of industries that have been located in this region for centuries, industries such as textiles, chemicals, metallurgy, and clothing. However, the diversity of the Paris basin has been increased by the location there of many foreign firms in a wide variety of sectors. The former could not be taken to be

Table 7.5: Emerging regional specializations, nine major regions

Region	Sectors attractive to FDI in France
Nord-Pas-de-Calais	Automobile
	Distribution-logistics
Île-de-France	Call centers
	Automobile, ECIa
	Distribution-logistics
Alsace	ECI, automobile
	Distribution-logistics
Rhône-Alpes	ECI, food processing, automobile
	R&D
Lorraine	Automobile, wood–glass–ceramics
Centre	ECI, electro-mechanic
	Call centers
Picardie	Electro-mechanic .
	Distribution-logistics
Provence-Alpes-Côtes d'Azur	ECI
	R&D
Poitou-Charentes	Wood–glass–ceramics

Note: a ECI refers to Electronic Communications Informatics.

Source: Les Echos, *l'Atlas des Echos: Régions*, 22 June 1998

the result of globalization but the latter certainly could. On the other hand, the lack of diversity of other regions could also be taken to be a result of globalization. For example, the concentration of French and foreign firms in the automobile and electronic sectors in Brittanny, Lorraine and France-Comté can be linked to the opening of the EU market and inward investment by foreign firms and the expansion of French firms to increase production to meet the needs of export markets.[48]

The Position of Paris

As has been mentioned above, the relation between Paris and the provinces has been an object of discussion since the publication of Gravier's book in 1947. During the 1950s and into the 1960s efforts were made to constrain the economic development of the capital and in particular to shift industry into provincial cities. Higher-level industrial and service sector activities could remain in Paris, but less-skilled activities were encouraged to move, albeit still to the north of a line from Bordeaux to Grenoble. Population figures indicate that the economy itself was moving things in this direction. The urban management plan of 1965 assumed that Paris would grow to a population of 14 million by 1990, but a revised plan in 1976 lowered this estimate to 12 million. After the census of 1982 the estimate for 2000 was lowered further to 10.5 million. The difficulty for Paris was that while the rate of natural population growth was above that of the national average, the capital suffered from outward migration.[49] This was particularly apparent during the periods 1975–82 and 1990–9 when Île-de-France ranked fifteenth and twelfth, respectively, among 22 regions with regard to population increase. More positively, the capital region has tended to have a net inflow of young people and a net outflow of its retired population. In the early 1990s the population of Paris was 18.8 per cent of the nation's total, but it produced 27.6 per cent of national output, 37.8 of the higher-level labor force, 30 per cent of national telecommunications activity, and 78 per cent of corporate headquarters.[50] So by any standard Paris dominated much of French economic life.

Government regional policy has been discussed above, both with respect to the efforts to use DATAR to build up provincial France and the decentralization efforts of the 1980s. However, as Lipietz notes, as policy became less dirigist and more liberal market forces were given greater leeway Paris came to be perceived as the primary if not sole 'growth pole' for France and France's only chance to insinuate itself into the high economic activity corridor from London to Milan – the rest of France was clearly in danger of becoming marginalized. In the 'blue banana' analysis London and Paris were virtually tied as the two primary cities in Europe; clearly if the right policies were chosen Paris could actually surpass London as Europe's primary urban economy. In effect this policy was that of creation of a French megalopolis that could compete on a global scale with London, New York and Tokyo.[51] In effect, the focus had shifted from seeking something that was beneficial with regard to France's internal economic space to the historic concern, from Louis XIV to de Gaulle, with the position of France in the larger international or global space.

Countering this view were two forces that were not necessarily in league with each other. Ecologists argued that continued growth of Paris would only lead to increased pollution, congestion that required more investment in the urban transportation infrastructure, loss of green space, socio-ethnic conflict, pressure on existing housing, and degradation of existing municipal services such as sewerage, water, and so forth. But Paris was only one example of what to them was an unacceptable situation to which uncontrolled growth could lead; they were also opposed to growth in general including decentralized growth of provincial cities. We have already mentioned the 1995 measures of Minister of the Interior Charles Pasqua that aimed to shift growth from Paris to the so-called fragile zones, rural areas, mountainous areas and the Atlantic littoral. Lipietz states that the Pasqua policies would virtually forbid growth in Ile-de-France and that all growth should be done elsewhere – but where?[52] So one of the two primary forces that sought to control Paris wanted no growth anywhere and the other sought to transfer growth from Paris to other cities, without any diminution of national economic growth. For the ecologists this latter approach merely pushed back the day of reckoning a decade or two.

Figure 7.1 and Table 7.1, at the beginning of this chapter, indicated both that population growth was greatest in suburbs and small cities and growth in the largest cities had stagnated and that Paris still dwarfs all other French cities. This situation is utterly unlike other EU members in which there are more secondary cities and they are all much closer in population to the country's primary city. In 1990, Paris accounted for over 16 per cent of the French population, the second-tier cities Lyon and Marseille had only about 2.2 per cent each, and only three others (Lille, Bordeaux and Toulouse) accounted for more than 1 per cent of the population. At that time only Lyon and Marseille had populations above 1 million. Recognition of the attractiveness of Paris to foreign and domestic economic actors generated a policy change in 1992 away from trying to constrain activity in Paris to that of extending Paris into the rest of France, at least to a distance of about 150 miles. Rapid transportation links by autoroute and TGV brought the populations of cities such as Caen, Rouen, Tours, Orleans, Chartres and Reims into commuting distance. Actually it has turned out that commuting goes in both directions, with individuals living in, say, Rouen and working in Paris while others live in Paris and commute to jobs in Tours. Thompson argues that as these peripheral cities gain greater access to Paris they gain 'a greater opportunity to develop their own initiatives, whether by indigenous or foreign investment, rather than to anticipate windfall decentralizations.'[53] In a moment we will examine the extent to which this has been possible in France's second city, Lyon.

At each of the major transformations of economic life it was Paris and other central cities in Europe that benefited. Increases in technology and the increased role played by relative prices resulted in redundant labor moving from agriculture in rural areas into the cities where the workers provided an abundant labor force for manufacturing. Similarly, the transition from a manufacturing economy to services privileged the large cities, and Paris most of all. In the broadest sense, global restructuring opened the developing world to relocations of manufacturing activities with low skill requirements, as was shown in Map 7.5 in which the slow-growing regions are those in the traditional manufacturing areas in the north and east of France. Services were attracted by agglomeration effects, access to the market, skilled labor, and so on, and Paris had these in abundance. As Thisse and Ypersele put it: 'the post-industrial city is associated with the growth of services and, more recently, with its role as a focal point of communication.'[54] This is clear from figures from 1993: Ile-de-France accounted for 25.1 per cent of French GDP, 24.4 per cent of industrial output, and 22.4 per cent of non-market services (public sector), but for 34.1 per cent of market services (private sector). This indicates that the higher skill and higher productivity activities are still, and one must note increasingly, located in the capital region.

The capital region was seen to be a national problem in the years following the crisis of 1974 during which time unemployment rose steadily to over 11 per cent. It was thought that Paris was draining vitality away from the rest of the national economy. But then two things happened. First, it became clear that in the evolving spatial economy of the EU a strong Paris was of benefit to the national economy rather than a drain on it and, second, as the effects of further opening of the EU market and the various reform and deregulation initiatives were realized the EU economy began to improve and unemployment began to fall.   More generally, in most industrialized economies population has begun to increase in second- and third-tier cities more rapidly than in the primary cities. This is helped by considerations of quality of life and a desire to avoid the urban disamenities that afflicted most of the largest cities during the last two decades of the twentieth century. So a rising sea seems to be lifting most of the city and town boats and the pressure for growth management is off Paris – at least for now.

The Entrepreneurial Policies of Lyon

As has already been noted, changes in the situation of France's provincial cities have been dramatic during the past two decades. While the distinctly pyramidal structure of the French urban hierarchy has not been converted to a flat-topped mesa the second-tier cities have unquestionably improved their position in that structure. Of these second-tier cities, including Marseille, Lille, Bordeaux, Toulouse, Nice and Strasbourg, Lyon has been the most active and the most ambitious. This entrepreneurial spirit may be in part due to the perceived need to assert itself as France's second city and to strike out on a path that has been given little support by the central government. The enormous gap between France's two largest cities is duplicated in no other EU member country with the exception of the United Kingdom.[55]   Another contributory factor may be that Lyon is an urban economy that is characterized by small rather than large firms. Its region, Rhône-Alpes, ranks ahead of only Limousin and Langedoc-Roussillion in the lowest percentage of firms with 500 or more employees, but is sixth from the top in firms with fewer than 50 employees.[56] This suggests a flexibility of maneuver that is lacking in economies dominated by large firms.

The first step was the creation of ADERLY (Agence pour le développement économique de la région lyonnaise) in 1974. In fact this was the first such initiative in any of the large French cities. ADERLY was given the task of promoting the economic development of the Lyon metropolitan area and on its own initiative did a study of the impacts of the Paris–Lyon TGV.

The decentralization initiative was introduced in 1982–3 and five years later Lyon had a strategy in place, with the document *Lyon 2010.*[57] The date of publication, October 1988, was just one year after the adoption of the Single European Act that signaled the beginning of the process of completion of the internal market. One part of the strategy focused on institutional and infrastructure changes in the agglomeration of Lyon itself, and the other looked to Lyon's place in the European and indeed the global economic space. The two parts of *Lyon 2010* are integrated since the local improvements are designed to make Lyon function more effectively as a connection between these macro-regions of Europe. The first page of the first chapter of the document places Lyon as the historic and natural conduit between the north of Europe and the Mediterranean world, including the Iberian and Italian Peninsulas and the south of France, and as the center of a dense regional network of important towns such as Grenoble, Saint-Etienne, and Geneva. The position of Lyon in the larger European economic space is captured in Map 7-6, which presents the three grand axes that define Lyon's potential reach as well as its link to Paris.

Quoting Fernand Braudel to the effect that Lyon had always based its development on an engagement that extended beyond France, a 1992 report of the Chamber of Commerce emphasized the disadvantage provincial French cities had labored under due to the position of Paris as the center of decision-making and power. However, it also noted that unlike most other French cities, Lyon was not situated in a 'desert' but was rather located on a historic transportation route, the Rhône River, and in a dense network of dynamic cities. These include the other seven cities in its greater metropolitan area, Chambéry, Grenoble, Saint-Etienne, Annecy, Bourg-en-Bresse and Valence, as well as Geneva. Lyon's international vocation was to be based on six objectives:

1. to develop decision-making functions at the national, European and global levels;
2. to affirm Lyon's place as a financial center;
3. to continue to support higher education and research in their international dimensions;
4. to enhance the cultural assets of the city;
5. to affirm Lyon's international image; and
6. to strengthen its position in international communication networks.[58]

Many cities throughout the world had similar ambitions, but Lyon's effort was continued with stronger political support than is the case with many city plans.

The major infrastructure initiative to insinuate Lyon into international networks was the development of the Satolas airport-LGV complex, recently renamed Aéroport Saint Exupéry, just east of the city. The airport has flights

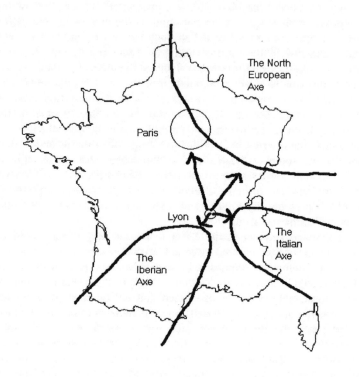

Source: *Lyon 2010: Une projet d'agglomération pour une métropole européenne*, Lyon: SEPAL, October 1988, p. 56

Map 7.6: The grand axes of Lyon's position in the European economic space

to 34 cities and with just under 5 million passengers in 1996 it ranked fourth behind Paris (almost 60 million), Nice with 6.6 million, and Marseille with 5.4 million, but is only the thirty-eighth busiest airport in Europe. The primary reason for the surprisingly low ranking of the airport is the success of the

TGV service. As was noted above, air traffic between Lyon and Paris has dried up due to the convenience of the rail service. Planned improvements to the TGV service to Turin, Marseilles, Nice, Bordeaux, Geneva and Toulouse should have much the same effect.

In its planning in 1989 Lyon emphasized five primary challenges.[59] First: the challenge of economic development. This noted the growing unemployment during the past 15 years in the face of a relatively rapidly growing active population, the restructuring of economic activity and the growth of the service sector, and the opening of the economy as a consequence of the Single European Act and a more generalized globalization. Second: the European challenge. Lyon had to recognize the growing competition among European cities and regions and it had to prepare itself to be more attractive in this environment and to develop transportation and institutional linkages with other parts of this developing economic space. Thirdly: the challenge of technological change. Given the advances of the recent past, one had to assume in 1989 that the foreseeable future was going to be marked by an acceleration of this revolutionary activity. Intelligent buildings, automated urban transport, automated production and distribution, astonishing new options for telecommunication, and unforeseen scientific breakthroughs would dramatically alter the economic environment in which Lyon would have to create its economic future. Fourth: the social challenge. Increasing inequalities among regions and disequilibrium among social groups, an aging population, increasing ethnic diversity of the population, and changing family structures would all have their impact on urban development policy. And, finally, fifth: the challenge of the environment. To meet the expectations of its residents Lyon would have to be more attentive to the values of beauty, health, and security. Urbanization and economic development bought pressures to cause the deterioration of each of these values.

These challenges were, of course, apparent to officials in other cities, but what is distinctive about Lyon's response is the continuity of the interest in achieving the stated objectives and in responding to the challenges of the city's mayors and of agencies at various levels of the urban agglomeration. These agencies include: the Agence d'urbanisme de la communauté urbaine de Lyon, the Agence pour le développement économique de la région lyonnaise, and the Chambre du commerce et de l'industrie. This continuity of focus can be seen in the report on economic development of the Agence d'urbanisme in 1997, and in the recent series of reports *Millénaire trois*, including 'Une agglomération compétitive et rassemblée' which sets out priorities for the twenty-first century that are very similar to those of *Lyon 2010*.[60]

The initiatives adopted are too numerous to be presented here in full, so only four major ones will be noted. First, one of the highlights has been the development of one of Europe's premier scientific research complexes, with the Gerland Scientific Pole, Porte des Alpes Technology, Biovision (an international bienial exposition of the latest research in this industry), and its own universities and other research institutes, as well as other facilities in other cities in close proximity such as Grenoble. These efforts have been concentrated in life sciences (bio-pharmaceutical and health), food processing, telecommunications and multimedia, and electrical equipment, while there has been continued support for Lyon's traditional strengths of textiles, chemicalsand automotive parts.[61] Second, an ambitious development of the transportation infrastructure has brought the TGV to Lyon with, as noted above, plans to make the city a cross-roads for traffic on a north–south axis from the Mediterranean to Paris, Brussels and the upper Rhine cities, as well as an east–west axis from Bordeaux to Italy (Turin) and Switzerland. Third, Lyon has been most active and imaginative in insinuating itself into functional relationships with other cities. The Alpine Diamond includes Lyon, Geneva and Turin and the Mediterranean Alliance brings Lyon together with Marseille, Genoa and Barcelona. Central to this initiative has been Lyon's central position in the EuroCities Movement, a group of over 40 major European cities which seeks to gain a stronger voice in decision-making circles in Brussels and in national capitals for policies and initiatives that are of benefit to them. EuroCities also meets to discuss common problems, from inter-modal transport and new TGV lines to the cultural sector and regional development funding. Fourth, in support of its desire to increase its position in the European urban hierarchy, to be attractive to the highly educated component of the labor force, and to make itself more attractive to international companies, Lyon has significantly upgraded its urban amenitites – the historic district and its cultural institutions. The Renaissance Quarter (Vieux Lyon) was given considerable attention and was declared a world heritage site by UNESCO), and the Opera was completely renovated. Lyon is one of the few European cities with a municipal dance space and its dance biennial attracts between 80,000 and 100,000 spectators during its two–week duration. Its Musée des Beaux-Arts was already one of the major collections outside Paris.

One must, of course, ask whether these efforts have paid off. Current data for large sets of cities are difficult to get in France, and even regional data are spotty for recent years. Rather more difficult to get are time series data, so one misses what is most important – movement over time. Nonetheless some understanding can be gained from the data that are available. In population there has been a definite turn-around. First, during the fifteen years following the crisis of 1974, the population of the city of Lyon declined by 8.9 per cent and that of the metropolitan area grew just 1.4 per cent. While Lyon has ceded second place to Marseille, of the most populous French cities, only Lyon, Lille, Bordeaux and Nantes did not have their population boosted by absorption of surrounding communties.[62] The rate of increase from 1990 through 1999 for both was about 7 per cent. Second, the employment picture for Lyon is very similar to that of other French cities. Employment in industry, construction and trade were down 5–15 per cent during 1990–9, but improved during the latter half of the decade during which time trade employment actually increased about 5 per cent. Services increased by 7–12 per cent for most cities during 1990–5 and by 10–20 per cent during 1995–9. Lyon's performance was in the middle of the pack with regard to employment during the 1990s. While employment does not appear to present a ringing endorsement of the success of Lyon's policy approach, a recent report by INSEE attributes much of the unemployment of Rhône-Alpes to the demographic structure of the region.[63] This same report also concluded that the strength of the Rhône-Alpes economy was in part due to the fact that it specialized in activities in which its productivity was higher than the national average. Third, the strength of the research infrastructure of the region is indicated by the fact that, using data for 1993, while Paris dominates in the number of patents filed, with 63.2 per cent of the national total, Rhône-Alpes is second with 16 per cent and is far ahead of the next region, Province-Alpes-Côtes-d'Azur, with 5.2 per cent. Lyon is responsible for 70 per cent of the region's patents and is strongest in chemical-pharmaceutical and manufacturing processes.[64] In 1991 the region of Rhône-Alpes was home to 450 research institutes with over 6,000 researchers and it appears that this latter figure increased to 6,500 by 1999.[65] This complex accounted for 50 per cent of French research in textiles, 40 per cent in non-ferrous metals, and 27 per cent in chemicals. Fourth, it is uncontestable that Lyon has greatly increased its profile as a center of culture, especially in opera and dance. Finally, it should be noted that economic activity in Lyon and its department, Rhône, is near the bottom of the rankings when it comes to reliance on the state for demand for its goods and for employment. Thus what has been accomplished has been done by meeting market demands from consumers and business.

Nonetheless, there is a feeling of frustration that not more has been accomplished. In his examination of the reasons why Lyon had not realized the potential it saw for itself in 1989, Bernard Sinou, Director General of Services for the Region of Rhône-Alpes, identified four: first, Lyon had not overcome its deficiency in infrastructure, training and services; second, the city had not yet achieved the image in other parts of Europe it had sought; third, in comparison with comparable cities in other EU countries Lyon labored under the heavy hand of centralized decision-making – French Jacobinism; and fourth, it lacked a coherent strategic vision.[66]

The conclusion that can be drawn from this admittedly incomplete picture of the contribution of municipal activism to the Lyon economy is that at the margin it has been reasonably effective. The boosterism of local authorities has undoubtedly raised the aspirations of local actors and enhanced its international reputation. In a decade of stagnation and restructuring of the French and European economies Lyon has managed to retain its strength in research and in its science- and technology-related industries. However, there remains a palpable sense that a combination of external and local factors has inhibited the city in achieving its objectives. One positive note is that after the first decade of operation of the Paris–Lyon TGV line fears that Lyon would become a suburb of Paris and that high-level economic activity would be transferred to the capital were in fact not realized.[67]

The Upper Rhine and Cross-Border Cooperation

Another type of sub-national activism in France has been that of the regional governments. As was noted above, Brussels has supported trans-border cooperation throughout the member countries of the EU. Partly this is because some of them have been far from the capital city in the interior of the country and therefore disadvantaged historically in their economic development. Another reason to support them is that the national border has truncated their natural economic reach and the lowering of barriers to interaction between contiguous trans-border regions has great potential for easy success. The final reason is that this hands-across-the border cooperation is at the heart of the economic integration initiative itself.

France has 11 separate trans-border zones that are comprised of 14 sets of cities and towns.[68] These extend from Kent–Calais–Boulogne on the Channel, along the Belgian, Luxembourg and German borders through Switzerland to Monaco on the Mediterranean border with Italy and, finally, the Pyrénées zone which stretches along the entirety of the border with Spain. *Régio basiliensis* was one of the first of France's trans-border regions to be established, in 1963. It extends from the Swiss city of Basel down the Rhine to include Alsace and parts of Baden-Württemberg and Rheinland-Pfalz in Germany. Alsace is one of the best performing of the French regions. During the 1990s its rate of unemployment was only about 58–60 per cent of that of the rate for France and for the last quarter of 2000 the rates for Alsace and France were 5.1 and 9.2 per cent respectively. At the beginning of 2000 the rate of unemployment for the 12 *zones d'emploi* in Alsace ranged from highs of 6.7 and 7.2 for the urban areas of Strasbourg and Mulhouse to 2.7–3.6 per cent for Altkirch, Saint-Louis and Wissembourg.[69] In 1998 gross domestic product per capita for Alsace was above the national average at an index of 102.9, the only region above it being Ile-de-France with 127.7. Finally, Alsace has been fortunate in the interest foreign investors have shown in it. The region is ranked first in France in the share of industrial employment that is in foreign-owned firms – 39 per cent in contrast with 24 per cent for France as a whole, and the absolute number of these workers is second among French regions at 54,000.

While, as was noted above, proximity to the 'blue banana' has not guaranteed good performance for France's regions, it does seem to have worked for Alsace; this is due to the strength of Baden-Württemberg, the German *Land* across the Rhine. While the ratio of German to French salaries in 1995 was 1.39, that of Baden-Württemberg to Alsace was 1.51, and both were considerably below that of the Basel region.[70] The two regions share some characteristics with regard to their respective national economies. Both are relatively industrialized and they share the same five dominant industries: construction, wholesale trade, retail trade, automotive products, and machinery and equipment, although not in the same order. As would be expected, this gap in earnings led to cross-border movements of labor with 45,000 of the Basel region labor force being resident in Alsace or Baden-Württemberg and 5,000 workers living in Alsace but working in Baden-Württemberg. For Alsace itself, the number of workers who travel to jobs in Germany has increased from 5,500 in 1968 to 13,300 in 1975, 16,900 in 1982 and 24,900 in 1990. The comparable figures for commuting to jobs in Switzerland are 7,400, 14,000, 17,600 and 30,500. Given the lower salaries in Alsace the reverse movements have been far lower.[71]

Given this rather advantageous situation, the primary task of the trans-border region is to improve its competitive position throughout Europe. The problem is rather more complex than that of Lyon due to the multiplicity of regional, departmental and municipal authorities. At the most general and relevant level there is participation in the INTERREG program of the EU, which has funded several programs throughout the upper Rhine region aimed at trans-border cooperation in zoning, environmental planning and economic development. Another initiative of the EU was establishment of the Association of European Border Regions (AEBR) in 1971 for the purposes of fostering contact and developing cooperation among border regions. The AEBR established the Observatory for Cross-border Co-operation in 1990 and through this several 'cross-border programmes for strategic economic development.'[72] But useful as these pan-European programs are, the ultimate objective of any region is to enhance its position relative to other European regions, and this can only be done through its own initiative. Here most of the action is done by the constituent sub-regions.

The smaller sub-region in the southern part of the region, Tri-Rhena, comprises a radius of about 40 miles or 60 km around the French city of Mulhouse, and includes territory in which are situated the northern part of Switzerland – basically the city of Basel – the German cities of Freiburg and Lörrach, and Belfort and Colmar in France. The initial enthusiasm of local authorities generated a set of other structures that had no decision-making authority. The three national governments brought some order to this situation with the 'Bonn Accord,' signed in 1975, and the agreement signed in Liestal (Switzerland) in 1991 which set up a tri-national structure of administration. Within this structure several working groups were established with mandates in areas such as transport policy, education and training, regional policy, environment and culture. In the administrative structure, positions were given to officials of some of the communities and departments, as well as representatives of the national governments.[73]

Given the recent history of the three participating national governments, the first priority for TriRhena was that of establishing amicable relationships among the peoples on both sides of all the borders. One of the most obvious initiatives to undertake is that of bilingual education and language instruction. This is being done at all levels of schooling. For example, there is a tri-national engineer education program, a program to develop bilingual instruction materials for students aged 8–15, and extensive cooperation among the universities and technical schools in the three countries. Dozens of other initiatives in the areas of culture, 'living together,' and sport and leisure round out the social aspect of the mandate.

The second objective of TriRhena cooperation is that of making the upper Rhine region competitive in the European context. To this end several interesting initiatives have been introduced. One of the existing competitive strengths of the region is its chemical and pharmaceutical industries. BioValley is an effort to create a primary Euro-region in this sector of the economy. The strengths of TriRhena in this area include a research and training infrastructlure that comprises 40 universities and institutes in the life sciences and bio-technology centers such as BioTechPark in Freiburg (Germany), the Bio-Pôle in Colmar (France) and the Innovations-zentrum in the Canton of Basel-Land (Switzerland). The objective is to link the existing universities, research institutes, large firms and small firms into a complex that can compete with other Euro-regions with strengths in this sector, such as that of Lyon–Chambéry–Grenoble and Copenhagen–Malmö–Lund. The EU has contributed over 2 million euros to this project.

An apparent success of TriRhena is the Basel–Mulhouse–Freiburg EuroAirport, an expansion of the existing airport at Basel. Serving the tri-national region, EuroAirport had over 3 million passengers in 2000 and is, in this regard, the third largest airport in Switzerland and the fifth largest serving France.

One of the obvious difficulties for TriRhena is the fact that Switzerland has chosen to remain outside the EU. This means that region-wide harmonization is not possible, although it must be admitted that even between France and Germany harmonization of taxes, wages and industrial standards has yet to be achieved. While France and Germany can be expected to come to some agreement on these matters it is not at all certain that Switzerland will be able to do so in a way that gives recognition to the fact that it must achieve cross-border harmonization with Italy and Austria as well as other border regions shared with France and Germany. Until this has been accomplished the economic potential of TriRhena will not be fully realized.

The northern part of *Régio basiliensis* is centered on Strasbourg and includes Baden-Baden and the eastern part of the Rhein-Pfalz in Germany. An administrative structure of cooperation similar to that of TriRhena was established in 1976. One of the most notable initiatives was that of the INTERREG program PAMINA (1989) which aimed at reducing cross-border inequalities. In addition to promoting bilingualism and regional tourism, PAMINA put in place a technology network, an institute to promote regional agricultural development, and structures for the exchange of information.

Similar initiatives have been undertaken throughout the other border regions of France. This discussion of what has taken place in Alsace should give us some idea of the extent to which regional policy in all EU countries has changed during the past two decades. Funding from Brussels has facilitated the development of regional entrepreneurial activity that is not totally subject to the control of the national government. As we have seen from the discussion of Lyon, this is also true for French cities.

NOTES

1. Daniel Noin, *Le nouvel espace français*, Paris: Armand Colin, 1998, p. 178.
2. DATAR, *Les villes 'européenes,'* Paris: La documentation Française, May, 1989.
3. The data presented in this section can be obtained from a variety of statistical sources, such as INSEE. They are also presented and discussed in Noin, *Le nouvel espace français*.
4. 'La population des regions (metropole): Recensement de la population de 1999,' *INSEE première*, no. 664, July 1999, p. 2.
5. 'Forte extension des villes entre 1990 et 1999,' *INSEE première*, no. 707, April 2000, p. 4.
6. John Ardagh, *France in the New Century*, Hammondsworth, Middlesex: Penguin, 1999, p.   261.
7. DATAR, *Débat national pour l'aménagement du territoire*, Paris: La documentation Française, April 1994, p. 20.
8. For a mapping of the universities of France and the linkages among them, see DATAR, *Débat national pour l'aménagement du territoire*, p. 50.
9. 'Les produits intérieurs bruts régionaux en 1998,' *INSEE première*, no. 754, December 2000, pp. 1 and 2.
10. Claude Dupuy and Jean-Pierre Gilly, *Industrie et territories en France: Dix ans de décentralization*, Paris: La documentation Française, 1993, p. 33.
11. Noin, *Le nouvel espace français*, p. 20.
12. Source: *Europe 2000+, Coopération pour l'aménagement du territoire européen*, Brussels: Commission of the European Union, 1994, pp. 175–215.
13. Jean-Luc Bœuf (ed.), *L'aménagement du territoire: bialan et renouveau*,

Problèmes politiques et sociaux, no. 750, Paris: La documentation Française, 16 June 1995, p. 9.

14. Jean-François Gravier, *Paris et le désert français*, Paris: Flammarion, 1972.
15. Noin, *Le nouvel espace français*, p. 184.
16. For an analysis of this period, see Catherine Grémion, 'Décentralisation An X,' *French Politics & Society*, vol. 9, nos 3-4, Summer-Fall 1991.
17. Jean-François Eck, *La France dans la nouvelle économie mondiale*, Paris: Presses Universitaires de France, 1994, p. 255.
18. Jean-Claude Thoenig, 'La décentralization: dix ans déja, et après,' *L'état de la décentralisation, Cahiers français,* no. 256), Paris: La documentation Français, May–June 1992, p. 73.
19. Gérard-François Dumont, *Économie urbaine: villes et territories en competition*, Paris: Editions Litec, 1993, pp. 135–136.
20. Thoenig, 'La décentralisation,' p. 73.
21. Grémion, 'Décentralisation,' pp. 36 and 41.
22. Albert Mabileau, 'La décentralisation en retard,' *L'état de la décentralisation*, pp. 66–72.
23. Ibid., p. 72.
24. Bruno Rémond, 'La loi du 6 février 1992: le second souffle' de la décentralization?,' *L'état de la décentralisation*, p. 87.
25. Ibid., p. 90.
26. Ronald Tiersky, *France in the New Europe: Changing Yet Steadfast*, Belmont, California: Wadsworth, 1994, p. 76.
27. Noin, *Le nouvel espace français*, p. 181.
28. This is developed in a work that pre-dates the 1995 law: Claude Lacour, *Espace Régionaux Nouvelles Métropoles International Nouveaux Déserts: Les Atlanti-Cités?*, Bordeaux: Université de Bordeaux I, Institut d'Economie Régionale du Sud-Ouest, Décision d'aide no. 88 V 0191, June 1991, and, with J. Le Monnier, *Prospective Arc Atlantique: analyses, stratégies, actions, Rapport final*, Paris: DATAR, September 1992.
29. Noin, *Le nouvel espace français*, p. 183.
30. Claude du Granrut, *Europe, le temps des régions*, Paris: Librairie Générale du Droit et de la Jurisprudence, 1994, p. 43.
31. Ian Thompson, 'The French TGV system – progress and projects,' *Geography*, vol. 79 pt. 2, no. 343, April 1994, p. 166.
32. Noin, *Le nouvel espace français* , p. 138
33. R.W. Vickerman, "Transport infrastructure and region building in the European Community," *Journal of Common Market Studies*, vol. 32, no. 1, March 1994, p. 16.
34. Jean-Pierre Arduin, 'Development and economic evaluation of high speed in France,' *Japan Railway and Transport Review*, no. 3, October 1994.
35. Mark Hart, 'Convergence, cohesion and regionalism: contradictory trends in the new Europe,' in Brian Graham (ed.), *Modern Europe: Place, Culture and Identity*, London: Arnold, 1998, p. 166.
36. Aadne Cappelen, Jan Fagerberg and Bart Verspagen, 'Lack of regional convergence,' in Jan Fagerberg, Paolo Guerriere and Bart Verspagen (eds.) *The*

Economic Challenge for Europe, Cheltenham, UK: Edward Elgar, 1999, pp. 131–134.
37. Reported in Hart, 'Convergence,' p. 177.
38. See 'Fonds structurels: un outil puissant de solidarité,' in Bœuf, *L'aménagement du territoire*, pp. 35-36.
39. du Granrut, *Europe*, pp. 42–48.
40. Robert J. Barro and Xavier S. Sala-I-Martin, 'Convergence across states and regions,' *Brookings Papers on Economic Activity*, no. 1, 1991, pp. 148–152.
41. Cappelen, *et al.*, 'Lack of regional convergence,' p. 133.
42. Roberto J. Camagni, 'Cities in Europe: globalisation, sustainability and cohesion,' in *European Spatial Planning*, Rome: Presidenza del Consiglio die Ministri Dipartimento per l'Informazione e l'Editoria, 1996, pp. 105–109.
43. Harvey W. Armstrong, 'European Union regional policy: sleepwalking to a crisis,' *International Regional Science Review*, vol. 19, no. 3, 1996, p. 202.
44. Luis Surarez-Villa and Juan R. Cuadrado Roura, 'Regional economic integration and the evolution of disparities,' *Papers in Regional Science*, vol. 72, no. 4, 1993, pp. 369–387.
45. From the EU website: http://www.europa.eu.int.comm/eurostat/ 'regional cohesion.'
46. Noin, *Le nouvel espace français*, p. 118.
47. Michel Houdebine, 'Concentration géographique des activités et spécialisation des départements français,' INSEE, September 1999.
48. Fréderic Lainé and Carole Rieu, 'La diversité industrielle des territoirires,' *INSEE Première*, no. 650, June 1999.
49. 'La population des regions,' p. 2.
50. 'Les fractures du territoire: surconcentration et dépopulation,' *Problèmes politiques et sociaux*, no. 750, 1995, p. 19.
51. Alain Lipietz, 'Face à la mégapolisation: la bataille d'Ile-de-France,' in Georges Benko and Alain Lipietz (eds), *La richesse des régions*, Paris: Presses Universitaires de France, 2000, p. 158–160.
52. Ibid., p. 162.
53. Thompson, 'French TGV system,' p. 166, and Lipietz, 'Face à la mégapolisation,' pp. 162–164.
54. Jacques-François Thisse and Tanguy van Ypersele, 'Métropoles et concurrence territoriale,' *Politique Régional*, Paris: INSEE, September 1999, p. 2.
55. This statement is based not on population but rather on the calculation of Roger Brunet and his team presented in Roger Brunet, *Les villes 'européennes'*, Paris: DATAR, 1989, p. 55.
56. 'La diversité industrielle des territoires,' *INSEE Première*, no. 650, Paris: INSEE, June 1999.
57. *Lyon 2010: Un projet d'agglomération pour une métropole éuropeenne*, Lyon: SEPAL, October 1988.
58. Pierre-Yves Tesse, *Charte d'objectifs: Lyon ville internationale*, Lyon: Chambre de commerce et d'industrie de Lyon, 14 June 1990, p. 4.
59. *Lyon 2010*, pp. 23–25.
60. *Développement économique dans l'agglmératon lyonnaise*, Lyon: Agence d'urbanisme, November 1997, and 'Une agglomération compétitive et rassemblée,' *Millénaire trois*, Lyon: Le Grand Lyon, 2000.

61. Jean Meilhaud, 'Industrie lyonnaise: l'alliance réussie de la spécialisation tranditionnelle et de l'innovation,' *Problems économiques*, no. 2.207, Paris: La documentation Francaise, January 1991.
62. 'Fort extension des villes entre 1990 et 1999,' p. 3.
63. 'Les produits intérieurs bruts régionaux en 1998,' p. 3.
64. *Premières illustrations des indicateurs comparatifs*, Lyon: Observatoire économique de la région lyonnaise, Sepember 1997, p. 43.
65. The uncertainty of this conclusion comes from the fact that the two figures for the number of researchers come from different sources: in Meilhard, 'Industrie lyonnaise' the source for 1991 is given as Agence pour le développement de la région lyonnaise, and 1999 data are from les Chambres de Commerce et d'Industrie Rhône-Alpes, *Chiffres Clés du Rhône: édition 2000–2001*.
66. Bernard Sinou, 'Comments,' *Rayonner dans l'Europe des grandes métropoles: les défis de la région urbaine de Lyon*, Lyon: Région Urbaine de Lyon, 1999, pp. 28–29.
66. François Plassard, 'L'impact territorial des transports à grande vitesse,' in Pierre-Henri Derycke (ed), *Espace et dynamiques territoriales*, Paris: Economica, 1992, p. 252.
68. Christian Estrose, *La coopération transfrontalière au service de l'aménagement du terrioire*, Paris: Conseil Economique et Social, 1996, p. 72.
69. 'Taux de chômage par zone d'emploi, 1er trimester 2000,' *DEFM 1: decembre 2000*, Observatoire Régional Emploi Formation Alsace, 2000.
70. Pierrette Briant, 'Bade-Wurtemberg: des salaires attractifs pour les Alsaciens,' *INSEE Première*, No. 660, June 1999.
71. Estrosi, *La coopération transfrontalière*, pp. 81–82.
72. Association of European Border Regions (AEBR) website: http://www.aebr-ageg.de/.
73. The source for this section is the website of TriRhena: http://www.regiotrirhena.org/.

8 Prospects for the French Economy

In the first quarter of 2000, the collected media, statisticians, economists and the French government congratulated themselves on the recovery of economic growth, after the short-lived slow-down in 1998–9. This growth was stimulated by strong domestic demand. They noted the 350,000 jobs that had been created in 1999, and the additional 500,000 new jobs in 2000, double the number during the entire decade 1986–96. By comparison, however, during the same time period the United States was able to create 11 million new jobs. As recently as 1996 French job creation was limited to no more than 4,800 jobs. From Figure 8.1 we can see both the pause of 1998–9 and the rising

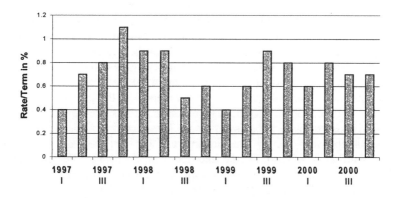

Sources: *Les Echos*, 7 July 2000, pp. 1 and 3; *Economie Française*, Paris: Direction des Etudes Economiques du CCF, December 2000, p. 9

Figure 8.1: Economic growth in France, 1997–2000

growth of 1997. Surveys of households conform to these movements and the majority of consumer sentiment became positive following the pause. After a brief examination of the near-term possibilities, of macro–economic conditions and of discernible directions in public policy, we will conclude this chapter by posing questions regarding the ongoing transformation of the French economy in the face of, and sometimes in opposition to, the forces of globalization that so strongly characterize the world economy and the adaptability of the French themselves.

FRANCE AND EUROPE IN 2000-01

In 2000 the French economy was still in the process of realizing its transition to a liberalized economy. It was alternately slowed by a succession of elections and stimulated by the old promises of transfer payments, of maintenance of privileged positions, and of the lure of the status quo. It must be remembered that the French economy is composed of two great parts: the private sector actors – heads of firms, salaried workers, liberal professionals, and so forth – and the public sector decision-makers – the government, the elected officials, and the bureaucrats. Paradoxically these two parts find they are in agreement regarding definition of their respective positions and responsibilities. Neither desires that anything be changed that would constrain their freedom of operation. This is an example of Milton Friedman's 'principle of the iron triangle.' In spite of all of the public discussion there has been one agreed-upon common ideology. Basically, it was agreed, first, that liberalism kills employment in France and that protectionism is required for both domestic and international exchange. Second, it was understood that the United States is invading Europe and the rest of the world with an unrestrained quest for profit, and that the counter of a 'French exception' is required in all spheres of economic, cultural and intellectual life. Third, the state has been accepted as the guarantor of social cohesion and security. Fourth, the corporate leaders are seen to wish to exploit workers through the guise of a social restructuring. It is clear that the oppositions between society and economy and between state and market are joined with that between France and the United States. Public opinion regularly gives evidence of supporting this negative position regarding increasing globalization, and it focuses almost exclusively on the negative aspects of movement toward a true market economy, as was suggested in Chapter 1. The French are repelled by the redistribution that is inherent in Schumpeterian creative destruction, and do not see the positive consequences of this movement. It is clear that French governments, whether of the left or the right, have had little incentive to alter this negative opinion, as this would put in jeopardy their own powers.

Two causes for the public taking this view can be discerned: (a) there is an attitude of fear in the face of the unknown and the perception that existing advantages or benefits would be lost; and (b) the political parties have found it to their advantage to promote this fear so as to entrench their position as the distributors of social programs. It is, of course, true that all dramatic transformations carry with them their own adjustment costs, which are referred to as social costs, because it is difficult to identify them at the level of the individual. The current acceleration of globalization is a revolution for all countries that do not completely close themselves off from the rest of the world. For France, this represents a combination of costs and benefits and must be seen as an opportunity that must be seized, in the way that many of the Asian countries have. At this date, the EU accounts for only 20.2 per cent of global GDP, in comparison with 25.8 for NAFTA, 25.9 for the developing economies of Asia, and 7.7 per cent for Japan.

The opening of markets, which was facilitated by progressive deregulation, is at the origin of a very considerable instability in the French economy, for several reasons. Information is a scarce commodity and the future is always obscure in a world in which pure surprise occupies a prominent place.[1] Furthermore, economic cycles are not synchronized between North America, which has tended to be ahead by two years, and France and the rest of the EU. This has had a favorable impact on the value of the dollar in relation to that of the euro, at least up to the time this is being written in May 2001. Capital movements, especially the withdrawal of Japanese funds from the European bond market, have contributed to this currency instability. Finally, even while the French economy has been experiencing record growth of GDP, the depreciation of the euro in currency markets in relation to the dollar and the yen has made import prices increase, most importantly that of petroleum. The slight increase in inflationary pressures and the more interventionist position of the European Central Bank (ECB) have suggested an end of economic instability and insecurity in Europe. But at the same time, both in France and throughout the world, the allocation of factors of production has been made more efficient through the liberalization of markets and is adapting continually to improvements in productivity. The latter is the fruit of important applied research increasingly being incorporated in finished products and services, as well as the continued extension and opening of markets.

Throughout Europe the most immediately pressing question is now how long will the growth last, rather than when will growth return? It is formulated in terms of the new economy. The context in which this question is now posed is a rate of economic growth of 3 per cent per year, a rate of unemployment that, while historically high, is being reduced, little inflation, and above all an expansion of investment and of employment of high-skilled labor. In 2001 the term new economy is centered on new technologies of information and communication. It brings together mobile telephones, the Internet, applications of computers, game technology, graphics, music, and programming. This growth is generalized throughout Western Europe and, at least within the EU, has given a positive result in the expansion of employment. The economy of France is presently serving as one of the primary locomotives of EU growth, with its own strong rate of growth and its

22 per cent share of the EU market. However, with Germany's fiscal reforms currently underway one can anticipate that this country will soon regain its position as leader of the EU economy. A short-term reduction of public sector deficits is crucial in this regard and would appear to be more credible for Germany than for France.

A quick look at the macro–economic situation confirms the general improvement in activity. At the beginning of 2001 the growth rate of GDP in France exceeded that of the other major EU member countries, With the exception of the United Kingdom, for the first time in many years. Since 1996 France has indeed been one of the primary engines of growth. However, the fact that the French government has not aggressively pursued the reduction of the public sector deficit does pose a problem. In 2000 public expenditures accounted for 3 per cent of GDP and the public debt 58.4 per cent. There exists a positive correlation between deficit in the government budget, on the one hand, and the rate of unemployment, on the other. But the tendency for public sector budgets to be lowered was reversed by the end of that year. The government decided to use the unanticipated fiscal revenues generated by strong economic growth for new social expenditures rather than for deficit reduction. In 2001 French economic growth weakened, as did tax revenues, and the government decided once again to increase expenditures, this time by 0.5 per cent in what was an election year. The policy of deficit reduction was indeed short-lived.

The year 2001 began with additional lay-offs (an increase of 2 per cent in February alone), authorized by law if done for economic reasons, while a reduction in unemployment is fully explained by increased training opportunities for the unemployed – these rose by 5.9 per cent in February.[2] In February 2001, unemployment was 8 per cent in the EU and 8.8 per cent in the Euro zone, while it was only 4.2 per cent in the US. In France, it was reduced to a low of 8.8 per cent in March. At the same time several large firms, such as Danone, Lu, and Marks & Spencer, accelerated their downsizing. The pressure of final demand as well as that of investment suggested continued growth for 2002–3, but the economic slow-downs, firings and corporate difficulties in the US and Japan reinforced growing pessimism in France. Public opinion polls indicated this change of mood among households and companies. In April *Les Echos* noted:

> while French opinion seems to be that for the next year unemployment will probably decline, the fourth edition of Démoscope [the opinion barometer of *Les Echos*] shows that beyond that year it is much less certain. At the base of this concern linked to the current situation one senses a note of anxiety that nibbles at the general optimism: will the employment picture be as rosy in the future.'[3]

Since 1997, the rate of unemployment has fallen from about 12.5 per cent to 8.8, but a slowing of growth is anticipated by the end of 2001 or the beginning of 2002.

Between 1996 and 2001 the budget deficit fell from 5.5 per cent of GDP to an estimated 1–1.4 per cent. Inflation was only 1.4 per cent in France in February 2001, while it was 2.3 per cent for the rest of the Euro zone. Germany and Italy have suffered from a cyclical slow-down during the middle of the 1990s and should continue to lag behind both the United Kingdom and France in 2001. Table 8.1 indicates just how well the French economy has been performing in relation to its EU counterparts. With regard to inflation, the picture is somewhat less satisfying with prices increasing in the EU more noticeably during 1999 and 2000. Petroleum prices, always a major cause of imported inflation, tripled in just one year to a price of over $30 by the end of 2000 and domestic taxes on petroleum products averaged in excess of 70 per cent.

Table 8.1: Macro-economic performance of major EU economies

	1996	1997	1998	1999	2000	2001
GDP growth						
France	1.1	2.0	3.2	2.9	3.2	3.1
Germany	0.8	1.8	2.3	1.4	2.5	2.5
Italy	0.9	1.5	1.3	1.3	2.3	2.7
United Kingdom	2.6	3.5	2.6	2.1	3.4	2.6
Inflation						
France	2.1	1.7	1.1	0.5	1.7	1.5
Germany	1.4	1.9	1.9	0.9	1.2	1.2
Italy	4.0	2.0	2.0	1.7	2.3	2.4
United Kingdom	2.4	3.1	3.4	1.6	1.5	3.1
Unemployment						
France	12.4	12.3	12.0	11.2	9.7	8.7
Germany	10.4	11.4	11.0	10.5	9.6	9.3
Italy	11.6	11.7	11.8	11.4	11.2	9.9
United Kingdom	8.2	7.0	6.4	6.2	5.0	5.1

Note: Figures for 2001 are estimates.

Sources: *Statistical Abstract of the United States*, various issues; *Annuaire Statistique de France*, INSEE, various issues; *The Economist*, various issues

Overall, however, the forecast must remain rather optimistic for the near future, if serious problems in the agriculture sector, such as foot-and-mouth and mad cow diseases, do not have a negative impact on EU exports. Both Italy and Germany have macro–economic performance data for 2000 that are as good as those of France. At the same time, as stronger economic growth exerts upward pressure on prices and inflationary pressure generated by the energy sector, the rate of unemployment in France has come down slowly, with its rate of decline hampered by persistent public sector deficits, high taxes, increased import prices and difficulties in agriculture. The forecasts of various French government offices as well as the Commission of the EU suggest weakness in both French unemployment and budget deficits. The slow-down of 2001 in other G-7 economies is not expected to have much of an impact on either France or the rest of the EU where the decline in stock prices has not been substantial. It is only in terms of GDP growth and inflation that France should do be able to better than the EU.

One can make the case that the French and German economies are increasingly tending to resemble each other, although it must be said that the fiscal revolution seems more apparent in Germany than in France. The United Kingdom has not suffered from the high value of its currency, but the pound has depreciated with reference to the dollar in 2000. In fact, the autonomy the United Kingdom has maintained in its monetary policy has probably helped to maintain its attractiveness to international investors. Last but not least, its fiscal and legal system are particularly supportive to the creation of new firms. It takes only a few days to start a new firm in the UK, whereas this can take 3–6 months in France, in addition to which French firms must pay higher taxes and social contributions.

The economy of the EU, and in particular of France, is in a good position at the start of the twenty-first century. Time will tell whether the euro can regain some of its lost value *vis-à-vis* the dollar and the pound, and if the monetary stability and reduction in transaction costs resulting from the single currency can overcome the uncertainties of the establishment of a single central bank, the end of competition among stock exchanges and the end of national monetary policies.

THE NEW CONTEXT FOR ECONOMIC GROWTH AND EMPLOYMENT IN 2000-01 AND POLICY OPTIONS

From 1998 to 2001 domestic demand fed economic growth in France, as had the positive external balance during 1991–7. This is shown in Figure 8.2. The last years of the 1990s, as was the case with the mid-1980s, were marked by several significant reforms, including the liberalization of financial and monetary markets, and the introduction of more competition to French markets. However, in France as elsewhere the good health of the economy was dependent to a considerable degree on the attitude of the government: the recent structural reforms, the market liberalization measures and the dynamism of investment have reinforced the growth potential of the French economy.[4] The privatizations of the 1990s stimulated both

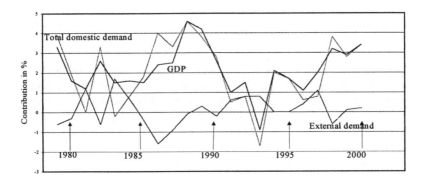

Source: *Comptes de la Nation*, Paris: INSEE, various issues

Figure 8.2: Contributions to French growth, 1979–2000

investment in plant and equipment and employment in the private sector. This has had a positive impact on the morale and purchasing power of consumers. However, the EU warned that not all of the unemployed will be absorbed into the expanding economy if the tax and social contributions system is not modified, if the public sector deficits continue, if the pension system is not reformed, and if contractual relations are not made more flexible and adaptable. In reality the return of a low rate of inflation and a slowing of growth have already appeared in the US and in Europe, and this will have the effect of slowing the pace of reform for the foreseeable future.

On the Verge of New Politics

Government economists are agreed on the consequences of 25 years of public sector deficits: the previous concern with external equilibrium has been replaced by that of solvency in the medium term, and also of the immediate requirement of budgetary discipline that is mandated by the single currency convergence criteria that the public debt be held at no more than 60 per cent of GDP. Furthermore, the return of economic growth allows one to imagine that policy will take a turn toward supply-side concerns with non-price competitiveness and emphasis on flexibility and elimination of rigidities in domestic markets, including the labor market. The improved conditions have led to a deficit in the international trade balance, something France has not known for some time. This deficit amounted to Fr6.2 billion in July 2000 and Fr1.6 billion one month later, although the current account has remained in surplus. In this new context French households remain optimistic and investment has held up very well in 2001.

In 1997 it was primarily the export sector that generated French economic growth. Since then this positive force has been weakened, in spite of the depreciation of the euro. The causes of this can be found in the Russian and Asian crises, and then in 1998 the Japanese recession, the consequences of the crisis in Latin America and the slowing of growth in the United Kingdom. The engine of growth in France was shifted from the export sector to an exceptional expansion of domestic demand. For example, the expansion of consumption rose from 0.9 per cent in 1997 to 3.8 per cent in 1998.

Investment and the Orientation of Economic Policy

The situation

Investment showed considerable strength in 1997 and was even stronger in subsequent years. It grew by 9 per cent in 1999, by 6.1 per cent in 2000 and is expected to rise by 6 per cent in 2001, fully regaining the ground that was lost prior to 1997. But problems do remain. The crowding out of private borrowers in the face of enormous public sector borrowing has had a depressive effect on investment in plant and equipment. Loanable funds at medium and long term have been directed to other countries, especially to those outside Euroland. The spread of returns between placements in France and Germany remains minimal. Fortunately the CAC 40 stock exchange gets 40 per cent of its business from foreign investors, thus adding to the supply of capital in France.

The contradictory impact of increased fiscal pressure has changed the behavior of savings. Non-monetary saving declined to roughly 10 per cent following increased state borrowing during the past decade, while total saving remains today at an elevated level of 15.5 per cent of GDP. The recovery of consumption and investment has been nourished since 1997 by the easing of credit, and consumers are now taking on additional debt. Some have described this as part of an Americanization of French society. It must also be remembered that household borrowing represents in effect a form of financing of firms and also of the state. The wave of borrowing by companies and households during the 1980s has been followed by a reduction of net debt, especially by companies. The recent return to borrowing during the late 1990s slowed noticeably during 2000, caused by the increases in interest rates which has caused them almost to double in 18 months. During the same time period the public sector debt has not been reduced in spite of a windfall tax gain as a result of renewed economic growth and an increase in marginal tax rates by 0.5 per cent in 2000.

The consequence of this new French context for investment is rapidly becoming apparent. The return of some inflation toward the end of 2000 led to a transfer from borrowers to lenders, and from the young to the older generation, and threatens the increase in growth itself. These negative signs are not yet alarming. The French economy has been stimulated by the increase in domestic growth in France and to a lesser degree in the other EU economies, by an accelerated modernization of plant and equipment, by reforms in the areas of education and research, by public investments in infrastructure, and by the operation of externalities inherent in endogenous growth.

The long-term trend of investment is clearly one of growth, having risen from -4 per cent to +4 per cent in 10 years. The 1990s were marked by three business cycles, with the peaks occurring in 1992, 1994–5 and 1998. It is possible that 2001 will be situated in the beginning phase of another downturn in investment. It is possibale that 2001 will be situated in the beginning phase of another downturn in investment. This slow-down, though it may not be very important in the short run, could mainly come from labor shortages of up to 18 per cent, and only in part from a higher rate of capicity utilization (87.5 per cent in 2000)

Policy options
Given the macro–economic situation at the time, the government thought it sensible in 2000 to direct and to facilitate domestic investment according to the following four intermediary objectives:

1. to encourage long-term saving and investments in plant and equipment;
2. to counter the cyclical slowing of investment even if the period of stagnation is only short-term;
3. to evaluate the efficiency of public expenditures and of economic policies; and
4. to create an institutional situation that is pro-growth, through stability, fiscal prudence, and social cohesion.

The improvement in employment suggests the wisdom of emphasis on the fourth objective in particular.

Consumption

The growth of GDP was accompanied by a growth of the purchasing power of consumers. This growth attained 4 per cent in the second quarter of 1995, but became negative by the end of 1996. In 1997 purchasing power grew by 3 per cent and its growth rate is now about 1 per cent per year. The increase in the price of oil and gas clearly slowed this growth as it both increased the prices of consumer goods and brought lower growth of salaries. The growth of consumption reached 3.8 per cent in 1998, up from 0.9 in 1997, and regained its strength by 2000 when it rose by 2.3 per cent. The fluctuation in expenditure on manufactured goods has been particularly noticeable.

If the government honors its pledge to reduce taxes and social charges, disposable revenue should increase by 0.8 per cent in 2001, following a rise of 1.2 per cent in 2000. By all evidence the current and future governments will have to commit themselves to the disappearance of budgetary deficits and will have to reduce the rate of growth of public expenditures. A new law in 2001 presents the budget by programs rather than by budgetary envelopes, and it is thought this will make it easier to control expenditures and will aid in slowing the proliferation of taxes and charges. It is expected that if this is accomplished, the burden on household budgets will be eased by 0.3 to 0.4 per cent of disposable income in 2002 and 2003.

Banks have also increased the funds they have made available to households and this has stimulated renewed growth of residential construction between 1996 and 1999. Credits allocated to consumers have also increased, from 0.4 per cent in 1995 to 4.9 per cent and finally to 7.5 per cent in 1999. Facilitating this development has been the reduction in interest rates and inflation.

The rise in final consumption began toward the end of 1997. Reduction in the rate of unemployment has helped as it has the psychological effect of better times. The rate of labor market activity remains lower in France than in the rest of Europe, in spite of new opportunities and new activities. Only 43 per cent of Europeans below the age of 25 are employed, as opposed to 66 per cent in the United States, and 38 per cent of those over 55 years of age are employed in Europe while in America the figure is 59 per cent. The current Jospin government has begun to implement measures favoring the return to employment of individuals living on welfare. This approach is helped by the increase in government revenues, and the rate of activity in France should improve in the near future. Furthermore, 91 per cent of the active population is on salary, and salaries have continued to increase more rapidly than have prices of consumer goods. It would seem likely that these changes in policies and programs would reinforce this expansionist trend in consumption.

Employment

The situation
The recovery of hiring in France is a recent phenomenon of considerable magnitude, explained essentially by strong economic growth which itself is pressed by the demand for consumer goods and for plant and equipment. The improved outlook of households translates into a climate of confidence for the near future, stimulated by promises of reduced taxes and new products and

services (especially those of the information-communication sector) and made concrete by the reduction of unemployment and of its duration. This has all been expressed in increased demand for leisure goods. The creation of employment began in 1994 when a positive figure of 200,000 followed losses of 220,000 in both 1992 and 1993. There was a decline in 1996 (of 50,000 jobs) but since 1997 each year has seen between 300,000 and 500,000 new jobs being created.[5]

In 2000 and 2001, employment in France gave the best results in the Euro zone, returning to the level of 1990. Unemployment fell by 1.6 per cent in 2000 as opposed to just 0.8 per cent for the rest of Euroland. At the same time bottlenecks appeared when several industrial sectors could not find suitable workers. More than half of industrial firms in France could not find the skilled workers they required and 30 per cent were not able to fill available positions for senior executives. The solution to this problem will come from the development of skilled workers by the national educational system, continuing and professional education, improvement in the mobility of workers, and dealing with factors that keep some workers in a state of inactivity. Regarding this last point, a negative tax or a tax credit scheme that is to be put in place during the autumn of 2001 should help some workers return to employment. Some have seen this, especially observers in Germany and the United Kingdom, as a moderation of the redistributive ideology in France and the development of a creative realism. Only the future will tell whether French thinking has changed this much. Nonetheless, 2001 remains remarkable for the positive dynamic of job creation in all sectors – 350,000 new jobs are expected.

The comparison between France and both Germany and Italy has remained favorable during the past five years, as is shown in Table 8.2. It should also be noted that estimates for Germany for 2001 are rather pessimistic, with the economy suffering more than does the French economy from the weakness of the American economy. France is stimulated more by

Table 8.2: Percentage changes in employment, 1996–2000

	1996	1997	1998	1999	2000
France	+0.3	+0.3	+1.2	+2.0	+2.4
Germany	−1.3	−1.3	0.0	0.0	−0.2
Italy	+0.1	−0.2	+0.3	+0.4	+0.8

Note: The 2000 figures for Germany and Italy are provisional estimates.

Source: Ministère de Finance, de l'Economie et de l'Industrie, 2000, in *La Tribune*, 10 November 2000, p. 2

its own internal demand and the contagion from Germany is weak even though Germany is France's primary trade partner.

The recovery of demand in France weakened a bit at the beginning of 2001 so it cannot be said that the problems with unemployment and with job creation have disappeared. One area of concern is that of employment for those with little or no skill development, even though this has been subsidized in France and throughout Europe since 1998. In the words of Gene Koretz: 'according to a recent [US] Labor Department report, job growth rates in high education sectors in Europe and America have been "roughly comparable." From 1980 to 1996, employment in such sectors (where at least 30 per cent of full-time US workers have college degrees) rose at a 2.6 per cent annual rate in the US and an average 2.2 per cent pace in France, West Germany, Britain, and Italy.'[6] The macroeconomic data that have been published indicate that, on average, during the 1980s employment was created when annual GDP growth exceeded 2.1 per cent. According to INSEE the figure was 1.4 per cent; ANPE found it to be 1.2 per cent. A study by Banque Populaire concluded that jobs could be maintained with growth of 1.2 per cent and that unemployment could be contained with 2.2 per cent growth.[7] Finally, the Commissariat Général du Plan was the most pessimistic, concluding that unemployment could be stabilized only with GDP growth of at least 2.7 per cent.[8]

To summarize, it is essentially the strong domestic growth that has resulted in job growth in France being more vigorous than in its neighbors. But the nature of productive activities, as well as the specialties and qualifications required for labor, has been profoundly altered. Thus, we see unemployment of lower-skilled workers at the same time as labor shortages in higher-skill sectors of the economy.

Analysis of 2000–01
Unemployment has been the great failure of the end of the twentieth century, especially in France where the average duration of being without a job was 16 months during the 1990s but only 3 months in the United States. It took the recent acceleration of the rate of GDP growth to reduce both the unemployment rate and its duration. It is, of course, human beings who produce value added and to participate in this process there must exist the combination of possibility and motivation. The French labor market has always been marked by rigidity and inflexibility, by over-regulation and by excessive taxes. For workers mobility is low because it is very costly for them to get the necessary education, because the costs of home ownership and of movement are high, and because of seniority clauses, salary structures and collective agreements. It is also true that the policies of government, primarily the low minimum wage and high social benefits, provide a strong

disincentive for unemployed workers to seek employment. The slow development of labor market flexibility favors not only, by definition, employment but also economic growth. The recently enacted 35-hour work week law increased costs significantly and was accepted only after certain aspects of flexibility were also adopted. Part-time employment and contracts of limited duration have accounted for 60 per cent of hiring since 1997. It is estimated that in 2000 approximately 25 per cent of salaried workers were not on long-term or permanent contracts. This has brought a strong negative reaction in public opinion, as French workers have become very attached to stable employment during the post-war years. Concerning the reallocation of factors of production by the market, the recent decision to reduce certain social contributions of some poorly qualified and poorly paid workers should increase further the flexibility that was obtained by reduction in long-term contracts as a share of total employment.

France creates less employment than its neighbors with the same rate of economic growth because of the accelerated development of service sector activities, many of which have been automated, the resulting rate of productivity growth, and the consequences of the introduction of the new information and communication technologies. Both France and the United States need low-skilled labor. This sector of the labor force does not develop because of the high cost/productivity ratio, the periodically increased minimum wage, and certain disincentives to work. The elasticity of demand for labor with regard to its cost remains high, certainly in excess of unity. It is therefore low-skilled labor that is in most need of assistance since demand for it continually decreases. In addition, the salaries of the active population increase more rapidly than inflation and this hinders employment and makes it more sensible to invest in plant and equipment. We must add to this rising salary the additional cost of social charges which have risen from 38.4 per cent of salaries in 1982 to 48.0 per cent in 2000. Finally excessive regulation of the labor market represents another, though hard to quantify, cost at the microeconomic level.

The minimum salary, social benefits and regulation of markets also create difficulties for supply to meet the demands of the labor market. Many companies in some cities cannot find the labor they need, even low-skilled labor, in the restaurant, construction and public works sectors. It is hoped that supply will develop under the influence of the new measures that have been enacted for the purpose of bringing back to the labor force the estimated 1 million individuals who are now living on welfare. During the 1990s many new policies were introduced aimed at reducing unemployment. Economists also argue that the non-inflationary level of unemployment is now below far 9 per cent. It remains difficult to estimate the impact these recent measures will have on French employment. The main impact of the measures seems to have been that of reducing the cost of employing a worker, for example the 1992 initiative to reduce by 30 per cent the charges on part-time employment which were extended to low-skilled workers in 1993, aids to the creation of new firms, assistance in gaining first jobs for young workers, and so forth. It is difficult to determine whether the 35-hour law has had a positive or negative impact on employment. Unfortunately, these and other measures tend to introduce distortions and modifications of behavior that are not always to the benefit of unemployed workers.

Policy options
Robert Graham has recently written in *The Financial Times*:

> In part, growth is coming from productivity gains and investment in high-technology plus internet-related activity. A boost has also come from the weak Euro which has aided experts. But the government with some fairness can claim that after three years in office, France is reaping the fruits of a well-executed macro-economic strategy. This has boosted domestic demand in three successive mildly expansionary budgets, raising minimum wages and introducing from the outset job creation stimuli. France has been less rigorous in observing stability pact discipline than most of the 11 in the Euro-zone. Nevertheless, its policies have created a virtuous circle of increased confidence, greater investment, declining unemployment, lower budget deficits and expanding household spending in a low inflation environment.[9]

The French government has yet to translate through concrete acts its expressed desire to reduce taxes and social charges, and above all public expenditures. Other reforms, in 2000 and also in 2001, which the government appears to recognize as necessary concern incentives for workers to move from the ranks of the unemployed to jobs and the replacement of public assistance by economic expansion. In this case as in so many others, the French social-fiscal system is atypical among EU members.

Another idea that was introduced in 1999 is the reduction of the charges employers pay for each employee – this amounts to the subsidization of employment of low-skilled workers. Some economists at the Commissariat Général au Plan, among others, argue that a reduction in charges to employers is the policy that is the most supportive of job creation. These are the sort of reforms that have been suggested by Brussels as they restore flexibility in the labor market.

In conclusion, the protection of workers as well as protection of the French systems of social security carry a price: the persistence of unemployment and the substitution of capital for labor. But in the end, labor productivity is improved as well as employment and wages. The increase in productivity should extend employment to low-skilled workers as long as the financing of social systems does not discourage hiring, and as long as measures to encourage the movement from welfare to employment are successful. If this takes place unemployment of low-skilled workers should finally begin to diminish during 2002 or 2003.

The European Union and the Euro in 2000–01

Full economic integration of Europe is far from being accomplished. The experience with the euro has left many economists skeptical and many investors wary. After the Single Market initiative, the Single Currency and the European Central Bank (ECB), projects such as Social Europe or Fiscal Europe suggest a Europe if not homogeneous at least different from the Europe of the twentieth century – one in which individuals will be in principle free to work or move or establish economic ventures anywhere they choose.

The increasing role for the EU, for better or worse

Two extremely important trends were developing in Europe in 2000. First, the continuous process of European economic integration accelerated with the adoption of the euro in 1999. This process of implementing a unified European financial market is just a beginning. Second, mergers and acquisitions in Europe have been the most active in the world. These new trends are changing the face of European corporate culture and the strength of European economies, including those of Central Europe. This is for the good.

As for the bad, the loss of value of the euro, growing anxiety about the ECB, and concerns about some European governments and their ability to manage their economies successfully have left a bad impression on many both inside and outside of Europe. Investors abandoned European stocks and bonds and this paved the way for the weakened euro and economic stagnation until the end of 2000. Loanable funds migrated to North America and Japan and to South East Asia's fast recovering economies. There has been a partial reversal of these flows in 2001, in large part due to the economic slow-down in the United States.

Reduction of European public sector deficits seems to be on the way, with the probable exception of France and perhaps Germany. Nevertheless, governments and publicly owned firms and institutions continue to have large borrowing needs. The questionable benign neglect of the ECB and some elected officials with regard to the exchange rate may have deterred world saving from being attracted to European financial markets. The detrimental result has been rising long-term interest rates, which rose by 1.5 per cent during 1999, and additional charges for both investment and consumption. As we have seen, in the long run a weaker euro generates increased inflation. It is then not surprising that the ECB increased interest rates to 4.75 per cent in the fall of 2000. Some capital has been attracted by this and long-term rates declined by 0.75 per cent in 2000.

The Fall of the Euro and Policy Options

The value of the Euro in terms of US dollars fell from its initial value of $1.18 in January 1999 to below $0.85 in October 2000. Thus the actual depreciation of the euro has exceeded 30 per cent in less than two years while interest rates fell significantly during 1999 and inflation was suppressed until the beginning of 2000. Furthermore, Greece will become the twelfth member of the Euro Zone in January 2001. An accelerated rate of growth and an increase in interest rates since 1999 have attracted short-term capital to the United States. During 2000 US long-term interest rates declined more than European rates so that the gap between the two is now quite minimal. The US stock exchange has become a risky place to put funds and Europeans have reduced their acquisitions of American firms. Capital has therefore been diverted to Europe while the risk of depreciation of the US dollar has increasingly become a concern. Refinancing remains a bit more expensive in the US than in Europe, with the Federal Funds (US) rate about 1.5 percentage points higher than the comparable rate in Europe. With the lowering of the US rate in April 2001 the US rate has come even closer to that of Europe. This convergence of interest rates can be seen as one of the predicted consequences of globalization. National borders are becoming less and less important as we move into the new century.

The decline in the value of the euro having taken place by mid-2000, the ministers of finance of the 11 members of the Euro Zone harmonized their approaches to monetary policy. The ECB was in danger of losing some if its independence in favor of (to use the term of Jacques Delors) a 'European economic government,' that would be somewhat more political in nature. Against this eventuality, it was argued that good fundamentals, strong growth of GDP and falling unemployment would make it less likely that there would be any political interference in ECB policy and that the Bank would be able to pursue a sound monetary policy.[10] This tendency on the part of European governments to intervene in monetary policy is explained by the fact that Keynesian fiscal policy does not work in a world of flexible exchange rates and capital mobility and by the burden of national budgetary deficits and debts. Some economists, such as James Buchanan and Richard Wagner, take this further by arguing that 'the Keynesian-inspired budgetary anarchy that we observe cannot continue.'[11]

Policy options
The attitude of the ECB seems to be that of doing nothing. Indeed, beginning in September 2000 the Bank has been responsible for the increase in French inflation. The price of petroleum rose sharply and while the key interest rate managed by the Bank rose to 4.75 per cent in two steps on September 9 and October 6, 2000, the rate of inflation for euro having increased from 1.2 per

cent to 2.8 per cent during the previous year. At the end of 2000 the French annual rate of inflation was 2.3 per cent and that of the United Kingdom, not a Euroland economy, was only about 1 per cent. European inflation was caused in part by the increase in petroleum prices, but above all by the rising cost of imports consequent on the depreciation of the euro during 1999 and 2000.

Economists have been concerned that a resurgence of an inflationary wage–price spiral would further put pressure on production costs, already burdened by the 35-hour law and the corporate charges that will pay for this initiative. Since the middle of 1999 French firms have lost a portion of the gain in competitiveness that had been progressively achieved since the beginning of the 1980s. Since only monetary policy is effective under the current conditions the ECB has become the key policy institution. In October 2000, *The Economist* judged the ECB to be 'short of credibility' just when 'what the euro needs now is credibility.'[12] Developments in the value of the euro, capital movements, and foreign trade all await decisions that are yet to be taken by the Bank. The suggestion made in April 2001, that the euro and the US dollar would soon find parity, cannot be taken seriously.

A SURVEY OF THE PRINCIPAL SECTORS OF ACTIVITY

Economic growth, having been regained by France in 1997, has slowed throughout Europe because of the petroleum price hikes, depreciation of the exchange rate and high interest rates. All sectors of the economy have been affected. In France, it is expected that GDP growth will reach 3 per cent in 2001, but more important may be the changes in the nature of production in these sectors that are anticipated as we pass into the twenty-first century.

Agriculture and the Primary Sector

Agricultural prices
The challenge of the near future is dominated by the liberalization of trade between France and the EU and the rest of the world (principally with the United States). The EU ministers of agriculture are united on this point and have focused their interest on protection of the environment and the health of consumers. The heart of the problems of agriculture remains the question of subsidies to the industry. The EU is, of course, not the only entity to subsidize agriculture and the US continues to be a heavy subsidizer of its own agricultural sector.

The situation of France is rather special in Europe. France's agricultural production of over €50 billion in 2000 accounts for 22 per cent of EU production. As is clear from Table 8.3, French production exceeds that of either Italy or Germany. The turnover of the total food sector puts France second behind Germany and ahead of the United Kingdom. French exports have averaged an annual rate of increase of 2 per cent since 1980. Since 1979, with the exception of 1994, France has been the second leading exporter of agricultural products behind the United States. Since 1988 France has also been the world's number one exporter of processed foods.

Table 8.3: Basic data on agiculture, 1996

	France	Germany	Italy	Spain	UK	EU
Populaation (millions)	58	81	57	39	58	371
Acreage (000 sq.km)	549	357	301	505	244	3240
GDP (Fr billions)	6560	9338a	5960	2750	5481	37533
GDP per capita (1994) (index)	109	107	102	78	99	100
Active agricultural population (000)	997	1350a	1572	1015	529	8085
% of active population in agriculture	3.9	2.9	7.9	7.9	2.0	5.3
Cultivated land (millions ha)	33.0	17.3	17.2	25.0	17.0	136.0
Cultivated land per farm (ha)	39.0	28.1	5.9	19.0	72.6	16.4
Farms (000)	735	540	2488	1280	234	7321
Share of agriculture in GDP (%)	2.4	0.8a	2.7	3.5	1.4	1.7
Total value of agricultural Production (Fr billions)	302	212a	203	178	136	1427
Rank	1	2	3	4	5	...

Note: a Estimates including the five new Länder.

Sources: ADEPTA (1996), *Le panorama de l'agriculture et des industries agro-alimentaires: Statistiques de l'introduction*, Paris:Association pour le Développement des Echanges Internationaux de Produits et Techniques Agricoles et Agro-alimentaires; also <www.adepta.com/Panorama>

In the EU, France is the largest producer of cereals, oil-producing seeds, sugar beets, beef, poultry and eggs. Food processing is the primary outlet for French agricultural production; however, its rate of growth has fallen from 4.2 per cent in 1995 to 0.6 per cent in 1999. Exports have shown an even greater decline, from 11.8 per cent in 1997 to −1.7 per cent in 1998 and 1.0 per cent in 1999. The food processing industry has expanded employment since 1996, but with a higher proportion of temporary and short-term workers than has been the case in other sectors of the economy. The decline in exports has naturally had a depressive impact on the incomes of farmers and the food processing industry. Costs of production have fluctuated due to the progressive liberalization of European markets, and in addition there has been unfavorable weather, long-term deterioration of demand, and short-term fluctuations of production of meat products internationally. For example, the price of pork was very low in 1976, 1988, 1993 and 2000, but abnormally high in 1985, 1989 and 1996, and these variations in price have been the magnitude of 50–70 per cent.

The general index of agricultural prices has declined by 4 per cent between 1995 and 2000, with vegetables being an exception.[13] The prices of cereals and oil-producing seeds have fallen by 10–20 per cent while the cost of investment has increased by 6 per cent. With regard to energy, petroleum products are generally tax-free for farmers and this has reduced fluctuations in their prices. All in all, French agriculture is currently experiencing a period of considerable difficulty although expectations are high for 2001. By contrast, the food processing industry has experienced a rather stable situation since 1990.

Genetically modified products are not a problem for France since the government has provisionally banned their production. In the US the expansion of their production has slowed even though the Food and Drug Administration has declared that the health risk from modified corn is remote.[14] On the other hand, organic farming has shown strong growth throughout Europe with an annual growth rate of 28 per cent since the 1992 reform of the Common Agriculture Policy. In France this industry accounts for only 0.5 per cent of the total number of farms and 0.36 per cent of cultivated land.[15] In the United Kingdom where this accounts for 3 per cent of cultivated land, 'farmers cannot keep up with the demand for organic food. The British farming community has reacted very slowly to this market, whereas other countries are modernizing their farms to produce organic food.'[16] It is therefore surprising that the French supply has not reacted more strongly to this new opportunity, especially since the British import so much of their consumption.

This French and European approach to food safety is based on the 'precautionary principle,' whereby restrictions or regulations on food imports are justified while the scientific risks to health remain unproven. The World Bank has calculated that this can in principle save two lives per billion (the population of the EU is 370 million) but that it is likely to cost African countries some $700 million in lost exports.[17]

The New Agriculture

If we are to present an accurate overview of French agriculture we must note that this sector is undergoing a rapid transformation and modernization under pressure from the EU as well as from the forces of globalization. As was stated in a report of the Food and Agriculture Organization, 'the opening of borders has gone hand in hand with significant structural changes in [most of the agricultural products and food processing] producer countries – operators in the various sectors are experiencing increasingly strong competition on a regional, national and international level.'[18] However, among EU countries French agriculture is changing comparatively rapidly at the outset of the twenty-first century.

The specific character that French agriculture is adopting is to a large part determined by the national government although the EU is playing a significant role as well. The model that is being adopted has been referred to as 'multi-functional.' It is defined in the very conservation oriented *Loi d'Orientation Agricole de 1999*:

> European agriculture will be heading for destruction if it sets as its sole objective the ability to sell raw materials on the world market at the same price as its keenest world competitors. This will only be possible at the price of destroying at least 300,000 French farms, and hundreds of thousands of European farms. This is a result no one wants. Government intervention is only justified if it promotes sustainable and balanced economic development – preserving farms over time, fostering the development of employment, thus allowing young farmers to establish themselves – and if it strengthens the role of farmers as producers of services and landscapes. [19]

The challenge to French farmers in achieving such policy goals is much broader than the sole and primary function of producing food.

Fishing is another important activity in the French primary sector, since the country is bordered by the Atlantic Ocean and the Mediterranean. The primary products are tuna, sole, lobster, cod, whiting, sea bass and shell-fish. The chief export market is the rest of the EU. Fishing accounts for 100,000 jobs including 17,000 sea fishermen with 8,500 boats (of which 2,500 are in overseas departments), generally less than 36 feet in length. It is an industry that has remained largely artisanal in its structure and operation. During the past two or three decades fishing has undergone a difficult restructuring in response to increasing competition from foreign producers, changes in patterns of consumption, and over-fishing of many of the world's fish stocks. Imports come from the United Kingdom, Norway and Denmark. Successive French governments have often been obliged to give assistance to the Atlantic fishery but the number of jobs has continued to decline. This too is a consequence of government policy in that a quota of small-scale producers is fixed annually by the Minister of Agriculture. Regulation by the EU was strengthened in November 1999 with regard to methods of fishing, the zones in which fishing is allowed, the quantities of various species that can be caught, destruction of excessive supply, and fines and taxes. This set of regulations and norms is at least as extensive and as complex as that for agriculture. These policies are aimed at creating an environment of stability or at least of minimizing the uncertainty faced by European producers.

Manufacturing

The progress of French manufacturing

The Economist noted recently: 'France is better known for its beautiful women and buildings, tasty wines and cuisine, grand art and culture, a country with a grand history and a capital, Paris, that is consistently rated as among the world's most beautiful. Business and commerce are sentiments not normally associated with France or the French. But they are doing pretty well.' Even, one could add, without the help of their still relatively centralized state.

The rate of growth of European industrial production slowed somewhat in 2001, after having achieved a figure of 5.5 per cent in 2000. After a sharp decline in demand in the second half of 2000, when it declined by 1.8 per cent in August and 1.2 per cent in September, it is expected to grow by 2.7 per cent in 2001 and by over 3 per cent in 2002.[20] The deregulation of the utility sector promises to change the situation for industry significantly. The recovery of job creation in manufacturing took both economists and governments by surprise. As in the rest of the economy, manufacturing investment regained the ground it had lost since 1990. In 1993, manufacturing investment fell by 18 per cent from the 1994 level, but since 1995 it has grown annually by 5–11 per cent. Unfortunately production has been slower to recover.

In 1995 the level of French industrial production was the same as it was in 1990 and the following five years saw growth of only 17 per cent. In the previous chapter we noted that this was in part caused by an acceleration of outsourcing by firms.[21] It is also clear that these aggregate figures hide major disparities among sectors of manufacturing. Overall, application of new technologies has separated many activities from manufacturing and the restructuring has not yet been completed. According to the Minister of the Economy: 'the new technologies account for 20 per cent of French GDP growth in 1999.' This explains the current concern of the government with regard to professional training, and the further development and opening to competition of sectors such as communication and energy. At the beginning of the twenty-first century one thing that is strikingly new in French manufacturing is the extensive development of networks and other relationships among small and medium-sized firms.

The impact of globalization and the New Economy
There are 3 million firms in all sectors of the French economy, of which 2.1 million are very small (fewer than 10 employees). Manufacturing is the sector that is the most concentrated. This structure has not changed much in recent years, in spite of the numerous mergers and acquisitions that have taken place. It resembles the structure of Germany in that there are a large number of small-sized firms alongside many very large manufacturing groups, and very few medium-sized firms. Concentration is strongest in the steel industry, with Usinor producing 90 per cent of French output. Output in this industry grew by 4.7 per cent in 2000. French manufacturing exports were €5.3 billion in 2000 while imports amounted to €4.7 billion.

French manufacturing consists primarily of aircraft, electronics, transportation, textiles and clothing, chemicals, machinery and steel. As is shown in Table 8.4 its concentration is similar to that of other industrialized economies.

Table 8.4: The Importance of small and medium-sized firms, industrialized economies, 1996

Country	Share of all employees	Share of all of total sales	Sales as a share
France	96.1	53.1	41.4
Germany	94.8	47.4	37.0
Spain	98.5	71.6	56.9
UK	96.9	62.6	49.7
USA	90.9	34.8	26.2
Japan	97.9	60.2	39.4

Note: Figures are for firms with 20–499 employees, and are in percentages. Food processing is excluded.

Sources: *Les Quatre Pages des Statistiques Industrielles*, Ministère des Finances, de l'Economie et de l'Industrie (2000), p. 139; *Annuaire Statistique de France* (1999), INSEE

France has been very receptive to the establishment of foreign firms, especially in chemicals, pharmaceuticals and certain branches of industrial equipment. Globalization has been marked by a variety of joint efforts, international mergers and acquisitions in which French firms have been most aggressive and successful during recent years. Firms in which foreign interests own over 50 per cent of the shares constitute 34.5 per cent of French firms, with the figures being 20 per cent for automobiles and 40 per cent for industrial equipment.[22]

The French 'new technologies of information and communication' sector is fourth in the world behind Japan, the US and Germany. The impact of these new technologies is not yet clear. One analysis of this issue suggests that the indirect effects, that is new relations among firms and labor productivity, will be greater than the direct effects in terms of value added production. The difficulty in determining this is that many of the new start-ups are not yet making a profit or have actually failed, perhaps as a result of the collapse of share prices on the NASDAQ. This is a global phenomenon and the sudden halt to economic growth could very well lead to a worldwide recession. At this moment, however, the primary concern of French business is the 35-hour law. The government was fully aware of the negative potential of this initiative but chose to accent politics rather than competitiveness of French firms, and went so far as to recommend flexibility in the application of the law. Fortunately, as we have seen, the return to a growth-oriented distribution of income has assisted in this effort. It was expected that the impacts of increasing globalization would exclude low-skilled workers. In actuality, many firms in sectors such as construction, hotels, restaurants, farming and artisanal activities (such as butchering and roofing) have not been able to find enough suitable labor.

The new nature of the restructuring in progress
The available data obscure a new phenomenon that is slowly becoming apparent. In 2000 and 2001 the French manufacturing landscape is in a process of transformation. The increasing presence of smaller firms in France is not significant in their numbers but rather by the fact that they are often components of a large industrial group, that groupings of a radically new character are forming and that smaller firms themselves are forming various sorts of networks.[23] Among all smaller firms, six workers out of ten are employed by one of 3,900 manufacturing groups, and one group in five is itself headed by a firm with fewer than 500 employees. These groups account for 88 per cent of French industrial production, 95 per cent of its exports and 98 per cent of R&D expenditures, and control 8,700 of the 23,000 firms with more than 20 employees. This phenomenon is a consequence of the numerous divisions and splits of firms taking place in the large groups. Thus, a new form of industrial concentration is taking place in France of groups of firms in which there is a leader firm, but not a parent firm, and they exist in areas in which there is a central activity, such as automobile construction.

These changes have had their most important impacts on the automobile industry, shipbuilding, electronics and electrical equipment, pharmaceuticals, perfume and chemicals. During the 1980s these industries increased their share of total employment, and smaller firms increased theirs from 51 per cent in 1990 to 53 per cent in 1997. These two events are not contradictory since smaller firms are so prominent in these industries and through restructuring many large firms have been split into several smaller ones which they continue to control. The presence of these groups does little to modify the concentration of these already heavily concentrated industries. On the other hand, it is evident that certain sectors that are not very concentrated in terms of enterprises become so when one considers the collections of many firms in these large groups. This is especially true in the case of pharmaceuticals, metals, wood and paper, as well as electronics and electrical equipment.

Furthermore, the smaller firms not controlled by these groups often form themselves into networks, some of which are based on geographical districts. The most common basis for these industrial districts is, of course, a specific product or sector of manufacturing. This structure is most common in Italy where they account for 10 per cent of national manufacturing output and 50 per cent of that output is exported. They constitute growth poles or technopoles of firms in the same region and product area and strengthen their role in the market by combining their capabilities, their relations and their know-how. They also join their efforts to lobby or influence policy in their national capital and in Brussels. This structure is becoming more common in France, and at the end of 2000 there were 13 French industrial districts.

This entirely new industrial landscape has been designed to deal with two distinct problems: the management of competition among smaller firms themselves and the difficulty in mastering the market in which they operate. In the globalized economic environment it is of utmost importance to exchange information rapidly, even through informal relationships when the partners are local and well known. As a report by the Department of the Economy put it:

> These swarms of smaller firms, where the activity is often of a high-tech artisanal nature, develop intensively, seeking more to increase value added, to differentiate their products by quality, and to pursue innovation than to reduce cost through economies of scale,…,Diversification, training, knowledge of markets, joint efforts in foreign markets, and establishment of a common presence in Brussels – the network of French industrial districts was established in 1998 with a dozen active districts. [24]

Some of these districts even cross national borders, such as that of Vallée d'Arve-Geneva which consists of 550 smaller Swiss and French firms in machine tools production.

The French state is only belatedly disengaging itself from productive activity and remains in control of many economic decisions through its direct or indirect control of many large enterprises. The newer firms and the smaller firms in France have learned how to circumvent the state and its financial institutions. They have access to international financial markets and the value of their shares is attractive to foreign investors. Their primary short-term anxiety is over the value of the euro in exchange markets.

Financing the new firms
As a financial center Paris is equal to Frankfurt, but it has only 1,135 firms (as of June 1, 1999) compared to Frankfurt's 4,004, 2,650 for the New York Stock Exchange, and 4,870 for NASDAQ. But the Paris Exchange in 2000 lost all of the gains of 1999 and the New Market of high-tech firms followed a downward path similar to that of NASDAQ (see Table 8.5).

Table 8.5: Capitalizations of principal exchanges (% national GDP)

	March 1998	January 2000
New York	159	195
Tokyo	50	117
Helsinki	74	268
Geneva	228	253
London	205	214
Luxembourg	180	200
Amsterdam	139	175
Stockholm	122	160
Athens	33	158
Paris	54	102
Dublin	82	78

Source: *Les Echos*, May 5, 1999, December 1, 1999, and March 16, 2000.

The state, companies and exports
A new role appears to have devolved to the state in France, that of facilitator rather than of principal actor (with Colbertism) or of general-in-charge (with state planning) as evidenced by a gradual easing of existing regulations and the creation of legal structures that are favorable to the appearance of new forms of relations among economic actors. The roles of the EU and of globalization have been crucial here. Economic growth in an open economy tends to spread to its trading partners. In this environment the French state cannot retain its capacity to intervene and it can no longer subsidize the exports of French firms as this contradicts the principles of the EU as well as agreements signed under the aegis of the World Trade Organization.

'All the large states assist their national firms in conquering external markets and in gaining contracts,' in the words of *Les Echos* in 1997. These old habits have hardly changed since that was written. The various initiatives of the OECD have not modified this policy. Japan and France are among the economies that resort most often to giving financial assistance to projects in difficulty. There is also the tradition of trade fairs or trade missions abroad in which the head of state or a minister plays the role of chief commercial representative. This, of course, is the practice of most of the other industrialized countries. *Les Echos* also argued that while 'France is ahead of the others in terms of subsidies to large contracts, the United States tends to prefer to finance specific projects.'[25] In addition to this the government has developed in the course of the last century a program of Conseillers de Commerce Extérieur, or foreign trade counselors, of whom there are currently 3,500.

What is new in this behavior of the French state is its recent interest in exports by smaller firms, virtually ignored until the end of the 1990s. While 300 firms account for more than half of French exports and 40,000 smaller firms the remainder, the 140,000 smallest companies have seen their exports grow from 3 per cent of total exports in 1997 to about 5 per cent in 2000. On the other hand, little has changed with regard to the complexity and the diversity of agencies and other ministerial services that compete among themselves. Figure 8.3 gives a very simplified depiction of this structure.

State intervention in the French economy is certainly less in 2001 than it was in preceding decades. However, 'opaque and closed off, the system of public financing benefited a handful of large companies, beyond any real control.'[26] The French government allocated to these companies Fr170 billion each year, as much as they pay in taxes. There are about 70 different systems of public support for companies, 18 for regional development, 13 for research, 60 for assistance to employment, 1,832 for creation of new firms, and so forth. If social transfers to households are added to this, France stands at the forefront of all countries regarding the importance and complexity of subsidies and other aids to companies, exports and consumption. There are many dozens of public and para-public agencies and organizations with mandates to redistribute a portion of the tax revenues of the state. But it remains the case that it is the largest industrial groups, such as Rhône-Poulenc, Thomson and Bull, that receive the most benefit from this system because they continue to maintain privileged relations with public sector decision-makers. According to a report of the Senate, 'smaller firms are ignored by the government's systems of support for research and development.'[27] Additionally, there are subsidies by local governments that are designed to promote companies to locate in their area. Another government report stated:

> The resulting excessive support is a result primarily of the myopia of the state. No one is in actual control of this diversion of state funds to companies,...,With regard to support for R&D and exports the wide variety of services charged with their management make is impossible to put in place a unified system of control; each service or organization acts just the way it wishes to.[28]

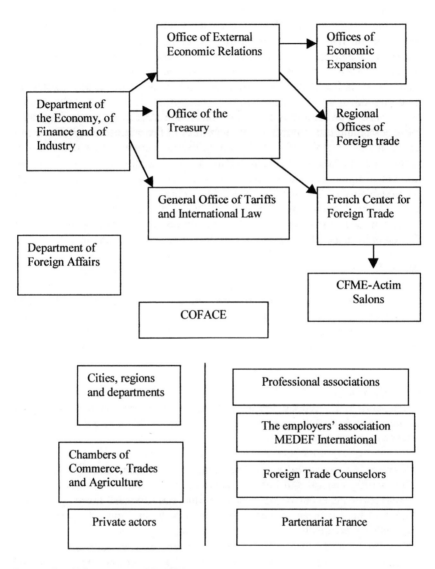

Source: *Les Echos*, January 29, 1999.

Figure 8.3: French state services and agencies assisting exporters

For half a century, the French State has had an important position in the financing and direction of R&D. After the Second World War the objective was that of regaining the slippage of France *vis-à-vis* other industrial economies, especially the United States. In the 1960s a large number of public research agencies were created on the initiative of the Direction Générale de la Recherche Scientifique et Technique. This agency instituted a new method of administration and of contractual relationships with private companies. The programs of innovation of the 1970s, in comparison, were more costly and less productive and subsidies to firms became something of a tradition. The method of R&D by administrative networks that was followed in the 1980s must also be considered to have been a failure. At the same time the government internationalized its research programs through multiple relationships with EU member countries. Finally, multiple-year support of *pôles technologiques* was introduced with the objective of enhancing European competitiveness. At the beginning of the twenty-first century French pubic support for research is essentially European in nature.

Services

This sector is by far the most dynamic in 2001 in that it creates the most employment and new firms of any sector. Each new firm is, of course, the source of new jobs. The distinction is made between specialized commercial services, on the one hand, and retail sales, finance, insurance, and transportation, on the other.

Private services
These services correspond largely to the activities of smaller firms and some of the larger firms. It is a very diversified sub-sector and consists of three categories of service:

- *Services to companies.* Post and telecommunications, consulting companies, general and business services, and research and development. This represents about 70 per cent of commercial services. More specifically we find here courier services, computing, software, system maintenance, consulting, architecture, engineering and publicity.
- *Services to individuals.* Hotels and restaurants, travel agencies, cultural activities, recreation, and personal services. These account for 23 per cent of commercial services.
- *Real estate.* This consists of real estate developers, agents, and managers of real estate.

The growth of commercial services has increased steadily since 1993, a year that saw a minor slow-down. As Table 8.6 indicates, it was services to companies that provided the growth most strongly. Services to individuals have developed most slowly, while the rate of growth of real estate services has been irregular. As a general statement we can say that the most traditional branches are as dynamic as those that are dominated by the new information technologies. In 1997 the commercial services sub-sector consisted of 250,000 firms and at least 2 million employees, and 97 per cent of these had fewer than 30 workers. However, the 2,200 firms with 100 or more employees accounted for more than 40 per cent of total revenues. One-third of all workers are on temporary contracts.

Table 8.6: Growth of volume of commercial services

Services	1985	1990	1999
Services to companies	100	115	130
Services to households	100	125	150
Total of commercial services	100	125	150
Value added (private sector services)	100	119	140

Source: *INSEE Première*, July 2000

The trends in 2001 are all favorable for commercial services, including an explosion of information processing and telecommunications activities. Many of these services are performed by sub-contractors and are often outsourced by larger firms. It is clear that the growth of these services varied dramatically from one branch to another under the impact of new technologies and ongoing changes in final demand. Commercial services have recently shown a rate of growth that was strongest in the areas of data processing, real estate, radio and television, telecommunications, and short-term employment agencies. By contrast funeral services, travel agencies, and beauty salons have seen diminished growth.

Retail trade, finance, transportation, and insurance
The activities of this sub-sector regained their vigor toward the end of the 1990s. One of the main reasons for this was the considerable amount of concentration and restructuring that took place, which affected both retail trade and financial institutions. Again, there was impressive application of new information and communication technologies here. Table 8.7 shows that recent growth of this sub-sector in the context of other sectors.

Table 8.7 Production by branch, volume, average annual growth

Sector	1999/1990	1999/1998
Commercial services	2.2	5.1
Commerce, banking and insurance	1.8	3.1
Manufacturing	2.5	3.2
Agriculture, food processing and energy	0.7	2.7
Value added (private sector)	1.8	3.2

Source: *INSEE Première*, July 2000

The strong growth of consumption after 1997 has been favorable for the largest retailers, both of food and specialties, and for department stores. The small traditional merchant has remained relatively stable for this three-year period. For the third consecutive year retail trade has shown significant growth of more than 7 per cent, especially in the area of sales of appliances and other equipment. The future, as it is in most of the other industrialized economies, is with the large retailers with large stores and with suppliers linked by the Internet. Transportation services are, of course, linked with that of retail sales. Transportation has also suffered in part by the slowness of liberalization regarding the French monopolies of air and rail transportation. Road haulage has also seen problems arising from restructuring, with the large companies developing to the detriment of the smaller independent firms, and the workforce is frequently confronted with the bankruptcy of their employer. The European trucking network is less and less adapted to heavy transport and successive French and Italian governments plan to complete this system and then to replace it by one of truck–train containers. The development of this sub-sector is therefore essentially difficult and uncertain. Intra-European competition has become quite intense.

The distinction between banks and insurance companies is less and less clear. Banks offer insurance services, often merging with insurance companies or developing a network of supply. The trend in 2001 is toward mergers and acquisitions, sometimes for protection or prevention of a takeover, and there is resistance to hostile takeovers by foreign or French competitors. At the same time French firms use the same techniques for gaining access to foreign markets. In the longer term, it is probably the case that transport and commerce will continue to develop at a pace that exceeds that of banking and financial institutions. The trend for the past 20 years has been a growth of 80 per cent for commerce, 74 per cent for transport and only 44 per cent for financial services.

CONCLUSION

Industry adapts to a New World – this could be the title of a new book on the French economy of 2001. Old-style manufacturers have become competitive again. This may be the Internet age, but France is a country that still has many of the old-style manufacturers. Trains, automobiles, aircraft, ships, semiconductors and clothing: all of them are still produced by French-based companies. It might have been the will of French governments to prop up diversified businesses. For instance, big companies such as Giat Industries or Thomson Multimedia had received huge subsidies until the end of the 1990s. However, it is clear that the last two years of the century were remarkable in that a 'normal' French capitalism emerged; that is to say, French capitalism now resembles that of other industrialized economies. The reason for this is partly the retreat of the state in economic matters, partly the liberalization of the economy and partly privatizations. Now French CEOs behave more or less the way their counterparts do on the other side of the Atlantic or in South East Asia.

For example, in 1999 and 2000 there were hostile takeovers or mergers of Elf Aquitaine by TotalFina; Alcatel and Canada Newbridge Networks; HSBC and Crédit Commercial de France; France Télécom and Orange; and Crédit Lyonnais and Société Générale; while others, such as Air Liquide and Air Products and Péchiny, Alcan and Swiss Alugroup, failed. *The Financial Times* commented:

> Even if a more aggressive corporate culture is developing, the most powerful influence on French business is still the French state. But the state's influence is no longer quite what it was – if it was, last year's battle of the banks would probably not have happened. Asked whether the state could have stopped a hostile takeover of Alcatel a while back when the company's shares were in the doldrums, many analysts and bankers would answered that it could not,...,There seems little reason to believe that the current pause signals the end of hostile takeover activity in France - although, as one observer put it, 'there are still very powerful protective networks. [29]

As for employment, France is on the way to modernity, keeping up with the most efficient industrialized countries. The tradition of fixed jobs is changing as employment opportunities open up and the labor market as well as work practices become more flexible. Flexibility has to some extent also been one of the unexpected outcomes of the 35-hour week law. In addition, the desire of the employers' association to renew the dialogue with the unions on the project of redesigning the French system so that it will be less rigid and more modern is very encouraging. For example, they have suggested joint management of the system of social security.

Finally, we must note that the economic reality facing the French economy does not conform to the conceptualization traditionally held by governments both of the right and the left. Robert Graham has stated that 'the Jospin government has managed to appease its left while playing the turn of the market and globalization.'[30] And John Andrews adds that 'in spite of all the strikes,…,which are so common in France and in spite of all the populist rhetoric directed against the world of business France has adopted a certain number of Anglo-Saxon traditions and practices, without seeming to have done so.'[31] France, its state, its economy and its inhabitants have entered into a new age. It resembles increasingly other successful societies that it has historically not wanted to resemble, such as the United States. Is France aware of this? That is another story.

NOTES

1. For a discussion of discovery and surprise in economic matters, see I. Kirzner, 'Discovery, private property and the theory of justice," *Journal des Economistes et des Etudes Humaines*, October 1990, pp. 209–223.
2. *Les Echos*, April 2, 2001.
3. *Les Echos*, April 3, 2001.
4. 'Bruxelles demand à la France de réduire plus rapidement ses déficits, *Les Echos*, January 25, 2001.
5. These figures are from the Ministère de l'Emploi, in *Les Echos*, February 19, 2001, p. 3.
6. Gene Koretz, 'Where Europe lags in jobs – low-education sectors have shrunk,' *Business Week*, 14 September, 1998.
7. *Le fait du jour*, Paris: Banque Populaire, February 8, 1999.
8. Commissariat Général du Plan, *Emploi, négociations collectives, protection sociale: vers quelle Europe sociale?*, Paris: La documentation Française, November 1999, p. 28.
9. Robert Graham, 'Forces of change in a conservative society: The Jospin government has managed to appease its left while playing the tune of the market and globalization,' *Financial Times*, June 14, 2000.
10. Fl. Aftalion, 'Les raisons fondamentales des faiblesses de l'euro,' *Les Echos*, May 29, 2000, p. 77.
11. James M. Buchanan and Richard E. Wagner, *Democracy in Deficit: The Political Legacy of Lord Keynes*, New York: Academic Press, 1977, p. 182.
12. *The Economist*, October 9, 2000.
13. Ministère de l'Agriculture et de la Pêche, *Les chiffres de l'agriculture et de la pêche*, and *Cahier AGRESTE*, Paris: Ministère de l'Agriculture et de la Pêche, 2000.
14. *The Financial Network* (2000), CNN, at <http://cnnfn.cnn.com> October 25, 2000.

15. Comité de Promotion des Produits Agro-alimentaires de Rhône-Alpes, *Organic Farming in Figures*, Lyon: R3AP, Comité de Promotion des Produits Agro-Alimentaires de Rhône–Alpes, 2000.
16. *The Independent*, October 26, 2000.
17. Tsunehiro Otsuki, John. S. Wilson and Virvat Sewadeh, *Saving Two in a Billion: A Case Study to Quantify the Trade Effect of European Food Safety Standards on African Exports*, Washington: The World Bank, Development Research Group, 2000.
18. Food and Agriculture Organization, *FAO Conference in Maastricht, 12–17 September 1999: Contribution de la France,* Paris: Senat, 2000.
19. *Loi d'Orientation Agricole de 1999*, adopted in 1999.
20. Crédit Lyonnais, *Revue économique*, October, 2000.
21. This comment of Minister Dominique Strauss-Kahn is found in *Les Echos*, October 13, 1999, p. 4.
22. *Statistiques et Etudes Industrielles*, 2000, *Implantation étrangère dans l'industrie française au 01/01/1998*, Paris: Ministère de l'Economie, des Finances et de l'Industrie, 2000.
23. *Statistiques et Etudes Industrielles, Les 4 pages*, Paris: Ministére de l'Economie, des Finance, et de L'Industrie, February, 2000.
24. Ibid.
25. 'Comment les etats aident leurs entreprises à l'export,' *Les Echos*, October 28, 1997, pp. 70–71.
26. *L'Expansion*, June 10, 1999, p. 70.
27. Sénat, *Rapport Guillaume*, Paris: Sénat, 1999.
28. Service des Etudes à la Direction de la Campatabilité Publique, cited in *L'Expansion*, June 10, 1999, p. 9. For the Department of Finance's view of administrative wastage see Jean Arthuis, *Valeurs Actuelles*, April 24, 1999, pp. 22–25.
29. Robert Graham, 'Economy, France Survey,' *The Financial Times*, November 10, 2000.
30. Ibid.
31. John Andrews, 'Petits pas vers une économie libérale,' in *Le Monde en 2000*, Paris: Courier international and The Economist Publications, December 2000, p. 24.

References

Abramovits, Moses (1989), *Thinking about Growth*, Cambridge, MA: Harvard University Press.

Adams, William James (1989), Restructuring the French Economy, Washington, DC: Brookings Institution.

Agence d'urbanisme de Lyon (1997), *Développement économique dans l'agglomération lyonnaise*, Lyon: Agence d'urbanisme. compétitive et rassemblée, *Millénaire trois*.

Allègre, Claude (2000), *Toute vérité est bonne â dire*, Paris: Fayard Robert Laffont.

Altman, Roger C. and Charles A. Kupchan (1997–98), 'Arresting the decline of Europe,' *World Policy Journal*.

Andrews, John (2000), 'Petits pas vers une économie libérale,' *Le Monde en 2000*, Paris: The Economist Publications, December.

Annuaire statistique de la France, Paris: INSEE, various issues.

Anon. (1997a), 'RMI et SMIC: étude sur l'apport financier de l'accès à l'emploi,' *Problèmes économiques*, Paris: La documentation Française, no. 525, 13–19.

Anon. (1997b), 'Comment les états aident leurs entreprises à l'export,' *Les Echos*, October, 70–71.

Anon. (2000), 'Fewer and wrinklier Europeans,' *The Economist*, January 25, 52.

Anon. (2001), 'Bruxelles demands à la France de réduire plus rapidement ses déficits,' *Les Echos*, January 25.

Ardagh, John (1999), *France in the New Century*, Hamondsworth, Middlesex: Penguin Books.

Arduin, Jean-Pierre (1994), 'Development and economic evaluation of high speed in France,' *Japan Railway and Transport Review*, October 3, 1–11.

Armstrong, Harvey W. (1996), 'European Union regional policy: sleepwalking to a crisis,' *International Regional Science Review*, 19 (3).

Arondel, Philippe (1997), *L'homme-marché*, Paris: Desclée de Broulwer.

Arthuis, Jean (1999), *Valeurs Actuelles*, April 24.

Ashford, Douglas H. (1982), *Policy and Politics in France: Living with Uncertainty*, Philadelphia: Temple University Press.

Askenazy, Philippe (2000), 'Les 35 heures, une clé inattendue,' *Les Echos*, March 28.

Asselain, Jean-Charles (1984), *Histoire économique de la France*, vol. II, Paris: Editions du Seuil.

Asselain, Jean-Charles (1992), 'L'ouverture à la concurrence internationale,' *Cahiers Français*, no. 255.

Association of European Border Regions (2001), website: http://www.aebr-ageg.de/.

Axford, Barrie, *The Global System: Economics, Politics and Culture*, New York: St. Martin's Press.

Banque Populaire (1999), *Le fait du jour*, Paris: Banque Populaire, February 8.

Barber, Benjamin (1996), *Jihad vs. McWorld*, New York: Balantine.

Barrau, Alain (1999), *Union européenne et Mercosur: mariage ou union libre?*, Paris: Assemblée Nationale.

Barro, Robert J. and Xavier S. Sala-I-Martin (1991), 'Convergence across states and regions,' *Brookings Papers on Economic Activity*, 1, 107–181.

Bauer, Joachim (1992), *Europa der Regionen*, Schriften zum Europäischen Recht, Band 9, Berlin: Duncker & Humblot.

Bean, Charles R. (1994), 'European unemployment: a survey,' *Journal of Economic Literature*, XXXII, 573–619.

Becker, Gary (1976), *The Economic Approach to Human Behavior*, Chicago: University of Chicago Press.

Beitone, Alain, Maurice Parodi and Bernard Simler (1994), *L'économie et la société française au second XXème siècle*, Paris: Armand Colin.

Bertola, Guiseppe and Andrea Ichino (1995), 'Crossing the river: a comparative perspective on Italian employment dynamics,' *Economic Policy*, 21.

Blanchard, Olivier and Jean-Paul Fitoussi (1998), *Croissance et chômage*, Paris: La documentation Française.

Blodget, Henry (2000), 'L'Europe a le même potentiel que les Etats Unis pour le commerce électronique,' *Les Echos*, February 25.

Bœuf, Jean-Luc (ed) (1995), *L'aménagement du territoire : bialan et renouveau*, Problèmes politiques et sociaux, no. 750, Paris: La documentation Française.

Briant, Pierrette (1999), 'Bade-Wurtemberg: des salaires attractifs pour les Alsaciens,' *INSEE Première*, (no. 660).

Brunet, Roger (1989), *Les villes européennes,*' Paris: DATAR, 1989.

Buchanan, James and R.D. Tollison (eds) (1984), *The Theory of Public Choice – II*, Ann Arbor: University of Michigan Press.

Buchanan, James and Bordon Tulock (1971), *The Calculus of Consent*, Ann Arbor: University of Michigan Press.

Buchanan, James M. and Richard E. Wagner (1977), *Democracy in Deficit: The Political Legacy of Lord Keynes*, New York: Academic Press.

Buigues, Pierre-André and André Sapir (1999), 'L'impact du marché unique sur les grandes pays européens,' *Revue économique et politique*, 109, (2).

Buzelay, Alain (1996) *Intégration et désintégration européennes*, Paris: Economica.

Cahiers AGRESTE (2000), Paris: Ministère de l'Agriculture et de la Pêche.

Cahiers AGRESTE (1996), Paris: Ministère de l'Agriculture et e la Pêche, October, no. 6-7.

Camagni, Roberto J. (1996), 'Cities in Europe: globalisation, sustainability and cohesion,' in *European Spatial Planning*, Rome: Presidenza del Consiglio die Ministri Dipartimento per l'informazione e l'editoria, 105–109.

Cameron, Rondo (1997), *A Concise Economic History of the World*, Oxford: Oxford University Press.

Cappelen, Aadne, Jan Fagerberg and Bart Verspagen (1999), 'Lack of regional convergence,' in Jan Fagerberg, Paolo Guerriere and Bart Verspagen (eds), *The Economic Challenge for Europe*, Cheltenham, UK: Edward Elgar.

Caron, François (1997a), *Histoire économique de la France, XIX-XXe siècles*, Paris: Armand Colin.

Caron, François (1997b), *Les deux révolutions industrielles du XXe siècle*, Paris: Albin

Michel.

Carré, J.-J.P. Dubois and E. Malinvaud (1975), *French Economic Growth*, Palo Alto, CA: Stanford University Press.

Cazes, B. and P. Mioche, (1990), *Modernisation ou décadence: Contributio n à l'histoire du Plan Monnet et de la planification en France*, Aix-en-Provence: Publications de l'Université de Provence.

Challenges, various issues.

Chambres de Commerce et d'Industrie Rhône-Alpes (2001), *Chiffres Clés du Rhône: édition 2000-2001*.

Chevalier, Jean-Marie (ed) (1999), *L'idée de service public est-elle encore soutenable?*, Paris: Presses Universitaires de France.

Cobban, Alfred (1965), *A History of Modern France, 1871–1962, Hamondsworth*, Middlesex: Penguin.

Cochet, François (1997), *Histoire économique de la France depuis 1945*, Paris: Dunod.

Cohen, Daniel (1997), *Richesse du monde, pauvretés des nations*, Paris: Flammarion.

Cohen, Daniel (1999), *Nos temps modernes*, Paris: Flammarion.

Cohen, Daniel, Arnaud Lefranc and Gilles Saint-Paul (1997), 'French unemployment a transatlantic perspective,' *Economic Policy*, 25, 267–285.

Cohen, Elie (1992), *Le Colbertisme hi-tech: Economie du grand projet des Télécom*, Paris: Hachette.

Cohen, Elie (1994), *La tentation hexagonale: la souveraineté à l'épreuve de la mondialisation*, Paris: Julliard.

Cohen, Elie (1996), 'Ne pas confondre service public avec service du public,' *Chronoiques Economiques DEDEIS*, 3.

Comité de Promotion des Produits Agro-alimentaires de Rhône-Alpes (2000), *Organic Farming in Figures*, Lyon: R3AP, Comité de Promotion des Produits Agro-Alimentaires de Rhône– Alpes.

Commissariat au Plan (1997), *Quelles politiques pour l'industrie française? Dynamiques du système productif: analyses, débats, propositions*, Paris: La documentation Française.

Commissariat Général du Plan (1999), *Emploi, négociations collectives, protection sociale: vers quelle Europe sociale?*, Paris: La documentation Française, November.

Commission of the European Union (1994), *Europe 2000+, Coopération pour l'aménagement du territoire européen*, Brussels: Commission of the European Union.

Concialdi, Pierre (1997), 'Income distribution in France: the mid 1980s turning point,' in Peter Gottschalk, Björn Gustafsson and Edward Palmer (eds), *Changing Patterns in the Distribution of Economic Welfare: An International Perspective*, Cambridge: Cambridge University Press, pp. 239–264.

Conso, Pierre (1997), 'L'apparition de nouveaux modes d'organisation industrielle et de management,' in Christian de Boissiu (ed), *Les mutations de l'économie française*, Paris: Economica.

Crédit Lyonnais (2000), *Revue économique*, October.

Crozet, Yves *et al.* (1997), *Les grandes questions de l'économie française*, Paris: Nathan.

DARES (1997), 'Les politiques de l'emploi en France depuis 1974,' Paris: La documentation Française, no. 509.

DATAR (1989), *Les villes 'européenes,'* Paris: La documentation Française.

References

DATAR (1994), *Débat national pour l'aménagement du territoire*, Paris: La documentation Française.

de Benoist, Alain (1996), 'Confronting globalization,' *Telos*, 108.

de Closet, François (1982) *Toujours Plus*, Paris: Grasset.

de Granrut, Claude (1994), *Europe, le temps des Régions*, Paris: Librairie Générale du Droit et de la Jurisprudence.

DePalma, Anthony (2001), 'U.S. and Europeans agree on deal to end banana trade war,' *New York Times*, April 12.

d'Irribarne, Philippe (1989), *La logique de l'honneur: Gestion des entreprises et traditions nationales*, Paris: Editions du Seuil.

Dumont, Gérard-François (1993), *Économie urbaine: villes et territoires en competition*, Paris: Editions Litec.

Dunning, J.H. (1983), 'Changes in the level and structure of international production,' in Mark Casson (ed), *Hegemony of International Business*, London: Routledge.

Dupuy, Claude and Jean-Pierre Gilly (1993), *Industrie et territoires en France: Dix ans de décentralization*, Paris: La documentation Française.

Les Echos, various issues.

Eck, Jean-François (1994), *La France dans la nouvelle économie mondiale*, Paris: Presses Universitaires de France.

Eck, Jean-François (1996), *Histoire de l'économie française depuis 1945*, Paris: Arman Colin.

Estrose, Christian (1996), *La coopération transfrontalière au service de l'aménagement du territoire*, Paris: Conseil Economique et Social, 1996.

The European Internet Report, New York: Morgan Stanley Dean Witter.

European Union (2001), website: <http://www.europa.eu.int.comm/eurostat/> 'regional cohesion.'

L'Expansion (1999), June 10, 70.

The Financial Network (2000), CNN, at http://cnnfn.cnn.com, 25 October.

Flockton, Christopher and Eleonore Kofman (1989), *France*, London: Paul Chapman.

Fontagné, Lionel and Michaël Pajot (1998), 'Investissement direct à l'étranger et commerce international,' *Revue économique*, 49, (3).

Fontaine, Pascal (2000), *Dix leçons sur l'Europe*, Luxembourg: Eurostat.

Food and Agriculture Organization, (2000), *FAO Conference in Maastricht, 12–17 September 1999: Contribution de la France*, Paris: Senat.

Forrester, Viviane (1996), *L'horreur économique*, Paris: Fayard.

Forrester, Viviane (2000), *Une étrange dictature*, Paris: Fayard.

Frydman, Roger (1992), *L'économie française: croissance et crise*, La Garenne-Colombes: Éditions de l'Espace Européen.

Généreux, Jacques (2000), *Une raison d'espérer*, Paris: Pocket.

Gourdon, Vincent (1992), 'Les étrangers en France,' *Histoire économique de la France au Xxe siècle, Las Cahiers Français, no. 255*.

Graham, Robert (2000a), 'Forces of change in a conservative society: the Jospin government has managed to appease its left while playing the tune of the market and globalization,' *The Financial Times*, June 14.

Graham, Robert (2000b), 'Economy, France Survey,' *The Financial Times*, November 10.

Gravier, Jean-François (1972), *Paris et le désert français*, Paris: Flammarion.

Grémion, Catherine (1991), 'Décentralisation An X,' *French Politics and Society*, 9

(3–4), 32–42.

Gueslin, André (1992), 'Les politiques économiques au XXe siecle,' *Cahiers Français*, no. 255.

Gueslin, André (1994), *L'économie ouverte 1948–1990*, Paris: Éditions La Découverte.

Hall, Peter (1993), 'Forces shaping urban Europe,' *Urban Studies*, 30 (6).

Hart, Mark (1998), 'Convergence, cohesion and regionalism: contradictory trends in the new Europe,' in Brian Graham (ed), *Modern Europe: Place, Culture and Identity*, London: Arnold.

Henriot, Alain (1997), 'Quelle place pour la France dans la novelle géographie des échanges internationaux?,' in Christian de Boissiue (ed), *Les mutations de l'économie française*, Paris: Economica.

Hirsch, Fred (1976), *Social Limits to Growth*, Cambridge, MA: Harvard University Press.

Hohenberg, Paul (1968), *A Primer on the Economic History of Europe*, New York: Random House.

Holcman, Robert (1997), *Le chômage*, Paris: La documentation Française.

Houdebine, Michel (1999), *Concentration géograhique des activités et spécialisation des départements français*, Paris: INSEE.

Hough, J.R. (1982), *The French Economy*, New York: Holmes & Meier.

Hrbek, Rudolf, 'The German Länder and EC Integration,' *Journal of European Integration*, XV (2 & 3).

Imbert, Claude (2000), 'La leçon de choses,' *Le Point*, no. 1462, September 15, 5.

INSEE (1999a), 'La diversité industrielle des territoires,' *INSEE première*, no. 650, Paris: INSEE.

INSEE (1999b), 'La population des regions (metropole): Recensement de la population de1999', *INSEE première*, no. 664.

INSEE (2000a), 'Forte extension des villes entre 1990 et 1999,' *INSEE première*, no. 707.

INSEE (2000b), 'Les produits intérieurs bruts régionaux en 1998,' *INSEE première*, no.754.

INSEE (2000c), *Répertoire des entreprises contrôlées majoritairement par l'Etat*, Paris: INSEE.

Izraelewicz, Erik (1997), *Ce monde qui nous attend*, Paris: Grasset.

Izraelewicz, Erik (2000), *Les Echos*, February 21.

Jack, Andrew (2000), *The French Exception*, London: Profile Books.

Kenen, Peter (1995), *Economic and Monetary Union in Europe*, Cambridge: Cambridge University Press.

Keynes, John Maynard (1933), 'National self-sufficiency,' *Yale Review*, 26, 755–769.

Kindleberger, Charles P. (1964), *Economic Growth in France and Britain: 1851–1950*, New York: Simon & Schuster.

Kirzner, Israel (1986), *Discovery and the Capitalist Process*, London: Routledge.

Kirzner, Israel (1989), *Discovery, Capitalism and Distributive Justice*, Oxford: Basil Blackwell.

Kirzner, Israel (1990), 'Discovery, private property and the theory of justice,' *Journal des Economistes et des Etudes Humaines*, October, 209–223.

Kirzner, Israel (1992), *The Meaning of Market Process*, London: Routledge.

Koretz, Gene (1998), 'Where Europe lags in jobs: low-education sectors have shrunk,' *Business Week*, September 14.

References

Kuisel, Richard (1984), *Le capitalisme et l'Etat en France: Modernisation et dirigisme au XXème siècle*, Paris: Gallimard.

Lacour, Claude (1991), *Espace Régionaux Nouvelles Métropoles International Nouveaux Déserts: Les Atlanti-Cité*, Bordeaux: Université de Bordeaux I,'Institut d'Economie Régionale du SudOuest.

Lacour, Claude and J. Le Monnier (1992), *Prospective Arc Atlantique: analyses, stratégies actions*, Rapport final, Paris: DATAR.

Lacroix, Robert (1997) 'Mondialisation, emploi et chômage,' *L'Actualité économique, Revue d'analyse économique*, 73 (4).

Lafay, Gérard (1996), 'Les origines internationales du chômage européen,' *Revue d'économie politique*, 106 (6), 943–966.

Lainé, Fréderic and Carole Rieu (1999), 'La diversité industrielle des territoires,' *INSEE Première*, no. 650.

Le Gall, Jean-Marc (1996), 'Emploi et chômage en Europe: une nécessaire clarification,' *Revue politique et parlementaire*, 98 (985).

Léger, Jean-Marc (1989), *La Francophonie: grand dessein, grande ambiguïte*, Lasalle (Québec): Hurtubise.

Le Grand Lyon (2000), 'Une agglomération compétitive et rassemblée,' *Millénaire trois,* Lyon: Le Grand Lyon.

Le Scouarnec, François-Pierre (1997), *La Francophonie*, Canada: Boréal.

Lesourne, Jacques (1995), *Vérités et mensonges sur le chômage*, Paris: Editions Odile Jacob.

Leterre, Thierry (2000), *La gauche et la peur libérale*, Paris: Presses de Sciences Po.

Lipietz, Alain (2000), 'Face à la mégapolisation: la bataille d'Île-de-France,' in Georges Benko and Alain Lipietz (eds), *La richesse des régions*, Paris: Presses Universitaires de France, 151–169.

Mabileau, Albert (1992), 'La décentralisation en retard,' *L'état de la décentralisation, Cahiers Français,* no. 256, Paris: La documentation Français, 66–72.

Malinvaud, Edmund (1998), 'Commentaire,' to the report by Olivier Blanchard and Jean-Paul Fitoussi (1998), *Croissance et chômage*, Paris: La documentation Française.

Malinvaud, Edmund (1986), 'The rise of unemployment in France,' *Economica*, 53 (210).

Marini, Philippe (1998–9), *La concurrence fiscale en Europe: une contribution au débat*, Paris: Senate.

Martin, Hans-Peter and Harald Schumann (1997), *Le piège de la mondialisation*, Paris: Solin-Actes Sud.

Masera, Rainer (1994), 'Single market exchange rates and monetary unification,' in Alfred Steinherr (ed.), *30 Years of European Monetary Integration*, New York: Longman, pp. 286–297.

McQueen, Matthew (1996), 'ACP–EU trade cooperation after 2000: an assessment of reciprocal trade preferences,' *Journal of Modern African Studies*, 36 (4), 669–692.

Meilhaud, Jean (1991), 'Industrie lyonnaise: l'alliance réussie de la spécialisation traditionnelle et de l'innovation,' *Problems économiques*, no 2,207, Paris: La documentation Francaise.

Mendras, Henri (1997), *L'Europe des Européenes*, Paris: Gallimard.

Milner, Jean-Claude (1997), *Le salaire de l'idéal*, Paris: Éditions du Seuil.

Minc, Alain (1997), *La mondialisation heureuse*, Paris: Plon.

Ministère de l'Agriculture et de la Pêche (2000), *Les chiffres de l'agriculture et de la pêche*, Paris: Ministère de l'Agriculture et de la Pêche.

Ministère de l'Économie, des Finances et du Budget and Ministère du Commerce Exterieur (1989), *Où en est la compétitivité française?*, Paris: La documentation Française.

Ministère de l'Economie des Finances et de l'Industrie (1999), *La politique économique de la France*, Paris: Ministère de l'Economie des Finances et de l'ndustrie*.

Ministère du Commerce Exterieur (1990), *La competitivité de l'économie française dan la perspective du marché unique*, Paris: La documentation Française.

Musgrave, Richard (1959), *The Theory of Public Finance*, New York: McGraw-Hill.

Naudet, Jean-Yves (1999), *Economie Politique*, Aix-en-Provence: Presses Universitaires d'Aix-Marseille.

Nickell, Stephen (1997), 'Unemployment and labor market rigidities: Europe versus North America,' *Journal of Economic Perspectives*, 11 (3), 55–74.

Noin, Daniel (1998), *Le nouvel espace français*, Paris: Armand Colin.

Observatoire économique de la région lyonnaise (1997), *Premières illustrations des indicateurs comparatifs*, Lyon: Observatoire économique de la région lyonnaise.

Observatoire Régional Emploi Formation Alsace (2000), 'Taux de chômage par zone d'emploi.'

OECD (1994), *The OECD Jobs Study*, Paris: Organization for Economic Cooperation and Development.

OECD (1996), *OECD Country Surveys: France, 1995*, Paris: Organization for Economic Cooperation and Development.

OECD (1997), *OECD Economic Surveys: France, 1997*, Paris: Organization for Economic Cooperation and Development.

OECD (1999), *OECD Economic Surveys: France, 1999*, Paris: Organization for Economic Cooperation and Development.

Otsuki, Tsunehiro, John. S. Wilson and Virvat Sewadeh (2000), *Saving Two in a Billion: A Case Study to Quantify the Trade Effect of European Food Safety Standards on African Exports*, Washington, DC: The World Bank, Development Research Group.

Oxley, Howard, Jean-Marc Burniaux, Thai-Thanh Dang and Marco Mira d'Ercole (1997), 'Income distribution and poverty in 13 OECD countries,' *OECD Economic Studies*, no. 29.

Parodi, Maurice *et al.* (1994), *L'économie et la société française au second XXème siècle*, Tome 1, Paris: Armand Colin.

Petiteville, Franck (1996), 'Europe/Amérique latine: La synergie des logiques d'integration?,' *Revue politique et parlementaire*, 98, (983).

Plassard, François (1992), 'L'impact territorial des transports à grande vitesse,' in Pierre-Henri Derycke (ed.), *Espace et dynamiques territoriales*, Paris: Economica, pp. 243–262.

Problèmes politiques et sociaux (1995), 'Les fractures du territoire: Surconcentration et dépopulation,' *Problèmes politiques et sociaux*, no. 750.

Redor, Dominique (1992), *Wage Inequalities in East and West*, Cambridge: Cambridge University Press.

Régniez, Jacques (1999), *Nouvel âge d'or ou horreur économique?*, Paris: Presses

Universitaire de France.

Reich, Robert (1992), *The Work of Nations*, New York: Vintage.

Rémond, Bruno (1992), 'La loi du 6 février 1992: le second souffle de la décentralization?,' *L'état de la décentralisation, Cahiers Français*, no. 256, 87–90.

Revel, Jean-François (2000), *La grande parade: Essai sur la survie de l'utopie socialiste*, Paris: Plon.

Ridderstrale, Jonas and Kjell Nordstrom (2000), *Funky business: Le talent fait danser le capital*, Paris: Les Echos Editions.

Rifkin, Jeremy (1995), *The End of Work*, New York: G.P. Putnam and Sons.

Rosenvallon, P. (1992), *L'Etat en France de 1789 à nos jours*, Paris: Le Seuil.

Ross, Kristin (1996), *Fast Cars, Clean Bodies*, Cambridge, MA: MIT Press.

Roy, Jean-Louis (1989), *La Francophonie: L'émergence d'une alliance?*, Lasalle (Québec): Hurtubise.

Sabel, Charles and Jonathan Zeitlin (1985), 'Historical alternative to mass production: politics, markets and technology in nineteenth-century industrialization,' *Past and Present*, 108, 133–176.

Safir, André and Dominique Michel (1999), *Avantage France: France S.A. contre World Corp.*, Paris: Editions Village Mondial.

Sancton, Thomas (2000), 'The French are on the roll,' *Time Magazine*, July 17.

Sassen, Saskia (1999), *Guests and Aliens*, New York: The New Press.

Schutte, Ofelia (1996), 'Cultural identity: the aesthetic dimension,' in Marina Pérez de Mendiola (ed.), *Bridging the Atlantic: Toward a Reassessment of Iberian and Latin American Cultural Ties*, Albany, NY: SUNY Press.

Sen, Amartya (1997), 'Inequality, unemployment and contemporary Europe,' *International Labour Review*, 136 (2), 155-172

Sénat (1999), *Rapport Guillaume*, Paris: Sénat.

SEPAL (1988), *Lyon 2010: Un projet d'agglomération pour une métropole éuropeenne*, Lyon: SEPAL.

Servan-Schreiber, Jean-Jacques (1967), *Le défi Américain*, Paris: Editions Denoel.

Sheahan, John (1963), *Promotion and Control of Industry in Post-war France*, Cambridge, MA: Harvard University Press.

Sinou, Bernard (1999), 'Comments,' in *Rayonner dans l'Europe des grandes métropoles: les défis de la région urbaine de Lyon*, Lyon: Région Urbaine de Lyon, pp. 28–29.

Sofaës, Christian (1995), *Services publics question d'avenir*, Commissariat Général du Plan, Paris: La documentation Français.

Statistiques et Etudes Industrielles, (2000a), *Les 4 pages*, Paris: Ministére de l'Economie, des Finance et de L'Industrie, February.

Statistiques et Etudes Industrielles, (2000b), *Implantation étrangère dans l'industrie française au 01/01/1998*, Paris: Ministère de l'Economie, des Finance et de l'Industrie.

Straus, André (1992), 'La croissance en France de 1945 à la crise,' *Histoire de la France au XXe siècle, Les Cahiers Français*, no. 255.

Surarez-Villa, Luis and Juan R. Cuadrado Roura (1993), 'Regional economic integration and the evolution of disparities,' *Papers in Regional Science*, 72 (4), 369–387.

Symes, Valerie (1997), 'Unemployment in Europe: a continuing crisis,' in Valerie Symes, Carl Levy and Jane Littlewood (eds), *The Future of Europe*, New York: St.

Martins Press.

Tesse, Pierre-Yves (1990), *Charte d'objectifs: Lyon ville internationale*, Lyon: Chambre de commerce et d'industrie de Lyon.

Thisse, Jacques-François and Tanguy van Ypersele (1999), 'Métropoles et concurrence territoriale,' *Politique Régional*, Paris: INSEE.

Thoenig, Jean-Claude (1992), 'La décentralization: dix ans déja, et après,' *L'état de la décentralisation, Cahiers français*, no. 256, Paris: La documentation Français.

Thompson, Ian (1994), 'The French TGV system: progress and projects,' *Geography*, 79 (343), 164–168.

Tiersky, Ronald (1994), *France in the New Europe: Changing Yet Steadfast*, Belmont, CA: Wadsworth.

Topel, Robert H. (1997), 'Factor proportions and relative wages: the supply-side determinants of wage inequality,' *Journal of Economic Perspectives*, 11 (2).

TriRhena (2001), website: <http://www.regiotrirhena.org/>.

United States, Department of the Treasury (1999), *1998 Investment Climate Statement: France*, Washington, DC: US Government.

Vickerman, R. W. (1994), 'Transportation infrastructure and region building in the European Community,' *Journal of Common Market Studies*, 32 (1), 1–24.

Vimont, Claude (1993), *Le commerce extérieure français: créateur ou destructeur d'emplois?*, Paris: Economica.

Wacquant, Loïc J.D. (1992), 'Banlieues françaises et ghetto noir américain de l'amalgame à la comparaison,' *French Politics and Society*, 10 (4), 81–103.

Yeager, Leland B. (1966), *International Monetary Relations*, New York: Harper & Row.

Zylberberg, Michel (1992), 'De la guerre à la depression (1914–1939),' *Cahiers Français*, no. 255.

Index